Fit For Life

Fit For Life

RANULPH FIENNES

LITTLE, BROWN AND COMPANY

A *Little, Brown* Book

First published in Great Britain by Little, Brown 1998

A CIP catalogue record for this book is available from the
British Library.

ISBN 0 316 64476 5

Designed and typeset in Stone Informal by
M Rules

Printed and bound in Great Britain by
Butler & Tanner Ltd, Frome and London

Little, Brown and Company (UK)
Brettenham House
Lancaster Place
London WC2E 7EN

Only the fit survive

Robert Service

Note of Caution

The programmes in this book are intended for people of all ages in good health. Before beginning this or any other exercise programme, it is advisable to obtain the approval and recommendations of your doctor. While you are following this or any exercise programme, it is advisable to visit your doctor for periodic monitoring.

Contents

Acknowledgements

My thanks to Mike Stroud, Jonathan Beevers and Brian Welsby for all their fitness and nutrition advice and expertise over the years. To my wife, Ginnie, for putting up with muddy trackshoes and absences in my ongoing pursuit of fitness. To Ed Victor, Philippa Harrison and Caroline North for the book. To Frances Pajovic and Gina Rawle for help with the manuscript.

To Jarrod Lupson and Mark Downs, the managers of the Queen Mother Sports Centre in London, Cephas Anderson, the manager of the Courtneys/Adidas Gym there, for the photographs and their technical advice – and of course to all the volunteers who demonstrated exercises for the book:

David Baran, Alison Bolding, Lloymore Butler, Michael Cownley, Alan Crowder, Joanne Eldridge, Steve Fabear, Janet Gunn, Scott Harbour, Scott Kay, Tim Matusche, Remelbo Price, Rachel Ramsey, Roberto Valeri and Ben Willetts.

All the photographs used have been reproduced by kind permission of adidas, unless otherwise credited.

To Steven Seaton of *Runners' World* for his advice, research and valuable time. To Joe Dunbar, David Smith, Dr Bernard Watkin, Dr Earl L. Mindell and Brant Richards for their help and expertise. And to my ancestors for any genes which have proved beneficial to my fitness potential.

Author's Note

I have received no remuneration from any commercial organisation in return for mentioning any product in this book, and material assistance only from Courtneys/Adidas and Versaclimber Ltd. The specific manufacturers and service-providers included are recommended purely because I have personally found their goods and/or services to be excellent. There may of course be other products as good, or better, which you may prefer to use.

Introduction

In the spring of 1996, aged 52, I set out in a blizzard towing a 500lb sledge in an attempt to cross Antarctica. Over 1,300 miles of hazardous ice lay ahead and my rivals, two of the fittest men in the world, were half my age.

The extreme cold, and the rarefied air of the 10,000ft-high south polar plateau, meant travelling for three months at an effective altitude of 16,000ft above sea-level. I would have to burn an average 8,000 calories a day, almost three times the rate of running a marathon, to stand a chance of success. Unlike a marathon-runner, who can rest in between races, I would have to strive constantly for three months at my peak performance with no rest days. Despite consuming 5,000 calories of sledge rations every day, I could expect to lose more than 25 per cent of my body weight (going from 220lbs to 140lbs) and to suffer ongoing pain from frostbite, gangrene, the rub of raw flesh and ulcerated blisters, while having to maintain maximum energy output. I knew all this because I had crossed the continent three years previously, with Mike Stroud, an ultra-fit doctor 11 years my junior. On that occasion we had become the first people ever to man-haul the great

frozen continent, from Pacific to Atlantic coast, unsupported.

Unfortunately, two factors unconnected with my physical fitness snatched the solo record from my grasp in 1996. One was a kidney stone which lodged in my system one night when I was exactly halfway to the South Pole and well ahead of schedule. The other was the advent of para-wings – lightweight, hand-held wind sails.

The nature of the prevailing winds in Antarctica, close to and after the Pole, ensures more following winds as the crossing progresses. The arrival of para-wings on the polar scene in about 1994 meant that 'unsupported' crossings became, in reality, wind-supported endeavours and the great difficulty of all previous journeys became a thing of the past. So for an expert para-wings-user, an unsupported Antarctic crossing is no longer a problem. In fact these days I would even hesitate to describe it as an ultra-endurance event.

In spite of my lack of experience with para-wings, I managed one day with a following wind to complete 117 miles to the south. This alone would have ensured the eventual success of my attempt – had it

An award for fitness: the Guinness Book of Records *World Hall of Fame Awards in 1984. David Frost (front row, second left) and Norris McWhirter (second right) present awards to Paul Macartney (far left) for music, Billie Jean King (back row, second right) for sport and to the author (far right), aged 40, for exploration.* Guinness Book of Records

not been for the kidney stone – because my normal daily average progress, 10 miles of enormous effort, necessitated the amount of heavy rations on my sledge. That one day of wind enabled me to eliminate nine days' worth of food and fuel.

Back in Britain, I received a barrage of letters inquiring about my fitness regime. I tried to respond helpfully, but soon realised that anything less than a complete answer was liable to prove of minimal benefit. There are many sides to maintaining personal fitness, just as there are to maintaining a garden, playing golf or being a successful farmer. Advice needs to encompass every facet of the relevant information. Keeping fit involves exercise, food

intake and mental approach, and I could not cover all this in a letter. Instead I decided to address the whole topic by writing this book, which covers all the elements of my fitness regime, aimed at people of any level of fitness, from couch potatoes to Iron Man racers.

So what makes this book different from all the others of its genre? Well, it works for me: this is my own system which has, to date, kept my body capable of responding well to extreme exertion over long periods. Many fitness books are produced by radiant actresses, musclemen with startling pectorals, Mr Motivators who perform gymnastic miracles or dieticians who make you suffer. I am neither beautiful, muscle-bound, greyhound-like, nor given to dieting. I have smoked on and off for years and only four years ago won the British Pipesmoker of the Year Award. I am a chocoholic and I dislike taking exercise for its own sake. My wife has to bully me off the sofa and into the garden on Sunday afternoons. I have suffered from arthritis, chronic lower-back pain, haemorrhoids, kidney stones, rheumatic fever, retinal sun-blindness, recurrent glandular fever . . . I will not bore you with the rest. But, by following certain rules, for more than 30 years I have kept such afflictions largely at bay in order to follow a physically demanding profession – the leading of expeditions – interspersed with the sedentary activity of writing books about them.

At the age of 49, I was subjected to a series of fitness tests at the UK Army Personnel Research Establishment, the centre which for many years had evaluated athletes and special forces individuals for demanding tasks such as NASA space missions. The APRE supervising officer summarised my fitness as being 'in line with that of a 21-year-old top athlete in peak form'.

I had not worked hard to achieve that level of fitness. Indeed, I was writing a book at the time and had spent most daylight hours for the preceding six months at my desk. To take exercise is to use up valuable writing time, so I have always kept exercise periods to the minimum necessary. Likewise, because I am a natural glutton, specialising in confectionery, roasts, fries and gooey cakes with clotted cream as well as chocolate, I keep my dieting activities to a level that avoids deprivation and longing whenever possible.

Many fitness books contradict one another over the simplest advice. Some say nuts are good for you, while butter is bad, and that you should swim and cycle but never run. Others preach apricots and

Fitness has helped me to withstand the rigours of polar exploration. This photograph was taken seven days before my departure for Antarctica in 1992. I weighed 15½ stone (217lbs). Roy Morton, UPPA

A week after returning to London three months later, weighing 10 stone (1401bs). I was 48. Rex Features

You never stop reaping the benefits of being fit, as the age range of the British squad which completed the 1996 Eco-Challenge in the Rockies proves. From left to right: Mike Stroud, David Smith, Rebecca Stevens, the author and Vic Stroud. At 52, I was 19 years younger than Vic Stroud. Moira Howell

yoga. My system is designed to maintain a level of fitness through exercise and food control on a *minimal-bother* basis. It is realistic and achievable. The following practical advice and information, which I have tried to keep straightforward, assumes that you, like me, are often prone to lapse from fine intentions and fall by the wayside. No matter: relapses are normal. As long as you know what you should be doing and do it whenever you can, your fitness level will increase accordingly.

This book is for people of *any* age and *any* state of fitness. The various elements of my regime are, of course, second-hand. I did not invent any of them; I merely garnered a host of tips from my time in the SAS and from working closely with doctors, athletes, nutritionists and exercise specialists over 30 years at the leading edge of the international expedition world. It is never too late to improve your fitness. If you don't believe me, just look at the example of the British team which took part in the 1996 Eco-Challenge Race in the Rocky Mountains in the USA.

The Eco-Challenge Race takes place annually in areas of wilderness. Advertised as the 'most challenging race on earth', it is not for the faint-hearted.

Introduction

Teams from elite special forces units, physical training instructors from American universities, marathon-runners and orienteering clubs enter every year. Some are sponsored by Nike, Reebok and the like, who pay team members $10,000 each if they win, so the competition is fierce. Participants are usually selected for their supreme fitness and capacity for great endurance. The average age of the contestants is 25.

In 1996 Mike Stroud, with whom I had completed five polar expeditions and set a number of world records, and who is an expert on nutrition and exercise, formed a British squad to enter the Eco-Challenge. He decided that his team should be different. His idea was to have an age range stretching over five decades, in order to prove that endurance is not the prerogative of the young. Rebecca Stevens, Britain's first woman up Everest, was in her 30s. Mike was himself 41, I was 52, Chris Brasher – the man who, with Roger Bannister and Chris Chataway, had run the first four-minute mile – was in his 60s, and Mike's father, Vic Stroud, a retired businessman and keen fell-walker, was 71. In the end Chris Brasher had to withdraw, to be replaced by David Smith, a 44-year-old cardiologist from Exeter.

On Day 1, at 5am, 74 five-person teams charged away to the echo of the starting-gun's signal reverberating through the forests all about us. On every side the broken silhouette of the Rockies reared above us until it was obscured by the dust cloud generated by the 370 competitors.

Each team had two mountain ponies for the first 26 miles. Vic and Rebecca rode our stocky steeds and the rest of us ran. Then, at a checkpoint, we wrapped up our gear in polythene bags and leaped into a raging river, the only way forward. Vic was swept away, and for several agonising moments we feared he would drown, until Mike rescued him. For four days we slogged up and down high mountains, through tangled undergrowth in forests, along streambeds, over crevassed glaciers and down cliffsides. Mike's face was so swollen from hornet bites that he could hardly see; Vic's backside remained badly blistered from the initial pony ride.

By Day 3 we had moved from 56th position to 49th. People from younger, tougher teams were dropping out. Next came the river section. The five of us crammed into two canoes and paddled hard day and night without pausing to rest, through some of the most beautiful scenery in North America. At the next checkpoint we exchanged the canoes for mountain bikes and, still unrested, pushed on all night and for most of the next day, suffering several falls in the process. But we completed the race, and our final position was 29th. Each of our team, including 71-year-old Vic – by far the oldest of the 370 competitors – lived busy professional lives and none of us were athletes or even keen sportspeople. However, what we had in common was that we all tried to keep fit by taking occasional exercise and by thinking about what and when we should eat. So can you.

1

The Benefits of Being Fit

So what are the benefits to *you* of keeping fit? Why should you bother to read this, or any other fitness book? Why subject yourself to the disciplines of exercise and food control? The two main answers are obvious and undeniable.

Longer Life

The majority of smokers in Europe die of heart-attacks or cancer. The other side of the coin is that those of us who do not smoke are highly unlikely to die of lung cancer, and those of us who keep fit are far more likely to reach a ripe old age with strong hearts and less risk of suffering from cancer.

Poor physical fitness is associated with cardio-vascular disease. A great many medical research studies over the years have shown that people who exercise by walking outlive those who take no exercise at all, and that those who walk the most outlive those who walk the least. Genetic disposition to early death from cardiovascular cause is unusual and can anyway be postponed by taking exercise. To say, 'My mother died young of a heart-attack, so there is no point in my taking exercise since I am doomed whatever I do,' is a load of codswallop.

One Harvard study of 10,000 graduates over 40 years (during which 470 died) showed that deaths from cardiovascular disease were proportional to levels of physical fitness, and moreover that the fittest individuals were also the least likely to die from *any* cause. Of special interest to those of you who think you cannot stop smoking, the same study found that fit smokers were less likely to die than less fit smokers.

Quality of Life

Nobody wants to live longer, let alone be 'old', if they are not enjoying life in the first place. If it means pain from arthritis, osteoporosis, viral illnesses and so on, then what, you may wonder, is the advantage of a longer life? I would agree. However, by keeping fit and eating healthily you dramatically increase your chances of escaping such painful afflictions.

Quality of life involves happiness, self-confidence and good health. Fitness will increase your chance of enjoying all three.

Self-Motivation

Most people hate the thought of taking exercise, despite the knowledge that it is good for them. But many of these same folk, including me, still manage to keep fit because we know the penalties of lapsing into a sedentary, or semi-sedentary existence. Thinking about the benefits of keeping fit should be enough to provide the self-motivation needed to take exercise and eat correctly. But you need to keep reminding yourself of the benefits each time your natural laziness, or busy schedule, tempts you to give exercise a miss or to unwrap another chocolate bar.

I conjure up visual images to fight my idle nature. I once had cause to visit a terminally ill relative I had not seen for six months. She was dying of cancer and I was shocked by the sight of her. Knowing that exercise helps minimise the likelihood of my sharing her plight is a great stimulus in preventing lapses in training. A friend of mine stops himself from reaching for a cigarette by keeping a colour photo on his desk showing the effects of nicotine and tar on the human lungs. He also has a tape-recording of the breathing of a 50 year old man with emphysema. The following are some instant remedies for flagging self-motivation.

- Remembering that your exercise session will be enjoyable, not a mere boring nuisance, will help get you off your backside. It is a scientific fact that exercise does make most people feel more alive, because it triggers the release of chemicals (endorphins) in the brain, thereby creating a sense of wellbeing.
- Boredom, if your exercise has to take place in the same area each day, can be alleviated by setting yourself simple goals. When I wanted to join the SAS, I knew I had to be ultra-fit, so for 12 months before the selection course I strove daily to carry a 50lb-load rucksack for 10 miles across broken country in ever-quicker times. That gave me an ongoing target to aim at. Nowadays, having no such career ambitions, I set myself simpler tasks, such as reaching a certain landmark on a run before turning back, or counting to 2,000 step-ups before switching to the runners' treadmill.
- If you have a friend, or friends, to exercise with, you can start up some team activity, such as football, which you know will stretch you. If you keep fit between each match, with or without your team-mates, you will be less likely to let them down on the day. This knowledge alone provides a strong incentive to train. Plan your short-term training schedule by putting it into your work diary. Treat your runs as scheduled appointments. Take a pair of running shoes and shorts with you when you go on holiday or travel on business so that you miss no opportunities.
- If, despite a sound overall motivational rationale, I still find my lazy persona is winning the day and sense that the Devil is about to claim a victory in the temptation-to-be-idle stakes, I resort to my last-ditch tactic, which is simply to *stand up at once*. This is usually successful because it interrupts the negative thought processes and is in itself a physical action. If you are already standing up – gardening or cooking, for instance – then simply stop what you are doing and head for your running shoes *without* indulging in further thought.
- The benefits of keeping to a regime of minimal training are far greater than those gained through bursts of exercise on a haphazard and intermittent basis. This begs the question: what is minimal?

Minimal Training For Fitness

How much or how little you train depends, of course, on how fit you wish to be. The US Surgeon-General recommends the burning of 150 calories a day (1,000 a week) through exercise. This you can do by running 10 miles a week. However, if you were to run 40 miles a week, your health benefits would increase dramatically. An *Archives of Internal Medicine* 10-year study of 8,200 males concluded that those who ran 40 miles a week had a 30 per cent lower risk of heart disease, lower blood pressure and better cholesterol levels than those who ran 10 miles or fewer a week.

Research in the 1990s clearly indicates that the occasional fitness sortie on an intermittent basis can do your body more harm than good. Too little exercise too seldom can be dangerous.

In the 1960s, during my early 20s, I swore by the 5BX Canadian Air Force training system, which involved about 12 minutes of set physical exercises daily. In those days, I was pretty active in strenuous Army activities most days, so the 5BX training proved adequate (even though I failed to perform it on at least six days out of 10). However, I now believe that, even if I had been more conscientious, the 5BX on its own would have been insufficient. Some research facts bear this out, and help to pinpoint the minimum training we need to achieve bodily benefit.

- Even without any exercise at all a body burns up about 1,000 calories a day. We use up some 95 per cent of our daily energy output merely to stay alive – by breathing, digesting and fidgeting. However, if 100 per cent of our energy output in calories burned fails to match our calorific input on any given day, the balance remains in the body's system as a weight gain, and often as unwanted fat. A mere 12 minutes' exercise daily is unlikely to shift this balance, bearing in mind the eating habits and sedentary nature of most individuals today.

- American veteran runner Ken Cooper advised runners aiming for basic aerobic fitness (exercise beneficial to the heart and lungs) who are not massively worried about their weight, that two-mile runs three times a week are sufficient. His famous running compatriot George Sheehan recommends three-mile runs three times a week.

- Exercise is beneficial to your heart only if it achieves between 60 and 90 per cent of your maximum heart rate (MHR). Details of how to calculate this are given in Chapter 5.

- Scientific studies have resulted in different dictates as to how long you should exercise. In the Parachute Regiment, soldiers are advised to train for sessions of not less than 20 minutes three times a week. If you add 30 minutes for changing clothes, getting to your training site and showering, that is just an hour out of your day thrice weekly. The results, in both the short and long term, will be well worth the effort.

To understand the principle of minimal exercise levels you need to recognise the function of glycogen. Most foods of plant origin contain carbohydrates which your digestive system breaks down into sugars, mainly glucose, your major source of energy. Some is stored in your liver and muscles in the form of glycogen, which will release new energy when your reserves get low.

For the first 20 minutes or so of your daily exercise you will use up your first-line glucose supplies and your body will not yet need to call upon energy reserves from elsewhere, such as energy converted from your body fat. If you want to lose fat, you will need to train aerobically for at least 30 minutes per aerobic session. After the age of 35 I had to increase this to a minimum of 45 minutes.

Scientific studies between 1970 and 1996 uniformly agree that body-fat percentage reduces significantly over a year for people training for 30 minutes or more three times a week, but not at all when their sessions are of only 15 minutes' duration. Body mass and loose skinfolds are likewise reduced considerably more in four-days-a-week runners than in their three-days-a-week colleagues.

It is important to remember that, even when you are still at rest, your body burns up energy at a ratio of two thirds fats and one third carbohydrates. Low-intensity exercise does not alter this ratio. As you increase the intensity of your exercise, sadly, the ratio changes in favour of carbohydrates. You can burn plenty of calories and lose some fat in a mere 20 minutes of moderate-intensity exercise. So remember that my minimal training times are aimed at aerobic benefit, not just fat loss.

The frequency of your exercise bouts should be spread over each week so that your muscles can recuperate and you are less likely to get bored. An hour once every other day is my ideal format, when business commitments allow. If a demanding expedition is looming, my training will increase.

For non-athletes merely wishing to stave off ill health while running busy lives, most current scientific advice encourages the taking of strenuous exercise for at least 30 minutes three times a week.

Balancing Aerobic and Strength Training

Your Heart: Aerobics is the Answer

According to the World Health Organisation, 25 per cent of the 11 million deaths occurring each year in Western society are due to heart disease. That amounts to 2,750,000 deaths annually. Additionally, they estimate that a further 13 per cent (1,430,000 people) die from strokes. Coronary heart disease is the greatest single cause of death in North America and in most European countries.

Coronary artery disease, usually brought about by fatty foods and insufficient exercise, often starts its deadly course in young, healthy individuals. As fatty cholesterol begins to 'fur up' their arteries, restricting bloodflow and the oxygen supply to the heart, the heart's work capacity slowly declines and heart-attack risk increases. Coronary heart disease starts when we are young and develops until we are middle-aged. Then, from the age of about 35 years for men and 45 for women, if we have constantly eaten the wrong foods and neglected to exercise, we die. Since it is a pain in the neck bothering about exercise and extremely pleasurable to eat delicious foods, we knowingly play Russian roulette with our lifespan and commit 'slow suicide'.

Our health is our single most important asset but often it takes the shock of a major illness to make us think seriously about spending some time preserving our health. The risk of heart disease is greater if you are male, past youth and have close relatives with a heart-disease history, but these factors might just as well be ignored since you can do nothing about them. What you *can* control, with a minimum of effort, are my **six demons**, which are:

High blood cholesterol
High blood pressure
Cigarette-smoking
Being overweight
High blood sugar
Lack of sufficient physical exercise

There is a good deal of confusion about cholesterol, mainly because some is good (the high-density lipoproteins) and some is bad (the low-density lipoproteins) for the health. High levels of the latter are responsible for clogging the arteries and putting strain on the heart, which has to work harder to pump blood around the body and can eventually lead to heart disease. High levels of bad cholesterol can be caused by genetic disposition in some unfortunate individuals, but in most people it is caused by eating too much of the wrong sort of fat – saturated animal fat. We can't change our genetic make-up, but we can improve our eating habits by avoiding saturated and trans-fatty-acid foods, which I call 'bad' fats in this book, and by eating foods which help to lower the risk of excess bad cholesterol, such as fruit, vegetables, oats, bran and wholemeal or granary bread.

The heart is a wonderful muscular pump, the size of a fist, wedged between the lungs and protected by the ribs. Its task is to force blood around the body bearing nutrients and oxygen to every living tissue. The blood travels out from the heart in arteries and back again via the veins. Like any muscle, the heart needs to be kept fit to do its job properly. The average heart beats at between 60 and 100 times a minute when at rest, pumping around nine pints of blood per minute. The amount pumped increases in response to the quicker heartbeat when we exercise. At about 200 beats, some 45 pints per minute (over 60 pints in the case of a top athlete) can be circulated by a strong heart.

Any clogging of the arteries, caused by fats, interrupts the blood circulation with potentially deadly results. If arteries supplying oxygen to the heart itself are blocked, parts of the heart muscle may fail, which you could experience as angina pain or eventually a heart-attack. Lack of exercise and food control is asking for trouble. The only excuse you have for killing yourself (and hurting anyone who loves you) is ignorance or sheer idleness. Once you've finished reading this book, only idleness will remain.

However busy you are, you find time for your favourite activities, hobbies and small pleasures like watching the television or reading the newspaper. On Sundays people make time for mowing the lawn or washing the car. Even weightlifters and bodybuilders can spend hours every day working on their chests and biceps, yet ignore their heart muscles. Finding time, or making time, to service your heart is infinitely more important.

The chest expands with increased bench presses; likewise, the heart grows with prolonged aerobic exercise. A well-exercised heart can be 40 per cent larger than a 'normal' heart and can pump 50 per cent more blood with every beat.

Once you have worked on it, your heart will have bigger chambers, so it will not have to beat so often to keep you 'ticking over'. The lower your heart rate, the better your chances of living longer and retaining good health. Regular aerobic exercise will reduce stress and high blood pressure, cut down the amount of 'bad' cholesterol in your system while increasing levels of 'good' cholesterol, reduce any excess weight and help you to suppress bad habits like eating chocolate or smoking.

If you have already had a heart-attack and do not improve your ways, you will soon die. Medically supervised exercise and food control can give you a new lease of life with no more heart-attacks and no more angina.

There are five additional perks for folk who treat their hearts correctly:

- A smaller acceleration of your pulse rate under stress.
- Your pulse rate returns more rapidly to its normal rate after suffering stress.
- Your heart pumps more blood per beat at rest and during exercise.
- The small blood vessels that supply your heart muscle are more richly developed.
- There is a far better supply of oxygen and 'food' to your muscles and a quicker recuperation after exercise, whether at work or at play.

Any exercise that helps develop heart and lung capacity can be described as **aerobic**. Certain training modes, such as weight-training and sprinting, are known as **anaerobic** exercises. The dictionary defines 'anaerobic' as 'capable of existing in the absence of air or oxygen'. These exercises are short, speedy burst motions demanding energy and power from the muscles once oxygen from the blood has been used up. The only track events, for instance, that are anaerobic are the 100- and 200-metres races, so short that sprinters can't take enough breaths to complete the distance without using all the oxygen from their blood supply. To make up the deficit they use anaerobic respiration, which, scientists believe, was developed to provide our cave-dwelling ancestors with short, fast bursts of speed to escape from hungry predators.

Each of us inherits in our genes a different muscular chemistry and varied sporting talents. Some of us are born to sprint. Physiologists describe such types as having 'fast-twitch' muscles. Others are born in the 'slow-twitch' mode and find long-distance running much more their cup of tea. The advice offered in this book will benefit anyone and everyone, but my system, like any aerobic stamina-training programme, will be easier for slow twitchers (like me) than for fast twitchers (like Linford Christie). Nonetheless, everyone, however they twitch, should train aerobically as this is the *only* way to improve the cardio-respiratory system. Folk with sprinters' genes might try interval training programmes (see pages 82–83), which will suit them better and achieve the same results. As far as food control is concerned, your twitch type is irrelevant.

Strength and Endurance

When selecting individuals for expeditions of great length through rugged terrain, lugging heavy weights in extreme temperatures, I look for people with muscular strength as well as a capacity for endurance. You may think that somebody capable of winning an international marathon or a long-distance mountain race is bound to be strong. But this is a misconception which has caused two of my expeditions to fail. The team members in question were in both cases able to ski long distances superbly – but not, it turned out, when encumbered with very heavy loads. I weigh 180lbs when at my fittest, but my polar sledge weighs 500lbs, so I need certain muscles to be massively trained to pull such a weight over 1,000 miles.

Only weight-training and/or body-resistance work, as practised by gymnasts, can develop many of your key muscles; aerobic training alone will not achieve this. So my system attends to both your strength and your endurance needs. It stresses the benefits of strengthening the muscles which govern your posture, above all the abdominal muscles that protect your lower back. It is a scientific fact that intensive endurance exercise will in itself do little to enhance strength. No matter how far you swim or run, or how hard you exercise, you are merely contracting your muscles against the same amount of resistance. Yet you do need strength in order to avoid injury. Strong muscles (and not necessarily the ones that can be seen) give protection to vital organs and ligaments. All competitive sports, from golf to fishing to tiddlywinks, demand the use of specific muscle groups.

To follow my training system, or indeed to perform any activity which requires you to exercise strenuously, you must protect yourself from injury. By performing a few basic strength exercises, most of which need no special gear other than a couple of dumb-bells obtainable from any sports shop, you can stay injury-free and feel the day-to-day confidence of greater body strength.

The strength of a muscle is measured by the amount of force which that muscle can exert and is dependent on the size and number of muscle fibres that can be brought into action at any one time, and on the frequency of the nerve impulses you send them from your brain. If you have to wear a plaster cast on your arm for a month you will notice, when freed from the cast, that your arm looks wasted and thin. The reverse happens when you exercise your arm more than usual.

Strength exercise, over and above the normal demands of most people's daily muscular functions, is necessary to develop the modicum of strength that you will need to fulfil your aerobic work without suffering from repeated niggling strains and muscle pains. Running, swimming or cycling will enhance certain muscles and ignore many others. This can lead directly to injuries which you might never have suffered had you remained sedentary.

The answer lies in a minimal amount of strength training.

Before I developed my aerobic and weight-training system and concentrated purely on endurance work, I used to suffer from non-stop minor pains in my back, legs and feet. In fact I picked up more small, irritating injuries during training bouts than I have ever suffered on an actual expedition. This went on for more than 10 years. My current programme has, thankfully, cut down such problems by maintaining muscle balance and flexibility, especially in my feet and lower back.

2

The Outside Factors

Before getting down to the basics of what you can do about *your* fitness and when, pause to consider the wider picture. Facets of outside events, often events beyond our control, impinge on just how fit we can hope or need to be. Our bodies respond to distantly implanted 'cave-dweller' impulses – the 'Neanderthal factor'. Our genes often have unwanted and 'unfair' control on our development. So do our schooldays and childhood. Stress affects our digestion, and therefore our health. Bacteria are developing a resistance to antibiotics so that an ever-increasing number of patients, even in the world's most sophisticated hospitals, are dying of germs which penicillin would have eliminated a few years ago. Even if we avoid bacterial contamination, hundreds of thousands of individuals in the West lose their fitness every year, some permanently, through injury and sickness.

These factors may not interest you. You may feel they should be labelled as negative thought. You might wish to skip this chapter altogether in your desire to leap headlong on to your newly acquired treadmill with bananas sticking out of your trendy Lycra tights and get down to the serious business of

fitness. That is up to you. But remember that an awareness of the traits you inherit from your forebears and the effects of your current environment may enable you to maintain a higher level of fitness.

Our Prehistory

Asked what lessons our prehistory can usefully teach us today, some of the more realistic professors of the subject would laugh and proclaim the definition of prehistory as the 'study of the unverifiable to prove the unwarrantable about what never happened anyway'. Yet very few animals have changed their habitats and lifestyles as much as humans have over the past 2,000 years *and* survived the impact of such changes on their body systems.

We spend much of our waking lives standing upright, despite a skeletal structure designed for ape-type activities. We are omnivores, despite a digestive system plainly planned to cope with fruit and vegetables alone, and, although we know our tissues degrade through lack of usage, we nonetheless allow our muscles to atrophy. As a result, *homo erectus* 100,000 years ago was in many ways much better off fitness-wise than millions of people alive today. Doubts about the reality of anthropologists' findings and their sometimes dubious theorising must diminish as, each year, more fossils are found and analysed by ever-more ingenious instruments. Laboratories can already trace and identify dietary remains in the matter of prehistoric bones, while fossil teeth tell experts whether their owners gnawed at meat, chewed on vegetables or crushed fruits five million years ago.

The digestive systems of carnivores and omnivores are quite different from ours, as are their fingers and toes, which are designed to grasp and rend flesh, not to reach up for and curl around fruits. We do not have the long incisors, the claws, the innate desire to kill when we spot a rabbit or cow, the rough tongue or the jaw action. Yet at some point, or over some period of time so far unspecified by anthropologists, we taught ourselves the new practice of killing and eating other animals, despite the enormous harm this increased intake of animal protein and fats caused and still causes to our unprepared digestive systems. Just one such result is the release of large quantities of uric acid each time we consume meat. This highly toxic acid can, and often does, do irreversible damage to our bodies, because human livers can only eliminate small doses of the acid, while carnivores' livers are designed to process 12 times the amount. The kidneys, as well as the liver, are put under considerable strain too.

Newspaper articles often tell us not to eat hamburgers due to BSE (which has killed a mere handful of individuals worldwide), and beef on the bone has been banned in the UK, but we continue to eat meat in general, as we have done for tens of thousands of years, without giving a thought to the basic fact that we are not armed with the correct digestive system to cope and so fill our systems with excessive amounts of protein and fat which leads directly to

lethal degenerating illnesses including furred arteries, arthritis and some cancers.

Yet our bodies remember prehistoric impulses far more subtle than those of self-preservation and sex. It is thought that life originated in water millions of years ago. The role of water as the main element of our body mass, and our need for water as sustenance, has altered over the course of evolution, but it has not disappeared altogether. Modern water-drinking habits can also reduce our chances of keeping fit in the long term. My fitness system is based on water control as well as food control.

Genetic Effects

Choose your parents carefully. This advice can only usefully be given to Buddhists about to be reincarnated, otherwise it would be included in all fitness books. Genes make you the way you are and that includes many facets of how fit, fat and well muscled it is possible for you to become. The very nature of your muscle fibre and your chances of suffering from cancer are genetic inheritances, as is your fat gene, your manic-depressive gene, your addiction gene and your cardiovascular-disease-susceptibility gene.

But before you slam down this book in disgust and declare how unfair life is; before you decide that you are wasting your time fighting against genetically stacked odds because your parents, who were fat and feeble, died young of cancer and a stroke respectively; remember the importance of fitness in significantly reducing these odds. Take identical twins. Many sets of twins with identical genes have been monitored by researchers in the USA, who have followed their separate lifestyles. Where one twin has lived in a sedentary way and the other has been keen on fitness, the latter has invariably lived longer and enjoyed better health than the unfit sibling, despite each having the same genetic tendency to obesity and early death.

Similarly, you will live longer and retain a better quality of life than your parents if you keep fitter than they did when they had their chance.

Your fat gene decides how much of the fat you eat will be eliminated as surplus body heat and how much is stored as body fat. As a result you may have to work a lot harder than somebody else to reduce your waistline. But the overall fact remains that if you eat less fat – whatever your genetic make-up – you will *be* less fat. Conversely, individuals who run very fast marathons or win Olympic sprint races may have been blessed at birth with the very best relevant genes, but only years of dedicated hard work and skill-development will have enabled them to make the most of their inherited talents. There is a tendency for genetic characteristics to revert to the 'average' over the generations.

In addition to our genetic inheritance of fast- or slow-twitch muscles which make us more comfortable with sprinting or long-distance activity, we are born also as one of three basic body types, which I like to classify as Cherubs, String beans and Tarzans. You may think you fit into none of these categories, but you will certainly be more akin to one than to the other two.

- Cherubs are **endormorphs**, who are short, stocky and well rounded. They are often good long-distance swimmers.
- Tarzans are **mesomorphs**, with broad shoulders, narrow hips and above-average strength potential. They usually end up carrying the heaviest backpack in any group of ramblers.
- String beans, **ectomorphs**, are tall and thin, with narrow shoulders and neat midriffs. They make the best long-distance runners.

All this is just another genetic injustice, you may sigh if you ache to be a great marathon-runner but were born an endormorphic Cherub. Never mind, with the right fitness training, you can end up the top marathon Cherub in the country – and well ahead of millions of String beans who do not choose to enhance their God-given advantage with as ambitious an exercise level as yours.

I have enjoyed working with Mike Stroud on many strenuous endeavours over the years and I know it would probably be impossible to find a more affable yet strong-willed and physically tough individual than he is. When I eventually did the 1996 Eco-Challenge endurance race with his father, Vic, I soon recognised exactly the same rare qualities in the older man, an example of uniquely superior physical and mental resilience passing from father to son.

Schooldays and Childhood

Inactive children nearly always grow up to become adult couch potatoes. Bad eating habits also mar life for many people from cradle to grave via the school canteen. Hamburgers with chips and mayonnaise washed down with cola, year after year, make for fat, flabby children. The fast-food bars of the 1960s and 1970s have cleaned up their act a touch over the past two decades by pushing fruit and salad on their menus as health crazes swept North America and Europe, but bodies nurtured on solid fats naturally take a lot more training to whip into shape.

The number of adults whose childhood inheritance hangs around their necks, albatross-like, throughout their lives is increasing. In Britain nearly half of all men are overweight and one in nine is obese (roughly more than 20 per cent heavier than their ideal bodyweight – see chart on page 21). A third of women are overweight and one in seven is obese. The get-fit fad of the late 1980s has gone the way of the hula-hoop, and as a result the national obesity figure has more than doubled over the last decade. It is, after all, so easy to give in to the pleasures of biscuits and pastries and so incredibly difficult to abstain for any length of time.

A 1998 survey conducted at the Science Museum discovered that the average UK child consumes over a 10-year period 723lbs of fat – over 10 per cent more than is needed to stay healthy. Ninety per cent of boys said their favourite activity was computer games, and 45 per cent – 65 per cent of girls – said

---

Some Current Statistics Show Worrying Trends

- **40 per cent of eight-year-olds and 70 per cent of 12-year-olds in the UK have at least one preventable risk factor for heart disease: obesity, lack of activity, high blood pressure, poor cholesterol level and, for over 10-year-olds, smoking.**
- **Obesity is increasing in children. Eighty per cent of obese children will grow into obese adults. A sedentary lifestyle is largely to blame.**
- **47 per cent of girls and 38 per cent of boys at secondary schools do not take even the recommended minimum 10-minute brisk walk three times a week.**
- **Physical-education lessons are steadily decreasing in duration.**

---

they would prefer to watch sports than to participate. Instead today children watch up to 28 hours of television a week. Only 35 per cent of children walk or cycle to school. (For information on children's fitness classes, see page 192.)

At school in the 1950s, I spent a minimum of 40 minutes six days a week at some form of supervised physical exercise. When I left school I subconsciously wanted to continue being active because my body had been programmed that way, just as today's children are developing bodies that are cer-

tain to balk at any suggestion of physical exertion for the rest of their lives.

Although many health advances are enjoyed by children born over the past two decades – bonuses which did not previously exist, such as fluoride in water systems and ever-stricter controls on harmful pesticides and fertilisers – they have at the same time been subjected to new health threats. The lack of disciplines that were taken for granted when I was at school (which to me seems not so long ago) is slowly crippling many thousands of them. Rare is the teacher who dares tell his or her class to sit upright and watch their posture. The predominant schoolchild's 'writing position' is now that of a collapsed balloon. The entire class appears to be asleep. Only their writing hands move, their heads loll on their crooked arms over their desktops and their eyeballs are twisted sideways a biro's distance from their exercise books. This is asking for early trouble with their backs and vision. If you recognise any of the above as being partly or wholly applicable to your own upbringing, do not despair: my fitness system will help you to redemption – if you stick with it.

As for the next generation, parents can encourage their children by telling them health facts and stressing the minimum body need of three exercise sessions weekly. Activities should be fun and should match each child's stage of development. Remember that adolescents in particular can be put off fitness for life if they are forced to compete, especially if they suffer from some real or imagined physical defect.

Digestion

Another outside factor which stops us keeping fit is a poor digestive system. Later on I will describe how to look after yours without becoming a food martyr. But right now, let us look at the basics of digestion.

After you eat a big meal, especially one full of fatty ingredients, you often feel sleepy, as a general rule. The older you are, the more this is so. One reason for this is that your body is using up a great deal of energy digesting your meal. Some things are much easier to digest than others. A banana, for instance, is broken down and passed through the entire digestive system in only 35 minutes, whereas fatty red meat takes 35 hours and a lot more energy.

The digestive system begins in the mouth with the tongue and its 10,000-odd tastebuds, which can detect the tiniest difference in flavour. I have worked with Arab guides fighting communists in the Omani deserts, who could tell blindfolded which water came from which one of 20 widely dispersed desert wells. French wine-tasting experts can detect over 1,000 different vintages and their tastebuds still work well into their 90s. Saliva starts the pre-digestion work, breaking down starch as you chew.

If you eat something rich in sugar, like a banana, digestion is fast, smooth and effortless. The sugar is stabilised on the stomach wall by your gastric juices and then moves onward in a trouble-free way through the system. If you eat both sugar and starch, which takes longer to digest, in the same dish or the same meal, much of the sugar will hang around in the middle of the stomach, away from the walls where the gastric juices are at work. This is because whatever is eaten last will always settle in mid stomach in the fermentation zone. The lesson is clear: sweet things should not be eaten on a full stomach or in a starch–sugar combination.

Along with the nose, which activates the appetite, our eyes also have a part to play, since the mere sight of food can trigger the digestive system. Even the thought of unseen food sets off reflex digestive actions and releases gastric juices. Six pints of different acids move about daily in our stomachs (one of which is hydrochloric acid), and normally they do a fine job of killing food bacteria, stabilising sugars and breaking down proteins. But if our thoughts are screwed up due to tension or distress, our digestion can be directly and often chaotically affected. Different emotions can cause too much gastric acid to flood the stomach, leading to ulcers, while too little makes for inconsistent digestion. Thus stress upsets the digestive activities taking place along the 4,300-square-ft surface of the digestive canal, and interrupts the daily production of the 2 pints of saliva necessary to lubricate the swallowing process.

Stress

The effects of stress do not merely make it more difficult for us to keep fit and healthy by digesting food properly; they can even lead to death. Under stress we become increasingly vulnerable to certain cancers. Stress can also be lethal for people with coronary troubles.

Dedication to any fitness regime we may be following is likely to be put to the test by stress. If we are reformed smokers, stress will tempt us to light up again; if we are dieting, stress will tempt us to pig out, and often the routine of even the most dedicated exerciser can be thrown to the winds by the sudden advent of a stressful event. Sleep often suffers, and depression and irritability then set in.

My fitness system includes the handling of stress. Three years ago I wrote a best-selling book entitled *Mind Over Matter* which dealt with thought control under great physical and mental pressures. Later in this book I will explain how I apply thought control to minimise day-to-day stress, whether in business or merely when overtaking a car when oncoming headlights are blinding you.

This chapter has looked at outside factors which affect our individual health, such as our genes, environment and stress points. The next three chapters will deal with what we can do individually to maximise our fitness potential while minimising interference from these outside factors.

When 20,000 individuals go to a marathon they know that the race organisers will have placed large signs, spaced out over the first 500 yards of the route, marked 'two hours', 'three hours' and so on. Entrants decide where to start from according to the time in which they each expect to complete the marathon. Yet many will start way back at the four-hour marker even though they may have done the race in a much quicker time in the past. Perhaps they have not run for a year or two, or they may be uncertain of their current fitness. At this stage, you might likewise choose to move on to a later part of this book because you already know all the basics about food control, and how best to elevate your fitness from couch-potato level, or you may decide to stay with it just in case you pick up something new, such as a different, easier approach to an exercise you may have been doing for years.

If you are one of those who have never before bothered with self-imposed fitness regimes or food control, read on. This initial stage is the hardest step on the road to reaching your maximum potential. Changing from a more or less sedentary lifestyle to an active one is a shock to the system, so you need to take a lot of basic information on board before you catch the fitness bus, or you will soon fall off it. Don't get frustrated and disgruntled because you have reached this page and still you are not leaping up and down all over the place.

Just as the point at which a marathon entrant starts cannot be cast in tablets of stone, so there is no hard and fast rule to tell you at which precise level of activity or food control you should begin your regime. That will depend upon your goals, your age and on the outside factors already discussed. But the following few chapters aim to cover all the information you will need to progress from a mostly sedentary life to becoming gently active and eating sensibly.

Later stages of the book will take you on to being fitter than the average human being and using food control to give you excellent health.

The last chapter of the book will try to tempt you to dabble in extreme sports like Iron Man and Triathlon, where you use mind over matter, complex carbohydrates-loading and programmed physical training to reach the top of the ladder.

3

General Food Control: What is Good?

First of all, let's consider the background principles to food control and its interaction with exercise. In the diet of the vast majority of people in the West, over 40 per cent of calorie intake comes from fat. This contributes hugely to their bad health and early deaths from cancer and heart disease.

Unfortunately, it is difficult to switch to the correct, safe fat-intake level, which is no more than 30 per cent, because nature has expressly designed our bodies to store fat in readiness for times of famine. You are not likely to run into a famine, of course, but your body does not know that. So it continues to make you crave for more fat than you need by telling you you are hungry when you are not. Non-nutritious junk food is the worst for telling our brains that we are still hungry. Waste products from junk food tend to clog up the filaments which line our intestines. This hinders the absorption of nutrients into our bodies which, in turn, triggers our brains to order us to eat more.

If you progress through life giving in to these 'fat need' cravings you will, as you age, become fatter. You can exercise as much as you like but your health and your silhouette will always leave a lot to be desired. So, in tandem with any exercise programmes, you need to clean up your act on the food front, at least when you are at home. When you cook a meal you can choose what ingredients you use, but when you go out to a party or a restaurant it is less easy to monitor what you are eating. And you may find it difficult, even embarrassing, for both you and your friends, if you make a big thing about eating only healthy food. However, the food you select when you shop for yourself can and should be controlled. Keep junk out of your house (and your car). If you can develop a sensible approach to your food intake on the simple basis of knowing what is good and what is bad, your overall fitness regime will be more efficient.

Office work, hotel-hopping and international travel are ways of life for many of us, but the lack of exercise and excess junk food they involve don't do our bodies any favours. We try to make amends with exercise on a haphazard basis, aiming perhaps for a gentle run when we can fit it in, but this is nowhere near enough to cope with the amounts of fat our brains will be constantly telling us to consume.

People living in Mediterranean societies are no

less greedy than anyone else, yet they suffer far less from heart disease, cancers and other fat-related degenerative diseases. In fact, the inhabitants of rural Crete live longer, healthier lives than any other localised group in the world. Their secret lies in the *sort* of fats they consume. The food-control systems which follow take this into account. Conversely, 65 per cent of all Americans are technically overweight, 44 per cent of them clinically obese. Many try to diet but end up confused because the great diet experts constantly contradict one another. I have tried a great many diets and none have worked because my natural desire to eat and the sheer pleasure I derive from food defeats my willpower every time. For this reason my system does not include a diet as such. Instead it identifies good and bad foods and steers you clear of the latter.

Much of what we eat today also contains chemicals with which our digestive systems were not designed to cope. Processed foods are anything but natural, and fresh foods are divested of much of their goodness when we cook them, especially if they are fried in fat. The chemicals which are not used by the body are instead stored as waste in fatty-tissue larders which include our buttocks, chins, thighs and upper arms.

The solution is to concentrate as much on quality control as on quantity. Experiments with rats and monkeys show that those kept in a slightly underfed state remain the healthiest and live longest. The unmistakable deduction, which in theory applies equally to humans, is that calorific restrictions are a factor in long, healthy lives. But the downside of calorific quantity control is putting up with a life of nagging hunger. Besides, few people can remember detailed information about calorific values and protein-balance factors, and nobody can be bothered carrying a food chart about with them. Fanaticism about food can in any case become obsessive and self-defeating. The answer, as with so many things, seems to lie in compromise. The best way of avoiding what is bad is to remember what is good and stick to it. At the same time, remember that, if you can bear it, less is better.

You can be perfectly healthy, fit and a capable marathon-runner despite being what you may think of as fat. So what body weight should you aim for? Is there an ideal weight for you? Fatness in terms of a firm but definite pot belly may not detract from your health or fitness but merely offend your vanity. This being so, the weight and shape that you crave will not be relevant to your health and is therefore both impossible and pointless to determine. However, the chart on the opposite page, produced by Australian fitness doctors, which pegs weight to height (even though it ignores everything else) can serve as a rough guide to avoiding obesity, if you define obese as being 20 per cent more than the weight which the chart recommends for you.

Once you have a good idea of the best foods to eat you need to develop a routine so that you eat your main meals in rhythm with your body clock – *not* at any old time when you feel like it. Through more than six decades of research, nutritionists have learned that the human body works best to a repeating eight-hour clock. Obviously it is not always practical to adhere to this rigidly but if you keep as close to it as you can, you will sleep better and digest more efficiently. The clock runs thus:

Midday to 8pm: The time for eating and digesting.

8pm to 4am: The time for assimilating food into the body.

4am to midday: The time to get rid of food wastes.

To enable this schedule to run efficiently you should do most of your eating between midday and 8pm. Most of us have developed the habit of eating three big meals daily topped up by snacks in between. Evening meals are often eaten much later

Height/Weight Chart

Example: On this chart a six-foot person weighing 13 stone would be close to the border between correct weight and overweight.

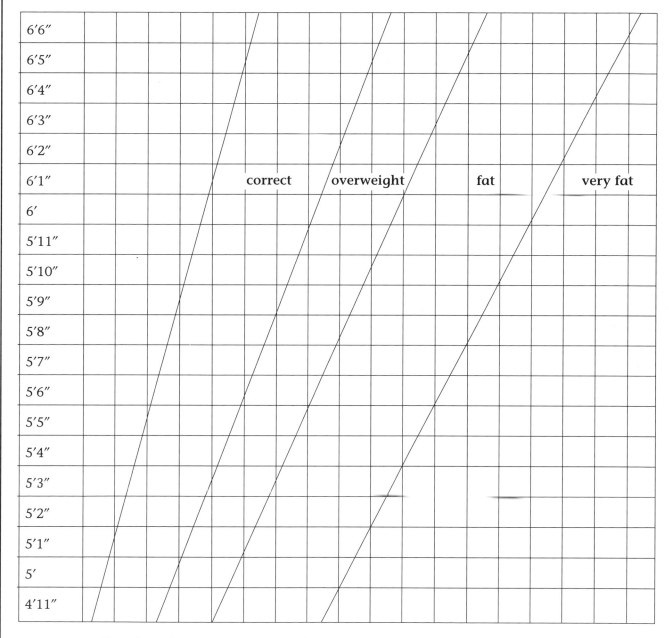

Note: 1 foot = 0.3 metres (12 inches = 1 foot)
1 pound = 0.45 kilos (14lbs = 1 stone)

than 8pm and breakfasts, especially in Britain, are traditionally heavy-duty events based on the Victorian advice 'Breakfast like a king, lunch like a prince and dine like a pauper'. There are some nutritionists who advise big breakfasts and others who agree with the eight-hour-clock system, which works best when breakfast consists of only fruit and water. I have tried both, and feel far fitter with the latter. Additionally, from a fat-loss point of view, the clock system with fruit breakfasts wins hands down.

Although fewer people nowadays go in for huge breakfasts, we still tend to eat first thing in the morning foods which are difficult to digest. And at the other end of the scale, some of us rush off to work without eating anything at all. The best possible stratagem to encourage efficient, uninterrupted disposal of food wastes is to extend the 'sleeping' period (obviously the easiest time to avoid snacks!) until midday, by eating only foodstuffs that digest easily, such as fruit. More about this later, but in general, try to eat nothing but fruit (or nuts) until midday, however much this goes against the grain, to eat your last meal of the day before 8pm, and not to mix fruit with other foods.

The food details which follow are accepted worldwide as being the best basis for nourishing the healthiest of bodies and for staving off degenerative illnesses such as cancer, heart disease and arteriosclerosis. I have listed foods which provide the vitamins and minerals we need without at this stage explaining what we need them for. It is enough for the moment to take an overview of our diet, cut out what is bad and focus on what is good. More specific dietary information for those who aspire to higher levels of fitness is given in Chapter 12.

Fruit

Fruit is *the* panacea for good health. There are a great many reasons why fruit is our best friend and our mainstay, not least that, as we saw in Chapter 2, the human body system, from hands and teeth to digestive juices, was designed to cope superbly with fruit and not with meat, or even cereals. The second main reason is that nothing fulfils our vitamin, mineral and toxin-cleansing water needs more effectively than fruit. Like the vast majority of other animals, we need to eat high water-content foods, ideally 70 per cent water, and fruits are top of the list in this respect. The quicker and easier food is to digest, the better it is for our health, and as we have already noted, typical digestion time for most fruits is 30 minutes, as opposed to 35 hours for red, fatty meat at the other end of the scale.

You must remember not to eat fruit either with or just after other foods. The common habit of having fruit as a dessert or an apple with lunch is not a good one, because the acid in the fruit causes any proteins or carbohydrates it meets in the 'mixing bowl' of the stomach to putrefy. This leads to more toxic waste heading towards our 'fat larders' and to stomach-aches. Fruit is absolutely the best foodstuff for our health, but only when kept an hour, or better still two, away from carbohydrate- or protein-consumption.

Bananas

Ripe bananas are one of your top weapons in food control. They are to chocolate biscuits what nicotine patches are to cigarettes. They are sufficiently filling to help stave off hunger pangs, yet at the same time they are beneficial to the body. Bananas are easy to store and rich in potassium, a mineral especially important to many of our bodily functions. They release natural sugars quickly into our bloodstream, which makes them ideal for runners and athletes.

Apples

Easy to carry to work or play, and less squashable than bananas or oranges, apples are high in vitamin C and beneficial fructose (a type of sugar). Always check with your supplier which are the sweetest type available as biting into a single sour apple can put you off them for weeks.

Oranges

Unlike bananas and apples, oranges, along with other citrus fruits, are not ideal for everyone. Arthritis sufferers should steer clear of citrus fruits, as well as pineapples, strawberries, gooseberries, blackberries, blackcurrants, tomatoes, damsons, plums and especially rhubarb, all of which combine with any lingering carbohydrates to form uric acid. But for non-arthritics, oranges and the whole citrus family provide vitamin C, and the B vitamins thiamine and folic acid. An orange, grapefruit or tangerine every morning is good news.

Pears

One pear contains some 72 calories including natural sugar, fibre, vitamin C and potassium. Pears are one of the least allergenic foods.

Peaches

Very tasty, and only 30 calories, rich in vitamin C and easy to digest. But beware of canned peaches in syrup, which are high in calories and will have lost most of their vitamin C.

Kiwi Fruit

Originally known as the Chinese gooseberry before it was popularised by New Zealand farmers, this furry, egg-shaped fruit is rich in potassium, vitamin C and soluble fibre which helps rid the body of 'bad' cholesterol.

Grapes

Always wash grapes before you eat them as their skins are especially prone to retaining traces of pesticides and fungicides. Grapes are relatively low in calories – a handful yields about 60 – a good source of potassium and a useful antioxidant (see pages 144–145). Red grapes can, however, give some people migranes.

Mangos

Messy to prepare and eat, but mangos are growing in popularity and widely available in supermarkets. They are rich in betacarotene and vitamin C, both active antioxidants.

Berries

Fresh berries, such as strawberries, raspberries and blackberries, are low in calories but contain plenty of vitamin C and potassium and have antioxidant properties. However, avoid berries if you suffer from arthritis.

Plums/Prunes

Rich in vitamin E and potassium. Prunes are the dried version.

Figs

High in fibre and help prevent constipation. Dried figs are rich in potassium, iron, calcium and natural sugar.

Dates

As an army captain in the 1960s, I spent many months in remote desert areas, living with Omani Arabs and eating what they ate. Dates and rice provided 80 per cent of our daily food intake and, despite non-stop, energy-sapping patrol activity, we remained fit and healthy. I have been keen on dates ever since. They are rich in nutrients, including vitamin C and potassium. I keep jars of them in my office at home to help me avoid chocolate biscuits between meals.

Raisins

Raisins are one of the best high-calorie, low-fat foods. I take them on man-haul expeditions as en-route snacks to ward off hypoglycaemia. They have a high natural sugar content, plus lots of iron and potassium.

Nuts

All nuts are packed with vitamins. Walnuts can help prevent heart disease by lowering 'bad' cholesterol levels and, like peanuts and hazelnuts, they are especially rich in those fatty acids needed for tissue growth. All nuts, except chestnuts, are extremely high in calories, but if you are worried about weight, choose chestnuts, which are best roasted or boiled. You do need to take care with nuts. Almond consumption can lead to food poisoning. Children can choke to death on nuts, and peanuts (especially those sold in bulk rather than in sealed packets) are prone to a fungus that can cause liver cancer and kill. Some individuals are allergic to peanuts and can become seriously ill from consuming even the merest trace of peanut extract.

Seeds

Like nuts, seeds make good snacks, especially pumpkin, sunflower and sesame seeds. It is best to roast them since raw seeds can contain toxins which cause diarrhoea. Beware of salted seeds if you are trying to avoid sodium. The carob pod is touted as a preferable alternative to chocolate since it contains no caffeine. However, it is just as fattening.

Cider Vinegar (made from fermented apple juice) I list cider vinegar high in the rankings because, taken with honey, it has rid me of the arthritis I suffered for years. If you have any reason for thinking you may be prone to arthritis, I strongly recommend **Honegar**, which is obtainable from most health-food shops. Cider vinegar bestows many other health benefits, too.

Vegetables

My food-control methods do not extend to any of the specific forms of vegetarianism, but I acknowledge the obvious benefits of them all. There are plenty of extremely fit vegetarians about, including a Mr Universe muscleman (Bill Pearl) and an Iron Man Triathlon champion (David Scott), and you do not see many fat vegetarians. They take in less 'bad' cholesterol and more fibre and antioxidants, thus greatly reducing their risk of succumbing to heart disease or cancer.

Weaning yourself off meat is surprisingly easy. Any yearnings that linger are as nothing compared with the lasting cravings suffered during cigarette or chocolate withdrawal. The problem with refusing meat is often more of a social thing, and it certainly does not help if your wife or husband or partner adores meat as mine does. If you do decide to stop eating meat, beware of the common trap: compensating with dairy products rich in saturated fats.

You should also be aware that a lack of vitamin B12, which is provided predominantly by animal sources, renders you vulnerable to tuberculosis, currently the world's greatest infectious killer. *Small amounts of dairy food and eggs are your best alternative sources of B12.* If you are pregnant and a vegetarian or a vegan (that is, you eat only foods of plant origin), it is especially important to check with your doctor that your food intake is not deficient in any key vitamin or mineral. A good vegan insurance against protein deficiency is to eat plenty of nuts.

Quite how fruit and vegetables protect the body from many cancers has not been established, but statistics show that this protection unquestionably exists. Scientists believe that phytochemicals (i.e., plant chemicals), found in all fruit and vegetables, contain antioxidants which neutralise marauding free radicals, which can be harmful to our DNA and to healthy cells (see Chapter 12).

Raw fruit and vegetables are usually better for you than cooked ones and undercooking is better than overcooking. Much of the goodness is often in the skin, provided that it has been well scrubbed to remove toxic spray residues. If you are able to grow your own, you can avoid the spray problem. Beneficial phytochemicals are found in abundance in cruciferous vegetables, which include **broccoli, radishes, cauliflower, brussels sprouts, cabbage, kale** and **turnips**.

Spinach

I used to eat huge quantities of spinach as a teenager in the misguided belief that, since Popeye and many contemporary nutritionists extolled the strength-giving magic of this vegetable so rich in iron, it rendered weightlifting unnecessary. In fact spinach is no richer in iron than many other similar vegetables, but it does contain an above-average supply of beneficial vitamins. People tend to plaster boiled spinach leaves with butter, which does not help weight-watchers. A good way to eat it is chopped up raw in a salad.

Because my body is inclined to manufacture kidney stones, I no longer eat spinach more than once a week because it is rich in oxalic acid, which can encourage stone-formation in susceptible individuals.

Broccoli

Even more healthy than the much-vaunted spinach. It is best eaten raw and cut up in salads, but still retains most of its goodness when frozen or cooked.

Beetroot

Beetroot is full of vitamins and has no known downside, save for its tendency to stain cooking pots. This can be avoided by cooking the vegetable unpeeled. Blended beetroot and carrot juice is an ultra-healthy drink, and I often have a glass of this at lunchtime.

Carrots

In my late teens, when I was hoping for selection by the SAS, who do much of their work at night, I ate a dozen or so raw carrots daily in the quest for better night vision. Scientists say that this does work, because of the high vitamin A content of carrots. During our continuation training in north Wales, suffice it to say that three of my SAS colleagues fell over a cliff at night and I did not. I have been a carrot fan ever since.

Raw carrots taste excellent, but they do need to be cooked if the betacarotene they contain is to be fully absorbed into our body systems. Betacarotene converts into vitamin A, a good free radical-fighter. Carrot-fly pesticide residues must be removed by slicing off the top and bottom and lightly scraping the rest of the carrot.

Peas

Peas are a good source of folic acid, thiamine, fibre and phosphorus.

Lettuce

There are many varieties of lettuce, and most of them taste rather bland. As a result we tend to drown them with oily dressings, which do not help our silhouettes. That apart, lettuces are an excellent source of vitamins, the darker the leaves the better. So you should resist the temptation to automatically chuck away the outer, possibly sad-looking leaves, since they are actually the richest in goodness.

Lettuces are 90 per cent water and can therefore help to satisfy your appetite without stacking up the calories.

Mushrooms

There is little to be said for eating mushrooms, wild or commercial, in terms of vitamin input. But they do add flavour to salads and they are not fattening. Eating them to excess can be dangerous because they easily absorb pollutants from the soil and the atmosphere, and they do contain elements known to be carcinogenic when consumed in large quantities.

Tomatoes

Although tomatoes are classified as a fruit, most people treat them as vegetables. They are chock-a-block with goodness, delicious in salads and low in calories. Recent research has linked them with the prevention of prostate cancer. Tomatoes should be avoided, however, by arthritics and anyone suffering from migraines, eczema or allergies found to be triggered by tomatoes.

Avocados

The wonderful taste and texture of avocados make them a must for delectable salads. Like tomatoes, they are a fruit in vegetable clothing. Weight-watchers must beware, since a single avocado can contain 400 calories. However, this includes a high percentage of monounsaturated fats which help fight against high levels of 'bad' cholesterol. No fruit has more protein content and few are packed with so much goodness, providing they are eaten before they get too soft and squidgy.

Garlic

Garlic is the number-one root vegetable. It contains allicin, which reduces blood pressure and protects against heart disease. Other ingredients help to ward off stomach and colon cancers. Recent scientific research indicates that garlic capsules designed to reduce tainted breath lose the effectiveness of their allicin. Other bulbs such as **onions** and **leeks** are also believed to slow down the development of cancerous cells.

Complex Carbohydrates

When I grew up, and certainly well into the 1960s, many people equated pasta and potatoes with hanging bellies and obesity. However, once nutritionists began to realise that people could be top athletes without eating protein, food control took a new turn which upset traditional thinking.

A typical Western diet contains 48 per cent carbohydrate, 10 per cent protein and 42 per cent fat. A healthy diet for non-athletes should be 58 per cent carbohydrates, 12 per cent protein and 30 per cent fat. Athletes (involved in heavy training) should have 70 per cent carbohydrates, 10 per cent in the form of simple sugars.

Over the past 30 years it has become accepted that energy is the key to athletic success, and that this is best obtained through a preponderance of carbohydrates.

Pasta

Wholemeal pasta is a low-fat high-energy food extremely rich in fibre and vitamins and made from semolina, the high-protein part of wheat. For lunch I pour a mugful into a lidless saucepan of boiling water and boil it for six minutes. After draining, I add olive oil and a touch of black pepper and eat with a vegetable salad. It is important to serve and eat the pasta quickly or it becomes sticky. Make sure you use wholemeal rather than ordinary pasta.

There are obviously other ways you may prefer to cook pasta, and boiling time is up to you, but do not succumb to the temptation of using butter, cream sauces or cheese to liven it up if you are worried about your shape. Vegetables such as spinach and tomatoes are a better choice.

Rice

In the SAS Officers' Mess in Hereford in the 1960s there were many old Malaya hands who adored curry and white rice, and I acquired a taste for it, especially for fried white rice. More recent complex-carbohydrate training has redirected me to boiled brown rice and wild rice. I take half a mug daily as an alternative to pasta. After washing and cooking the rice I rinse it in hot water in a sieve to prevent the grains from sticking, and again add olive oil and a touch of pepper and eat it with a fresh vegetable salad.

Endurance and Complex Carbohydrate Requirements

I never select individuals for long man-haul expeditions who are under 32 because they rarely reach their peak of endurance ability from a mental point of view before that age. Neither do I look at any new candidates above the age of 38, because, physically speaking, they are usually over the hill by then. With a team of keen, fit individuals between the ages of 32 and 38 we stand a good chance of success against our international rivals, usually younger men, on any expedition requiring extreme endurance. My problem, of course, has been that when I passed the age of 38 myself I was applying one rule to me and another to the rest of the team. This has been embarrassing, so I needed to find some way of staying as fit or, if possible, fitter than the others. By the time I reached 40 I realised that exercise alone was not enough. I needed to build my body up in a way which would enable me to cope well with extreme cold and hypothermic vulnerability, despite months of starvation and physical toil.

And for my post-1990 expeditions, it was clear that I was going to have to be super-fit. Up to the mid-1980s our polar journeys had involved travel supported by parachuted supplies, which meant that the loads we had to tow by sledge were not too heavy. But by 1990 we had set new world records for polar travel, beating our rivals to achieving the first journey via both poles and crossing both icecaps. To keep ahead of the competition, our next challenge had to be the race to cross the Antarctic continent – bigger by far than both India and China stuffed together into a single, vast and unpopulated land mass – *without* outside support. To succeed in making such a crossing each team member would need to drag sledge-loads of 500lbs, practically three times our body weights. The weather, the temperatures and the short summer allow only 100 travellable days in Antarctica, so we would have to complete an average of 16 miles every single day for over three months. Just one rest day could lead to failure.

A typical marathon-runner carrying nothing at all uses up 3,000 calories during the 26-mile race. He or she will wear light clothes, usually run in moderate temperatures and rest for many days before attempting a second marathon. To man-haul the Antarctic continent, we would need to wear heavy clothes and boots, climbing to 11,000ft above sea-level, and burning an average of 6,000 calories a day. We would therefore need unprecedented reserves of stored energy (glycogen) in our muscles. Only *complex carbohydrates*, consumed regularly over a period of time, could build up such reserves. The feat appeared physically impossible, even for young, very fit ski experts. My colleague Dr Mike Stroud and I were aged 38 and 49 respectively and, being British, we were indifferent skiers. It was apparent that our only chance of success was to become ultra-fit. On paper, it seemed unlikely that a man of my age, who was not a trained athlete, could achieve such a condition. However, there was no alternative but to try. So, in addition to a six-month regime of strenuous training, I followed the advice of a sports nutritionist, Dr Brian Welsby, and began to prepare a bowl of complex carbohydrates for lunch every day in addition to my normal food intake.

With my much younger rival Erling Kagge of Norway, waiting for the airlift to Antarctica from Punta Arenas in Chile. Mike Stroud

Potatoes

Potatoes are high-carbohydrate and protein-rich with potassium and fibre. Baked potatoes in their jackets are healthiest and not fattening, so long as you don't add mayonnaise or butter. Low-fat cheese or avocado provide tasty fillings. Eat with a salad.

Bread

Wholemeal bread is far better for your health than white bread. I eat four slices a day between lunch and tea. The complex carbohydrates of the wholemeal reduce 'bad' cholesterol levels and the fibre helps guard against some cancers. Iron, calcium and various key vitamins are important additional benefits. Bread is not fattening if you don't smear it with a thick layer of butter and jam. Marmite makes a great topping.

Lightly toasted bread helps to break down the gluten, which makes digestion easier.

Bran

Bran is the outer husk of wheat, oat or rice grains. Apart from its value as a complex carbohydrate, it is a rich source of fibre or roughage. I eat a bowl of cereal daily to which I add a maximum of three teaspoons of oatbran.

Cereals

Many popular brands of cereal are low in fibre and a waste of space. Concentrate on wholegrain cereals which are as natural as possible. Go for low-sodium and low-sugar kinds, for obvious reasons. I usually eat my cereal at teatime, about an hour after taking exercise. If I am having a business breakfast, and cannot stick to fruit, I will take cereal then. I use good helpings of Jumbo Porridge Oats and Jordan's standard Muesli Crunch, my three teaspoons of oat-bran, semi-skimmed milk and a tablespoon of runny Exmoor honey. Oatmeal lowers blood pressure and reduces 'bad' cholesterol levels. My cereal bowl packs a high carbohydrate punch and contains loads of protein, fibre and B vitamins.

Proteins

The protein portion of our diet should be selected with care. High-quality proteins include fish, poultry, meat, soya beans and eggs. We can obtain the same nutritional benefits from the proteins of beans and wheat eaten together as we can from meat.

Eating protein is vital because all body cells need it for growth and tissue repair. However, the necessary daily dose is a mere 2oz (55 grams) for a robust adult male, and most of us eat far more than that every day of the year. This is bad for our health because since the body has no means of storing the excess protein, it merely converts it to acidic urine and glucose, which puts great strain on the liver and kidneys and can cause arthritis and osteoporosis. I have spent many months on physically demanding expeditions when our high-calorie, lightweight food packs have contained no meat or fish at all, just soya-bean substitutes – vegetable protein is less harmful than animal protein.

Protein is made up of amino acids, and our digestive system breaks it back down into these vital derivatives, many of which perform key individual functions, so we need all of them all the time, just as a car needs brake fluid and engine oil as well as petrol. Key sources of protein include:

Fish

Fish-eaters around the world, such as the Japanese, live longer than the rest of us and have a lower incidence of senile dementia. This could be a giant coincidence, but nutritionists put it down to the life-giving properties of Omega 3 fatty acid, which is present in all oily fish. These include **salmon**, **sardines**, **tuna**, **oysters** and **rainbow trout**, fresh or canned. Eat fish grilled with a salad or vegetables – not in batter with chips. I eat fish three times a week, usually canned because fresh fish is unavailable where I live. If you are travelling or cannot for some other reason get hold of fish, you can always carry Omega 3 fish-oil capsules (take 1,000mg daily).

Fish canned in brine is preferable to that in sunflower oil. If you can only get the latter, pour the oil away before eating the fish.

Poultry

Chicken, **duck**, **goose** and **turkey** all contain plenty of protein, vitamins and minerals. The browner meat is richer than the white. You should always avoid the skin, which is full of the kind of fat that does you no good and raises 'bad' cholesterol levels. I always go for free-range chickens (and eggs) to minimise the risk of salmonella food poisoning.

Soya Beans

Soya beans contain genistein, which fights cancer and other degenerative diseases. When choosing soya products, go for soya protein *foods*, but avoid hydrogenated soya-bean oil, or even plain soya-bean oil, as they contain harmful fats.

Tofu

Tofu is a bland-tasting curd much favoured in Asia. It is made from cooked soya beans, ground to produce soy milk, which is then solidified with calcium sulphate. Healthfood shops and many supermarkets sell tofu as a cure-all, high in protein and low in bad fats, which fights arthritis, cancer and heart disease. Their claims are genuine; however, tofu is a pain in the neck to store, does not keep for long and is difficult to render even remotely interesting to the palate unless you doctor it with fatty 'nasties'. But if you can find a way of liking it, tofu will do you a lot of good and no harm.

Protein Requirements *(grams per day)*						
	up to 1 yr	*1–3 yrs*	*4–6 yrs*	*7–10 yrs*	*11–14 yrs*	*15–18 yrs*	*19+ yrs*
Male	14.9	14.5	19.7	28.3	42.1	55.2	55.5
Female	14.9	14.5	19.7	28.3	42.2	45	45

Fats

Fat, of all foods, is the most concentrated source of energy. Reducing fat intake is the most effective way to reduce your calorie count. There are 'good' fats and 'bad' fats. What I mean by 'bad' fats are the saturated fats from animal foods such as fatty meat, butter or full-cream milk, and poly-unsaturated fats. The bad ones often taste the best and are the most satisfying when contained in foods like biscuits, chocolates and ice-cream. Sadly, these bad fats lead to raised blood levels of bad cholesterol, obesity, heart disease, cancer and arthritis, and they will kill you (albeit slowly if you are lucky and if you take exercise). They will also very effectively counteract your best attempts to reach peak performance. It is better to eat low-fat alternatives like lean meat and skimmed milk which contain fewer of these fats. The best fats are monounsaturated, which are easiest for our digestive system to break down, and there is evidence that they lower levels of bad cholesterol in the blood.

Free radicals, the chemical compounds that wreak havoc with our body tissues (see Chapter 12), can enter our systems as rancid fat or fat that has been oxidised. Oxygen will be absorbed in seconds by saturated and polyunsaturated fats, so we must learn to avoid like the plague all foods containing them in order to keep free radicals to a minimum. Frying and cooking in butter, margarine, or any animal fats is courting trouble. By far the least damaging cooking fat is **extra-virgin olive oil**, which contains only 8 per cent of bad saturated fats, compared with 16 per cent for plain olive oil and 76 per cent for regular safflower oil. Swedish research indicates that use of olive oil can halve the risk of breast cancer, whereas a study of 61,000 women aged between 40 and 76 who ate polyunsaturated fat from corn oil and sunflower oils showed that they increased their risk of the disease by 69 per cent.

I lived for many months in Inuit villages in northern Canada and Alaska, and I used to wonder why they have such a low death rate from heart disease. They consume horrendous helpings of seal, whale and fish fat, often soaked in greasy blubber soup. The answer is, of course, that whereas bad fats kill, good fats are beneficial, indeed vital. They provide support and protection for our organs as well as an insulation layer under our skin to prevent heat loss. They help produce hormones and they delay the time the stomach takes to empty out digesting food, thus prolonging our sense of satiation. In addition fat yields more than twice as much energy per ounce as carbohydrates.

Water

Water is the one thing our bodies need above all else. An adult male is made up of 60 per cent water and females 50 per cent. To achieve weight loss before a weigh-in jockeys, boxers and other sports-people often stop drinking and dehydrate in saunas. Since every pint we drink weighs about 1lb this seems the quickest possible way to reduce weight. However, water loss can cause so much damage to our system that any water dieting is potentially dangerous. Water is the basic solvent for all the products of the digestive system and a shortage will lead to all manner of afflictions caused by toxic wastes in the body.

In 1993 I was asked to start the London Marathon. A few days earlier the Grand National starter had made a mess of things and the race had been abandoned as a result, so Chris Brasher, the marathon organiser, warned me to be careful. 'If you get it wrong,' he said, 'we will never be able to halt the forward momentum of over 20,000 runners!' The start was fine, but later, on Tower Bridge, as I watched the finish – Eamonn Martin won the race – I saw a very fit veteran entrant, whose time was about three hours, stagger and fall some 400 yards short of the finishing line. He tried to continue, but he was in a bad way. In spite of medical attention, he died within minutes. He had let himself become dehydrated. It is possible to lose 8 per cent of your entire body mass while running a marathon or performing some other equally strenuous activity.

When man-hauling in Antarctica, where the atmosphere is as dry as that of any hot desert, I lose a great deal of moisture through exertion: two thirds of a pint daily merely by breathing. Water lost in such a manner must be quickly replaced as even quite small changes in the water content of our body cells can cause serious bodily functional changes. One such is dehydration, which can lead to heat-stroke. When fluid loss exceeds a mere 2 per cent of

body weight, physical performance is impaired, and body temperature and heart rate increase. A water loss of just 9 per cent of our body weight can and often does prove fatal, yet we can survive a 40 per cent loss of our body weight in protein, fat and carbohydrates.

A marathon-runner is advised to drink about a pint of water every 30 minutes throughout the race, whether he or she feels thirsty or not – human thirst always underestimates water loss. Our built-in thirst sensation fails progressively as we age, which leads to our bodies becoming increasingly dehydrated. We often confuse thirst with hunger for food, so we eat when we should be drinking. One easy way to avoid this is to drink two glasses of water before every meal, ideally 30 minutes or more before eating, though even if it is only a few seconds earlier it will help.

Whether or not you are taking exercise, the way to maximise benefit from water intake is to drink small amounts often rather than, say, three pints in one go.

The colour of your urine can indicate whether or not you are drinking enough water. It should be colourless to light yellow: dark yellow is a sign of dehydration and means you should drink more.

In addition to eating fruit and vegetables with a high water content, I drink eight glasses of water a day. This flushes out my system, rinses sugar from the fruit off my teeth, helps clean my kidneys to prevent urinary infection and stones, lubricates my joints and eyes and keeps down my hunger for food. Indeed, together with fruit, water forms the basis of my food-control habits. When I wake up I run the cold tap (never drink from the hot-water tank – there may be a dead rat in it. Harmful metals from pipes also leach into the hot water) and drink two glasses of water slowly. By lunchtime I will usually have drunk two more. If you dislike the taste of your tap water, keep stocks of bottled water (still, not sparkling) at home.

It is a common myth that daily liquid input can be taken in the form of coffee, cola or alcoholic drinks which are, after all, over 90 per cent water. These all contain dehydrating and often carcinogenic ingredients and are harmful unless taken in extreme moderation. Coffee and cola contain caffeine, which increases the risk of heart disease, and cola is especially bad for anyone worried about weight. Alcohol, on the other hand, does have some benefits.

Alcohol

Although alcohol contributes to 24,000 deaths in Britain annually, *moderate* amounts (one or, at most, two glasses of red wine daily) help protect against heart disease. You should drink wine (or any alcohol) before a meal, ideally 30 minutes or more earlier, to prevent it fermenting food within the stomach. Red wine contains antioxidants which may reduce certain cancer risks and, like aspirin, reduce the blood clotting which leads to heart disease. Other alcoholic drinks have lesser anti-clotting effects and are more addictive.

For some reason Royal Tokaji wine from Hungary (see page 195) has enjoyed a remarkable reputation for helping to remedy a variety of illnesses for over three centuries. It is, however, quite expensive.

Tea

Although tea contains two thirds as much caffeine as coffee, it also has powerful antioxidants, like those in red wine, which mitigate heart-disease risks and fight cancer. Many hospital research studies evaluate tea-drinking in moderation as good for the health, whether black, green or herbal leaves are used. Drink two cups daily at most, unsugared, and with as little milk as you can manage.

Storage and Preparation

Poor storage of fresh fruit and vegetables can lessen their nutritional value. I keep fruit and vegetables in a standard 'larder' fridge, which has a temperature range more suitable to chilling fruit and vegetables than a typical domestic refrigerator. If you find it easy to shop for fresh food every three or four days, then you can probably manage without a 'larder'.

As a general rule you should eat fruit and vegetables within three days of buying them (as fresh as you can) and keep them chilled in the interim. Bananas are best kept in a cool room, and if purchased just ripened (more yellow than green, but unblotched), they will retain their full range of nutritional benefits for a good five days. If possible shop for fruit and vegetables in small quantities and often, rather than buying so much that they will spoil before being eaten.

- Cut vegetables into big chunks. The more surfaces you expose, the more vitamins leach out.
- Do not leave vegetables standing in water. Prepare, serve and eat in as short a period as possible for maximum benefit.
- Do not store any absorbent foods (such as butter or cut fruit) in clingwrap which contains soluble carcinogenic chemicals.
- Boil cooking water – as little as is practical – then add the fruit or vegetables and cook them as quickly as possible. Use the cooking water as a juice or for soup as it will be full of goodness. Cook skins whenever you can, as they often contain much that is beneficial (wash them first). You should not boil vegetables if you have the option of microwaving, steaming or, best of all, eating them raw. The enzymes in fruit and vegetables which do our bodies the most good are destroyed at 55°C (129°F).

Checklist of Foods For Your Larder

Apples	Figs	Peppers
Artichoke hearts	Fish (oily)	Plums
Asparagus spears	French beans	Potatoes
Aubergines	Garlic	Prunes
Avocados	Gherkins	Pumpkins
Bamboo shoots	Goose	Radishes
Bananas	Grapes	Raisins
Beansprouts	Herbs	Red wine
Beetroot	Kale	Runner beans
Berries	Kelp	Seeds (pumpkin, sunflower,
Bovril	Kiwi fruit	sesame)
Bran	Leeks	Soya protein foods
Broccoli	Lemons (to squeeze on fish)	Spices
Brown rice	Lettuce	Spinach
Brussels sprouts	Limes	Spring onions
Cabbage	Mangos	Stock cubes
Carrots	Marmite	Swedes
Cauliflower	Milk (semi-skimmed)	Sweetcorn
Celeriac	Mint sauce	Tabasco sauce
Celery	Mushrooms	Tangerines
Cheese (low-fat)	Mustard	Teriyaki sauce
Chicken (free range)	Mustard and cress	Tofu
Chicory	Nuts (hazelnuts, walnuts,	Tomatoes
Chillies	brazils, pecans, cashews)	Tomato puree
Cider vinegar	Okra	Turkey
Cod-liver oil capsules	Olive oil (extra virgin)	Turnips
Courgettes	Onions	Water (tap or bottled, still)
Cucumber	Oranges	Watercress
Curry powder	Pasta (all types)	Wild rice
Dates (seedless)	Peaches	Wholegrain cereals
Duck	Pears	Wholemeal bread
Fennel	Peas	Yeast

4

General Food Control: What Is Bad?

Foods to Avoid

Dairy Products

Milk

Almost half of the adult population of the UK is overweight and one in eight is obese. Dairy products are a major cause, because our digestive systems simply were not designed to cope with some of the constituent chemicals of cows' milk, butter, cheese and even yoghurt. Children are armed with the digestive enzymes of rennin and lactase, which enable them to digest milk, but they are designed to digest human rather than cows' milk, and after some four years these enzymes decrease, leaving children incapable of digesting all the lactose content of human milk, let alone that in cows' milk, which is 300 times greater.

Milk is also mucus-forming and can aggravate respiratory conditions like asthma. It may also contain chemical residues that can cause big trouble for our body systems.

Cattle are often inoculated against infectious diseases such as blackleg and anthrax, as well as being given hormones to increase their growth rate. These chemicals and 'bad' cholesterol from animal fats can enter our bodies from milk. If you add up all these potentially lethal factors, you might be forgiven for looking askance at the next milk bottle that comes your way. But there is a good side to cows' milk too, for it is rich in calories, vitamins and calcium.

The answer is to drink semi-skimmed milk (except young children and nursing mothers who need full-cream milk) and get in your daily pinta by adding milk to tea and cereal rather than drinking it on its own. (Breast-feeding mothers need 1.5 pints a day to ensure that their babies get enough calcium for bone growth.)

Semi-skimmed milk tastes just as good unless you are being ultra-fussy, but contains only half the fat; skimmed milk is virtually fat-free. But both retain most of the nutritional goodness of full-fat milk.

Cheese and Butter

The benefits and dangers of milk apply also to butter

and cheese. There are plenty of delicious low-fat cheddars and cottage cheeses available which can enable you to continue to enjoy the uniquely satisfying taste of cheese while reducing the amount of saturated fat in standard cheese (35 per cent in Cheddar or Stilton compared with 4 per cent in cottage cheese).

After years of expensive advertising campaigns and medical wrangling, butter- and margarine-promoters seem to have ended up in a no-win situation. Both substances are undeniably fatty and bad for you except in tiny quantities, so try to get used to spreading less and less of them on bread and toast and using a mere smidgen in cooking (whatever Delia and co. dictate). Cream, mayonnaise and ice-cream, however delectable, sadly come under the same 'beware of killer fats' umbrella.

A tiny butter tip: if you spread the smoother side of crispbread you will use less butter. It all mounts up.

Meat

Beef was for centuries the favoured meat of most developed countries, but BSE and heart-disease scares have led to a panic preference for white meat. This is not entirely rational since beef contains most of the nutrients we need and does not necessarily endanger our hearts. Lean meat from organic beef is far less likely to cause harm than a roast chicken which has come from a chicken factory, with its fatty skin and high salmonella risk.

My wife is a farmer on Exmoor of pedigree, organically fed Aberdeen Angus beef cattle, so you may think that it is fear of my wife's vengeance that stops me from pronouncing 100 per cent against red meat. I can assure you that this is not the case. Eating properly cooked, lean, red meat once or twice a week – not more often – may be as beneficial as drinking one or two glasses of red wine a day. Cut off any fat and avoid gravy. When you buy beef, ask

about its origins. Meat from a local butcher almost always comes from a known regional herd, whereas many supermarkets seem unable or unwilling to name their meat sources. Meat from some obscure country with dubious abattoir controls might not be what you had in mind when you asked for 'some beef'.

When preparing meat dishes you can diminish the likelihood of ingesting harmful HCAs (heterocyclic amines) by never undercooking. This is important since HCAs stimulate the free radicals that can cause cancer and heart disease. Oven-roasting, baking, stewing, boiling and microwaving are all excellent ways of eliminating HCAs, provided the meat is cooked thoroughly. Cut away the visible fat – and that means *all* the delicious roast skins and crackling. The worst animal fats to be found in meat are present in pâtés, pasties and sausages. You cannot physically remove the fat from these products, so give them a wide berth.

Nitrates are sometimes used to cure certain meats: sodium nitrate is often used in the curing of bacon, ham, salami and frankfurters. Nitrosamines, which can form in your stomach when you eat such nitrate, cause cancers such as leukaemia and brain cancer. Such cured meats are, therefore, best avoided.

Eggs

Egg yolks contain a high level of 'bad' cholesterol. Eggs are an allergenic and a high risk in terms of salmonella poisoning if not cooked properly.

My wife breeds free-range bantams, ducks, guinea fowl and quail. We would not expect salmonella to thrive on our farm but, like any responsible chef dealing with anaemic battery eggs in an urban restaurant, my wife sticks to the safety rules:

- Boil eggs for at least seven minutes. If you like them runny, you risk salmonella.

- Poach for at least five minutes.
- Fry for at least three minutes on each side.
- Cook omelettes and scrambled eggs until they coagulate.
- Use duck eggs only for baking.
- Avoid sauces, dressings and mousses which involve raw eggs.

In Antarctica my wife and I lived with two friends at 6,000ft above sea-level, in a base under the snow, for eight months. Our originally fresh eggs, kept frozen in snow tunnels, still tasted fine to us up to the end, but a polar scientist who flew in to see us was violently sick upon being given a fried eight-month-old egg. We called it lack of eggclimatisation. If you keep eggs in the main part of your refrigerator rather than in the less-cool door compartments, you can expect them to keep fresh for about three weeks at most, so be especially careful of 'best before' dates.

Due to the 'bad' cholesterol content of eggs, I knowingly eat only two egg yolks a week and not more than six whites. Omelettes can be made using only the whites.

Fast Foods (aka Junk Food)

Convenience foods come in two different guises: honest burgers and cunning 'healthy' lines which con you into thinking that eating or drinking 'lite' this and 'diet' that will be to your greater benefit. Once you have ladled fatty dressings on to your 'diet' salad because it is so tasteless you have gained nothing. Burgers, of whatever shape, size or content, are designed to fatten your bottom. Most hamburger 'dives' will give you a special price for a whole 'meal' including French fries and a cola. An average-sized special deal of this type will cost you 1,290 calories and 1.75oz in body weight. If eaten only once a week, such a meal will add 5.5lbs to your body weight over a year.

Biscuits, Cakes and Chocolate

Polyunsaturated and hydrogenated fats, which go rancid inside our body systems and can cause cancer, are to be found in most biscuits, pastries and cakes, as well as in fast food. Few such goodies avoid flour, sugar, eggs, milk, cream, salt and fats as basic ingredients.

Hydrogenation is the process of converting plant oil to a creamy margarine texture. All such fats are potentially lethal, but the danger is greatly increased when they are turned from liquid to solid (or semi-solid) and become trans-fatty acids, found in common foods such as margarine. These are a kind of man-made fat that is not found in any natural food. Disturbingly, the scientists simply do not know how the body deals with TFAs nor how harmful they are.

Coffee

According to the *British Medical Journal*, people who drink five cups of coffee daily have a 50 per cent greater risk of heart-attacks than non-coffee drinkers. There are at least 800 chemicals in coffee, and 19 of the 27 which have been analysed are carcinogens. One of these is caffeine, which is found in more than 60 species of plants, including cocoa beans, tea, coffee and cola nuts, and is therefore present to a greater or lesser degree in all the drinks made from them. Caffeine stimulates the heart and skeletal muscles, increases respiration levels and enhances alertness. Indeed, it is on the list of substances banned by many athletics bodies. Many people find they get insomnia if they take any caffeine drink at all after lunchtime.

Caffeine also increases the risk of heart disease, osteoporosis and many other unpleasant illnesses.

Before a 10-hour man-hauling stint through blizzards and vistas of never-ending, never-changing whiteness, I drink coffee and eat chocolate. I do the

Caffeine Content per 150ml cup	
Instant coffee	60mg
Roast or ground coffee	40mg
*Tea	40mg
Cola	20mg
Hot chocolate	3mg
Decaffeinated coffee	3mg

*The cancer-fighting antioxidants in tea outweigh the caffeine downside, if taken in moderation.

same on long car journeys to lecture at conferences. I know both are bad for my health – but not as bad as contracting hypothermia after dozing off during a blizzard, or crashing my car because I have fallen asleep at the wheel.

However, when I'm at home, I drink coffee only twice a week on average, and when doing business I keep coffee-drinking to a minimum conducive to politeness.

Unfortunately, even decaffeinated coffee is not risk-free. The removal of caffeine from coffee beans usually involves highly caustic chemicals which can themselves cause damage to our systems.

Soft Drinks

Many soft drinks contain a nightmarish mix of phosphoric, malic, citric and carbonic acids, in addition to caffeine, harmful sugar substitutes such as aspartame and carcinogens. Most of them also erode tooth enamel. If you wish to keep healthy, steer clear of them.

Sugar

Sugar could be described as addictive because it provides an immediate 'sugar rush', a rapid rise in blood sugar, which kills our appetite. This is why children should not eat sweets just before a meal. Unfortunately, the rapid rise is quickly followed by a steep fall which, of course, triggers hunger pangs. So we eat another chocolate and repeat the cycle. The healthiest form of sugar is fructose, which is supplied unprocessed by fruit, and which the body quickly assimilates.

Additives

Over 3,000 additive substances can be legally added to foods and the vast majority are merely flavourings. The additives used in officially retailed foods in the UK are closely controlled and well researched, and many of them actually make food safer by inhibiting the growth of bacteria.

Other Bad Habits

Smoking

Smoking causes cancer of the lungs, mouth, throat, larynx, stomach and bladder. If you smoke you are doing irreparable damage to your lungs, which cannot be transplanted. Each lung has 250 million tiny air sacs called alveoli. Flattened out they would cover half a tennis court. These incredibly delicate structures are where oxygen enters the bloodstream and the waste product carbon dioxide is expelled from the body through the lungs. Just to enable you to walk, your lungs require six gallons (27 litres) of air per minute – and that air is full of potentially harmful bacteria and viruses. Polluting acids and poisons which can slowly eat away stone statues and melt nylon stockings would be sucked non-stop through your lungs but for the hairs in your nose and the billions of microscopic hairs within your lungs' air passages, which are called cilia. Unfortunately, some airborne particles are too small to be filtered by the cilia.

Smoking slowly destroys the cilia and allows enormous damage to be wreaked within the complex structure of your lungs. Mucus and tar slowly advance into the air sacs and the lungs begin to drown. Your smoker's cough will do its best to shift the mucus, but your slow death has begun. This is what happens with emphysema, the most common smoking-related disease. Meanwhile, your blood will be cleaned and reoxygenated less efficiently and, slowly but surely, cancers will invade your system. Only immediate cessation of smoking can save you and rehabilitate the good health you could still enjoy. Decide *now* the date you will stop.

To keep fit is normally unrewarding in terms of seeing immediate results for lots of hard work. Months of food control and exercise often achieve only a moderate improvement in your overall health and shape. But the single act of giving up smoking achieves enormous benefits speedily and lastingly. If this book has a single vital message for fitness, then 'Stop smoking!' is far and away the front runner.

'Yes,' you will say. 'I know all that, but I have tried and failed to give up. It is impossible.' That is exactly what I once thought, but after 30 years of cyclical periods of smoking and not smoking, I have finally cut down the habit to a single roll-your-own cigarette after supper when I am at home, the occasional puff at high-pressure business meetings and none the rest of the time. On expeditions I no longer smoke at all. I feel enormously better for it. Many people who have stopped smoking find it best, like reformed alcoholics, never to touch a cigarette ever again, and obviously this is healthier than the solution I have arrived at.

Because smoking is the most important health factor in this book for those who indulge in it, my list of smoking 'dos' and 'don'ts' is a long one.

- Remember that smoking is making you a high-risk heart-disease candidate. Your heart-attack risk starts to fall only eight hours after your last cigarette. After five years of not smoking you face only half the risk you did when you smoked. After 10 years the risk is no greater than it would be if you had never smoked.

- Think how it would feel to be tested for lung cancer. Think how you would dread the diagnosis. Think of your reaction should you then be told that you do have the disease – or another life-threatening lung disease such as emphysema. Think of having to live with the knowledge that you will soon die in hospital on painkillers, a self-inflicted death, and of the effect it will have on those who love you and depend on you.

- Remember that, if you carry on, you are likely to join the UK death list of 100 people killed every day by lung cancer. The more cigarettes you smoke, the greater the risk as the days and weeks go by.

- Remember: one in 270 non-smokers dies of lung cancer. One in eight smokers dies of lung cancer.

- Cut out tea, coffee, alcohol or any daily habit which triggers your desire to smoke. Keep clear of places where you would normally have a cigarette and avoid other smokers.

- Remember that smoking makes you, your skin, your breath and your clothes stink.

- Do not forget that you are also causing those who live and work with you to risk developing lung cancer through inhaling your poison.

- Remember that smoking will progressively make you sick in 100 small ways. You will sleep less and less well as the months and years go by. If you are female, you enormously increase your chances of slow death by osteoporosis. And the list goes on.

- Do not try to kid yourself that stopping smoking will increase your blood pressure and thus your risk of heart-attack. Any temporary increase at the time of cessation will be more than outweighed by the ensuing benefits.

- Remember the cost of smoking, and what you will be able to buy with that money once you have given up.
- Look at films of people dying from smokers' diseases. Visit cancer and emphysema victims dying in hospital. You will see your own future in their dreadful suffering. Listen to their advice.
- Do not tell yourself, 'If I stop smoking, I will get fat.' This is pathetic. When you have stopped smoking you can decide whether or not to start a food-control regime.
- Remember that you are slowly but surely blocking up your arteries. Even if you are one of the lucky smokers who escapes lung disease, you are hugely increasing your chances of restricting the bloodflow to your brain or to your kidneys or, more frequently, to one of your limbs. Forty thousand amputations a year are necessitated by smoking.

When you have decided that you would like to stop smoking, take the first critical step at once. Say to yourself:

'I will give up all cigarettes after Sunday night,' or whichever day you choose. Ring a friend or relative who has given up successfully and warn him or her to expect more calls from you and to be ready to bolster you and help your determination. Then prepare your arsenal for the war to come. Lay in a store of ammunition, including nicotine patches, sugar-free chewing gum, ready-to-eat fruit and vegetables. Get supplies of fresh bananas and a big, bright mug that shrieks at you from which to drink cold water. The night before you start, throw away cigarettes, lighters, ashtrays and any paraphernalia you associate with smoking. For instance, if you usually smoke when reading the paper or listening to the news, get rid of the radio and cancel the newspaper order.

- When Monday morning arrives, constantly remind yourself that you are on Day 1 of a war.

This is the first battle which will rage between the temptation of your thoughts and your own common sense.

- Use every possible piece of the ammunition you have prepared in advance. Whenever you feel the urge to smoke, rush off and drink more water than you need from your special mug and eat a banana. Then chew some gum.
- Leave signs around the house and office proclaiming in large letters: 'IF I SMOKE AGAIN, I HAVE NO SELF-CONTROL' or 'I DO NOT WANT TO DIE SLOWLY OF SUFFOCATION' – whatever hard-hitting messages have the most effect on you.
- Master your thoughts. Do not allow defeatist thoughts to rule you and lead to smoking 'just one' cigarette. Think positively and enjoy each new victory as you survive another whole hour without smoking, then another whole day.
- Don't think about tomorrow; concentrate on no cigarettes today. When I crossed the Antarctic continent on foot in 1993, I realised by the third week that the distance ahead was so vast, the experiences to come so difficult and the hour-by-hour struggle so painful that the quickest way to failure would be to allow myself to think beyond the next hour on my watch. I could cope with 60 minutes, and when that ended I could cope with the next 60 minutes, and so on. That approach brought success and the first-ever unsupported human crossing of that vast, frozen continent. The same approach can be a powerful mental tool in the equally difficult no-more-smoking battle.
- Realise that your body may well feel awful as a result of nicotine withdrawal. This may go on for two or three weeks. The basic urge to smoke again (though not the physical effects of initial withdrawal) may remain with you intermittently all your life, just as a successful diet does not necessarily mean you will not experience future food cravings. If you expect such ill effects, and possibly moods of depression, you will be prepared to

fight them. Stay especially alert for those moments of stress, such as an argument at work or at home, which might trigger the need for a cigarette. Be ready for this and do not give in.

- Buy yourself things with the money you have saved and use them to help you in the ongoing battle. Non-fattening food goodies, music, new running shoes, indoor games, dice, cards, tickets to the cinema or theatre (but not somewhere which will offer renewed smoking temptations).
- Call the friend or relative who is helping you, or find a helpline in the Yellow Pages. They will give you many other tips to help you avoid buying another packet of coffin nails.

Cigars, Snuff, Chewing Tobacco

Some folk, including health wonders like Arnold Schwarzenegger, enjoy a single cigar a week and call themselves non-smokers. But many cigars contain 30 times the nicotine of a medium cigarette, which makes them even more addictive. Putting an unlit cigar in your mouth, a practice of wannabe quitters, is inadvisable since the nicotine is absorbed quickly under the tongue, with a consequent high risk of oral cancer. Snuff and chewing-tobacco-users face the same hazards.

Remember that smoking one medium-sized cigar a day increases your risk of heart disease by 300 per cent and of lung cancer by 500 per cent.

Alcohol

Although, as we have seen, moderate drinking can stave off heart disease, heavy drinking is the second biggest cause of premature death in the West, after smoking. Alcohol, even in slight excess (and this includes beer) destroys vitamins and has a slow but deadly toxic effect on many body organs, especially the kidneys and liver. So you need to get it right. The safest bet is to drink one glass of red wine most days and otherwise give all alcohol a wide berth. Drinking just to feel at ease socially, or because you are lonely, will lead sooner or later to increased consumption and, like hypothermia, alcoholism can claim you before you know it.

Never drink beer straight after taking exhausting exercise – rugby players please note – until you have first drunk plenty of water.

Checklist of Foods to Keep Out of the House

All trans-fatty acids and hydrogenated-oil products (especially margarine)	Coffee	Ice-cream
	Confectionery	Instant desserts
Alcohol (except for one glass of red wine daily)	Cooking oils (except olive and macadamia nut oil)	Milk (full-fat)
	Cream	Pastries
Bacon	Crisps	Pâtés
Biscuits	Eggs (eat 2 yolks a week maximum)	Pizzas
Butter		Salami
Cakes	Fast food	Sausages
Cheese (full-fat)	Ham	Salt
Chips	Hamburgers	Sweetened fizzy drinks
Chocolate	Hot dogs	Sweet sauces

Salt

Blood is full of minerals and sodium (salt) is the most abundant. But modern-day foods provide far more than our daily needs (0.5 grams) and these excess amounts may be a prime cause of lethal heart disease. Athletes often take salt tablets to replace sweat lost at exercise. This is a mistake, except in the most exceptional circumstances – such as a Saharan summer marathon – because pure, unadulterated water is all your body really needs to replace sweat if you are eating a normal diet.

Because frozen and processed foods, cereals, butter and any foods containing preservatives are laden with sodium, there is no need to add salt when cooking or eating out. We have acquired a taste for salty food but, with a small effort, losing the habit is as easy as cutting down on sugar. If you do not reduce your salt intake, as you approach 60 years of age, no matter how fit you may consider yourself to be, you will be running an increasing risk of high blood pressure, kidney failure, stomach cancer and ulcers. If you find it impossible to cut down, then at least go for low-sodium salt or coarse-ground sea salt.

5

The Fitness Basics

Your larder is by now stacked with good foods, smoking (even if you are still at it) is a dirty word and you want to start thinking about an exercise regime. To get the best out of any training, you need to ensure that it is tailored to your end goals. There are four factors to be taken into consideration:

- **Mode of exercise**
- **Intensity of exercise**
- **Duration of exercise**
- **Frequency of exercise**

Mode of Exercise

There may be a variety of reasons why you want to keep fit: merely to lessen the chances of ill health and disease; because you enjoy the confidence exercise gives you; because you want to lose weight or because you are keen to increase your muscle strength. Choose your particular exercise schedule accordingly: there is very little muscle-strength gain to be had from running and very little aerobic improvement from weightlifting. And long runs will help hardly at all if you need swimming training to cross the Channel. Advice on different kinds of exercise is given in Chapter 8.

Intensity of Exercise

There is, of course, a minimum amount of exercise required to produce an improvement in your fitness but this will depend on how fit you are at any given time. If you have been an idle toad for years, indulging in constant depraved binges, then a gentle 10-minute walk every day will be better than 10 minutes would not even register from an aerobic or strength point of view.

Each of us, depending on our fitness state and our weight, has a different level of training intensity, a minimum amount of exercise, below which taking exercise at all is a waste of time. This is called the **training threshold**. Yet there is no point in training too hard, either, because, at a certain level – the **overload point** – your heart rate will be too high, aerobic benefits will taper off and no extra improvement will be accrued from an aerobic viewpoint. Your body will let you train harder than is actually beneficial, so an element of control is needed.

An easy way to tell when you have reached your overload point is to try to carry on a conversation or whistle a tune without interrupting your activity. If you can't, you are there.

The area for which you need to aim is known as the **training zone**, which lies between the training threshold and the overload point. Within this 'zone' any time and effort you spend training will be effective.

Duration of Exercise

Duration and intensity of exercise are interdependent: an increase in one is likely to involve a decrease in the other. There is a marked difference between the number of calories burned when you slowly walk a mile and the number you use up when you run that mile at a fast pace. Running faster simply uses up more fuel, even though the time required to complete the task is less.

As a general guide:

• Running slowly (11 minutes per mile, or 5.5mph) uses 110 calories per mile.
• Faster running (8 minutes per mile, or 7.5mph) uses 113 calories per mile. So there is very little difference at this speed.

These figures assume you weigh 150lbs. Add or subtract 10 per cent for each 15lbs you weigh over or under 150lbs for a more accurate personal gauge. Use these figures to decide how long to exercise for if your primary aim is to lose calories. If, for instance, your target expenditure is 1,000 calories a day and you run a mile in 11 minutes you will need to run nine miles a day. Calorie expenditure in other sports

is not always as easy to assess as it is with running, but see the chart on page 78.

If you are exercising to improve your general aerobic fitness, then bear in mind the 'minimum' advice given in Chapter 1. If you are exercising within your training zone, each session should last for at least 30 minutes and any increase over that time will further benefit your athletic potential.

Frequency of Exercise

Fitness improvements are directly related to frequency of training, independent of the effects of intensity, duration and fitness level. Training six days a week is, for example, more than twice as beneficial in terms of aerobic fitness and weight control as two days. However many days you train, your exercise should be regular, not bunched and spasmodic. If you train three days a week, choose alternate, not consecutive, days.

Should You See a Doctor Before You Begin an Exercise Schedule?

If you are in any doubt about the condition of your health then it is better to be safe than sorry. Government health advice in Canada is that any citizen over 45 years should see a doctor if they intend to start an exercise regime after a period of sedentary existence. However, before rushing off to your GP, remember that moderate activity is less harmful to health than inactivity, so, in general, people who take no exercise are likely to be in greater need of a doctor's attentions.

If you are free of any danger symptoms or risk factors (such as high blood pressure, high cholesterol, a smoking habit, genetic disease history or advanced old age), then you should not feel bound to see a doctor. A good way of allaying any lingering doubts is to give yourself the pre-fit exam used in

Canada, which is designed to identify those individuals who should seek medical advice. If you answer 'yes' to any of the following eight questions, then it would be a good idea to talk to your doctor before you start exercising.

- Have you ever had heart trouble?
- Do you frequently have pain in your chest?
- Do you often feel faint or have spells of severe dizziness?
- Has your doctor ever said your blood pressure was too high?
- Do you have a bone or joint problem which has already been or could be aggravated by exercise?
- Is there any other physical reason why you should not follow a physical activity programme?
- Are you over the age of 65 and unaccustomed to vigorous exercise?
- Are you using drugs which might alter your response to exercise?

Measuring Your Progress

Once you are ready to begin your exercise programme, how do you establish just how fit – or unfit – you actually are, and what rate of improvement should you be aiming for? Keep your expectations moderate to avoid disappointment. Rome was not built in a day. If you have come to fitness late in life, remember that top athletes train religiously for many years. You can hardly hope to undo long periods of inactivity and muscle wastage in a few weeks or months of overdone fitness fanaticism, so do not go overboard.

Your improvement rate will be governed by your age, by outside factors such as genetics and by your initial level of fitness. If you are in your teens your improvement rate will be optimal. From about 20 onwards, it will decline slowly. As a young adult you can expect to improve your fitness by as much as 25

per cent; by the time you are 70, this will have decreased to a 10 per cent improvement. However, all improvements will greatly exceed these percentages if large body-weight losses are also involved. Even an 80-year-old body is still highly trainable in percentage terms. It is in absolute terms that the gains are small in comparison with those of younger people.

The more active you have been in the past, the smaller the improvement rate you should anticipate. If you have been sedentary for a year or more, you may improve your performance by 40 per cent, but if you are simply recovering from a two-month holiday after years of exercising, expect a mere 5 per cent improvement at best. Once your progress arrives at a fitness plateau, after several months of uninterrupted training, you should aim to maintain that peak rather than head back down the slippery slope as a majority of the once-fit brethren do.

A good way of establishing your initial fitness condition, monitoring your progress and maintaining fitness is to self-assess your performance on a regular basis in the following five categories:

- Heart rate/pulse
- Body fat
- Muscular strength
- Flexibility
- Abdominal strength

If you decide to join a gym or health club, the staff or your personal trainer will be able to keep tabs on your progress, but these simple tests will be particularly useful if you choose to go it alone.

For some of the following self-assessment tests, you will need to prepare by **warming up**. A finely tuned racing car with many interdependent components needs to be run from cool to warm before a race. The human body has many more complex and fragile parts that can easily be damaged by sudden movements, especially when switching from inaction to exertion without preparation, so you must always warm up to ready the muscles and joints for exercise.

Your Heart Rate/Pulse

The easiest way of assessing your general health and wellbeing is to monitor the speed at which your heart beats. This increases with age and with lack of exercise, but will improve to a slower rate as you become fitter. Your waking heart rate (WHR), taken when lying down, will be slower than your resting heart rate (RHR), measured while sitting. Most average, middle-aged marathon-runners will show a WHR in the low 50s and a RHR in the low 60s. A middle-aged person whose work involves exercise but who has no fitness regime may have a RHR in the mid-70s.

My WHR, measured in bed on waking, is currently 50 beats per minute (bpm). At midday, sitting at my desk, my RHR is 58 bpm. If I train hard for a week my rates lower to 49 and 55 respectively.

It is a common misconception that the RHR is an indicator of fitness. Unfortunately, this is not the case, but it is an excellent gauge of your general state of health.

Measure your RHR by taking your pulse, using your fingertips, not your thumb. Some people will find their pulse difficult to locate when their heart rate is slow; others will have easily readable pulses. Two good places to take your pulse are the neck (just off the windpipe) and on the wrist (just below the base of the thumb). Or use a heart-rate monitor. Most monitors come in two parts, a wrist receiver, which you put on like a watch, and a transmitter band which you strap on like a bra but just below your sternum. You need to ensure that the manufacturer's logo on the outside of the transmitter is the correct way up and that you moisten the inside of the transmitter band with water or spit before fitting it.

- **The heart rate of individuals over 40 is generally about five bpm higher than that of younger folk.**
- **A woman's heart rate is typically eight bpm higher than a man's.**
- **Rates as low as 28 to 40 bpm have been reached by some highly trained endurance athletes (aka freaks). Conversely, though, many world-class athletes have RHRs in the mid-60s or even 70s.**
- **Sedentary individuals may record 100 bpm.**
- **These general guidelines may not apply to everyone, so treat this method of self-assessment with caution. The standard medical rating of resting heart rate is:**

60	=	**slow rate (Congratulations!)**
60–100	=	**normal rate (The lower the better.)**
100	=	**fast rate (Watch it!)**

- **The normal Army rating for resting heart rate is:**

50	=	**very fit**
70	=	**fit**
80	=	**normal**
100	=	**unfit**

  There are a great many podgy persons serving Her Majesty these days, so this is not a spectacularly testing rating.

Try to take your RHR at the same time of day and record it in your diary. Once you have established your RHR, treat any daily increases from this baseline as a possible indication of fatigue or impending illness. Ease up on your training for a while to be on the safe side.

Exercise is beneficial to your heart only if it achieves between 60 and 90 per cent of your maximum heartbeat rate, your MHR. So you need to know right away, if you don't already, what your MHR is.

The most commonly advised method of establishing your MHR is to subtract your age from the number 220. I am 54, so by this method my MHR is 166. When I am training my heart therefore needs to be beating at about 70 per cent of 166, which works out at 116 beats per minute. However, this system is useless for serious and safe fitness training. Most people differ from the so-called norm. Gender is a major factor for a start. For males, 214 is more accurate than 220, and females should use 209.

To use your heart rate as a gauge in your training, you must therefore take the trouble to complete a simple maximal test which will give you a much more accurate MHR than the 220-minus-your-age system.

1. Run as fast as you can, evenly, without bursts of speed, for three minutes. You can either run free or use a treadmill.
2. Rest for two minutes by running gently.
3. Do another three minutes of your fastest running.
4. Count your heart rate at once. This is your true MHR.

Body Fat

Your health status does not depend on your weight. You may think that to be thin is to be attractive, but plump people may well be healthy, strong and very fit, whereas anorexics are certainly not in good health. The best approach to monitoring weight is to bear in mind what type of body you were born with – whether you are a Cherub, String bean or Tarzan, and the nature of your bone structure – and then decide on your own ideal weight goal. Any body-fat ready-reckoner chart should always include adjustments to be made for your specific bone structure.

Your total body weight is less important to your health than the proportion of fat-to-lean muscle on your body. This you can and should, if you are serious about fitness and health, identify and keep checking as you train. The best way of doing so is to use a Bodystat fat monitor (many health clubs stock them), which is extremely accurate and will quickly tell you your personal fat–lean ratio. The Bodystat body composition theme is summed up by the photographs below.

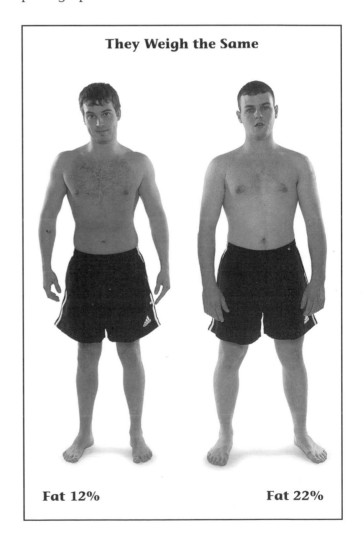

They Weigh the Same

Fat 12%   **Fat 22%**

Muscle weighs more than fat, so after a couple of months' training, you may weigh the same but have less fat and therefore be more healthy.

The *Reader's Digest* Ideal Body-Fat percentage is 15 per cent for men and 25 per cent for women. Below 5 per cent for males and 15 per cent for females is too low. To know that your fat–lean ratio is improving as you train, even if your overall weight is not changing significantly, is highly motivational. At Shell Research Centre over 200 female employees plan their personal training round Bodystat results. The following is a typical example taken of a 36-year-old Shell lady over a 12-month period.

Date	Total Weight in lbs	Fat Weight in lbs	% Fat
27.10.94	185	79	43
09.05.95	170	64	38
18.08.95	141	41	29
29.11.95	130	28	22

Buying a Bodystat or other 'fat-detector' is a relatively expensive option. An alternative is to enlist the help of your partner or a friend and use a simple pair of calipers to record the measurements of the 'fat folds' at particular points on your body where subcutaneous fat is stored (see photographs on page 48).

The following areas of the body may be used:

1. Triceps: the skinfold should be taken midway between the top of the shoulder and the tip of the elbow. Keep your arm beside your body.
2. Biceps: at a point midway between the elbow and the armpit.
3. Subscapular: at a point just below the tip of the shoulder blade.
4. Suprailiac: just above the top of the hip.

For maximum accuracy, the measurement should be taken three times and an average of the three results recorded. The test should be performed by the same person each time and at the same time of day, preferably in the morning.

1. Take all skinfold measurements on the right side of the body and record them in millimetres.
2. Pick up the skinfold between the thumb and the index finger and make sure that two thicknesses of skin and subcutaneous fat are included.
3. Apply the callipers about 1cm from the fingers and at a depth about equal to the thickness of the fold.

Now check your measurements against the relevant column in the chart on page 49 to obtain your body-fat percentage.

Muscular Strength

There are a good many ways of assessing your muscular strength but most of them require equipment. The simplest method to use if you do not have any gear is the push-up test (or press-ups, in Army terminology) – provided that you do not have an injury-prone lower back, in which case you should not do push-ups.

Make sure you know how to do a push-up correctly. Most men use their hands and feet and most women use their hands, knees and feet, as shown in the photographs on page 50.

1. Having warmed up, position yourself on the floor so that your body is straight and all your weight is on your hands, knees and feet (women), or hands and feet (men). Ensure that your hands are flat on the floor and directly under your shoulders.
2. Lower your chest until it touches the floor. Then push your body back up to the starting position. Exhale each time you push your body up, but do not hold your breath. Keep your body straight and fully extend your arms at the end of each push-up.

Areas of the body which may be used to measure 'fat folds'

1. Triceps: the skinfold should be taken midway between the top of the shoulder and the tip of the elbow. Keep your arm beside your body.

2. Biceps: at a point midway between the elbow and the armpit.

3. Subscapular: at a point just below the tip of the shoulder blade.

4. Suprailiac: just above the top of the hip.

Body-Fat Percentage Figures

Skinfolds (mm)	Men				Women			
	17–29 yrs	30–39 yrs	40–49 yrs	50+ yrs	17–29 yrs	30–39 yrs	40–49 yrs	50+ yrs
15	4.8	—	—	—	10.5	—	—	—
20	8.1	12.2	12.2	12.6	14.1	17.0	19.8	21.4
25	10.5	14.2	15.0	15.6	16.8	19.4	22.2	24.0
30	12.9	16.2	17.7	18.6	19.5	21.8	24.5	26.6
35	14.7	17.7	19.6	20.8	21.5	23.7	26.4	28.5
40	16.4	19.2	21.4	22.9	23.4	25.5	28.2	30.3
45	17.7	20.4	23.0	24.7	25.0	26.9	29.6	31.9
50	19.0	21.5	24.6	26.5	26.5	28.2	31.0	33.4
55	20.1	22.5	25.9	27.9	27.8	29.4	32.1	34.6
60	21.2	23.5	27.1	29.2	29.1	30.6	33.2	35.7
65	22.2	24.3	28.2	30.4	30.2	31.6	34.1	36.7
70	23.1	25.1	29.3	31.6	31.2	32.5	35.0	37.7
75	24.0	25.9	30.3	32.7	32.2	33.4	35.9	38.7
80	24.8	26.6	31.2	33.8	33.1	34.3	36.7	39.6
85	25.5	27.2	32.1	34.8	34.0	35.1	37.5	40.4
90	26.2	27.8	33.0	35.8	34.8	35.8	38.3	41.2
95	26.9	28.4	33.7	36.6	35.6	36.5	39.0	41.9
100	27.6	29.0	34.4	37.4	36.4	37.2	39.7	42.6
105	28.2	29.6	35.1	38.2	37.1	37.9	40.4	43.3
110	28.8	30.1	35.8	39.0	37.8	38.6	41.0	43.9
115	29.4	30.6	36.4	39.7	38.4	39.1	41.5	44.5
120	30.0	31.1	37.0	40.4	39.0	39.6	42.0	45.1
125	30.5	31.5	37.6	41.1	39.6	40.1	42.5	45.7
130	31.0	31.9	38.2	41.8	40.2	40.6	43.0	46.2
135	31.5	32.3	38.7	42.4	40.8	41.1	43.5	46.7
140	32.0	32.7	39.2	43.0	41.3	41.6	44.0	47.2
145	32.5	33.1	39.7	43.6	41.8	42.1	44.5	47.7
150	32.9	33.5	40.2	44.1	42.3	42.6	45.0	48.2
155	33.3	33.9	40.7	44.6	42.8	43.1	45.4	48.7
160	33.7	34.3	41.2	45.1	43.3	43.6	45.8	49.2
165	34.1	34.6	41.6	45.6	43.7	44.0	46.2	49.6
170	34.5	34.8	42.0	46.1	44.1	44.4	46.6	50.0
175	34.9	—	—	—	—	44.8	47.0	50.4
180	35.3	—	—	—	—	45.2	47.4	50.8
185	35.6	—	—	—	—	45.6	47.8	51.2
190	35.9	—	—	—	—	45.9	48.2	51.6
195	—	—	—	—	—	46.2	48.5	52.0
200	—	—	—	—	—	46.5	48.8	52.4
205	—	—	—	—	—	—	49.1	52.7
210	—	—	—	—	—	—	49.4	53.0

Push-ups for men (hands and feet) and women (hands, knees and feet).

3. Stop when you need to rest. Record the total number of completed push-ups and compare your result with the table below.

This system will test mainly your body strength. The majority of people, even fit people who do not specifically indulge in strength training, will find they rate as low.

If you are interested in similar self-assessment tests for other muscle groups, such as your upper legs, ask a health-club adviser for details. But

remember that you do not have to go overboard on muscle strength in order to become super-fit.

Flexibility

Flexibility is critical to avoid injury when training. As with muscular-strength self-assessment tests, there are a great many flexibility tests to choose from for different body areas, but the sit and reach test by Golding, Myers and Sinning is a good all-round indicator of your flexibility progress in the

For Complete Push-Ups

Age	20–29 yrs	30–39 yrs	40–49 yrs	50–59 yrs	60+ yrs
Men					
High	>45	>35	>30	>25	>20
Average	35–44	25–34	20–29	15–24	10–19
Below average	20–34	15–24	12–19	8–14	5–9
Low	<19	<14	<11	<7	<4
Women					
High	>34	>25	>20	>15	>5
Average	17–33	12–24	8–19	6–14	3–4
Below average	6–16	4–11	3–7	1–5	1–2
Low	<5	<3	<2	0	0

important hamstrings and lumbar region. You will need a simple carpenter's yardstick (make your own by marking out inches on a piece of wood at least 48 inches long) and some adhesive tape. NB: Do not do this test if you have lower-back problems.

The Sit and Reach Test

1. Sit on the floor with your legs stretched out. Place the yardstick between them so that the 15-inch mark is level with the soles of your feet (keep your feet about 12 inches apart) and the zero mark is nearest to your crutch. Tape the stick firmly to the floor.

2. Placing one hand over the other so your fingertips overlap, slowly stretch forward, keeping your knees as straight as possible, and slide your fingers along the yardstick as far as you can. Hold to a count of three and record the distance.

3. Do this three times and use and compare your best score with the examples in the table below.

The simple stretching exercises (see pages 57–69) you will complete after your main exercise should initially improve your flexibility by at least four inches a month. The rate will then steady and reach an optimum for you to maintain.

Abdominal Strength

This is not a test to try if you are feeling down-hearted, because few of us, including marathon-runners, have strong abdominals. It is important to try to develop them as a protection against lower-back injury. If you work hard daily at your abdominal crunches you will reach a stage where this assessment test becomes useful.

The majority of relatively fit individuals cannot

Sit and Reach Test					
Age	*20–29 yrs*	*30–39 yrs*	*40–49 yrs*	*50–59 yrs*	*60+ yrs*
Men					
High	>19	>18	>17	>16	>15
Average	13–18	12–17	11–16	10–15	9–14
Below average	10–12	9–11	8–10	7–9	6–8
Low	<9	<8	<7	<6	<5
Women					
High	>22	>21	>20	>19	>18
Average	16–21	15–20	14–19	13–16	12–17
Below average	13–15	12–14	11–13	10–12	9–11
Low	<12	<11	<10	<9	<8

touch their thighs with their elbows until they have worked hard at their abdominals for months. So to start with be proud if you can manage even one thrust!

1. Set up a clock with a second hand where you can see it.
2. Lie down with your back flat on the floor and your feet on a chair so that your knees are bent at right angles.
3. Fold your arms so that your hands are on opposing shoulders and point your elbows forward.
4. Raise your shoulders off the ground and thrust forward till your elbows touch your thighs.
5. Drop back until your shoulders touch the ground. Immediately return to another elbows-to-thighs thrust.

See how many thrusts you can complete in exactly 20 seconds – no cheating. If your elbows fail to touch or your shoulders do not ground, do not count that thrust.

You can use this simple test to monitor the improvement in your abdominal strength every month (it is suitable for men and women). If you are very strong abdominally, raise the 20 seconds to 30 or more.

For Complete Sit-Ups (Per 20 Seconds)

	up to 29 yrs	30–39 yrs	40–59 yrs
High	>17	>15	>13
Average	12–17	11–15	10–13
Low	<12	<11	<10

6

Warming Up, Stretching, Cooling Down

Warming Up

Before undertaking your main exercise you need to prepare by warming up. Afterwards you need to allow for a short period to stretch and cool down.

Most people find that they cut out warming-up periods if they are at all short of time (that is, usually). The best way to stop this from happening is to plan a schedule which incorporates this important preliminary as part and parcel of each training period, rather than treating it as a mere optional frill.

One idea is to start your chosen main exercise slowly and then gradually increase the tempo. So if you lift weights, start with easy loads for a while and complete half a lift movement several times before attempting the entire movement. If you are doing push-ups, first try several which involve only half the rising and falling motion. If you are going for a run, start out very slowly until you have warmed up before beginning to increase your speed.

However much of a hurry you are in, you cut out your warm-up at the very real risk of sprain injury, especially if you are over 40.

'Warming up' consists of any moderate exercise which raises the pulse. A gradual pulse rise is all that is required. A couple of minutes' running on the spot usually does the trick. This will prepare your cardiovascular system for work. Other body changes will also take place which will help minimise the likelihood of exercise strains and muscle tears occurring during the main activity to follow. These changes will include increases in:

- Your body and tissue temperature.
- The bloodflow through your active muscles.
- Your metabolic rate.
- The speed at which your nerve impulses travel (this facilitates your body movements).
- The speed and efficiency with which your muscles contract and relax.
- Your physical work capacity.
- Your psychological ability to accept the workload ahead.
- The ability of your connective tissues to elongate.

The duration of your warm-up should be sufficient to increase your body temperature to the point at which you begin to feel warm. So in cold weather the warm-up may need to be longer.

Stretching and Cooling Down

It is as important to cool down after exercising as it is to warm up beforehand. A gradual return to normal of your heart rate and circulation will help remove waste products, such as lactic acid, from your muscles.

Doing stretching exercises to cool down will help your muscles to return blood to your heart rather than allowing it to stagnate in the muscles, as it will if you go from full activity straight to zero. Reduce your exercise gently: for example, if you have been running, slow down to a walk. Ensure that your body does not become cold during the cool-down stage. Have a tracksuit ready to put on. Do your stretching exercises while your muscles are still warm at the end of your work-out.

The benefits of stretching include a significant reduction in:

- Muscular soreness and tension.
- Painful menstruation for women.
- Back problems, joint sprains and muscle strain.

Additionally, once you learn to feel the specific effects of each stretching movement on your body tissues, you will begin to enjoy the relaxing sensation of stretching (just as a cat or dog does), and you will become more aware of your body's potential and your own ability to increase your range of movements. The stretch reflex is a basic operation of your nervous system and is designed to help maintain flexibility and prevent muscle injury.

If you are someone who sits behind a desk for long periods or who does a good deal of running (and therefore uses the leg and back groups of muscles and joints for long periods in the same activity pattern), then you should include stretching exercises specific to your hamstrings and lower-back muscles to counteract the tautness you will have developed there. Flexibility exercises increase overall muscle length and reduce the incidence of muscle tears and strains.

Flexibility is the range of motion through which your limbs are able to move. Your elasticity limits, your connective tissues and the presence of excessive body fat will restrict this range of motion. Trauma occurs when a limb is forced beyond its normal range, so improved flexibility reduces this danger. Flexibility decreases year by year after adolescence due to lessening elasticity in the body's soft tissues, but exercise increases flexibility, so the older you are, the more important are your stretching exercises.

Most of your muscles work in pairs like piston arms. When one set of muscles is contracted its opposite set is relaxed. For the most effective stretching exercises, those parts of the muscle which perform contraction should be totally relaxed. Slow, steady stretching will achieve this best. You should aim to stretch the muscle as far as you can and then hold that position for two or three seconds. This is called the **static stretch**. Holding the stretch for 10 or even 30 seconds is advised by some experts and criticised by others.

Sports like gymnastics, karate and wrestling involve the **ballistic stretch**, which uses the body's momentum to induce a stretch by bouncing, rebounding or bobbing. Stay away from these movements as they can cause soreness and injury.

Many health clubs display instructions for a well-known stretch exercise known worldwide as the **Plough**. My advice is to steer well clear of the Plough. It compresses your heart and lungs as well as placing excessive pressure on your discs and lower back.

Do not stretch if you have had a recent fracture to a bone, if you have any pain or swelling around a joint or if you have a history of osteoporosis.

Correct Posture

The importance of working on the muscles which control posture – especially the abdominals, lower-back gluteals and hamstrings – cannot be over-emphasised, and my exercise system recognises this vital point.

By far the most valuable element of stretching is the maintenance of good posture by constantly nagging yourself, throughout your life, into avoiding the slouch. Good posture affects your whole body, including respiration, digestion, circulation and structural stress.

As we grow older the law of Isaac Newton increasingly applies – and it is not only our stomachs that respond to gravity. Our shoulders tend to slump forward, compressing the ribcage and pushing the upper part of the torso downwards. As a result our waists thicken, shoulder and neck muscles tighten and the hunchback-and-double-chin silhouette begins to appear. The resultant body-tissue collapse causes stiff joints, backache, arthritis, headaches

---

How to Avoid Exercise Injury

Thousands of runners and gymnasts are injured every year while taking exercise. That number could be cut dramatically through the observance of the following basic precautions:

- **Consider seeing a doctor or exercise professional before starting to exercise, especially if you are over 40.**

- **Make sure that you warm up before taking exercise.**

- **Plan in advance how hard to train and for how long.**

- **Always stretch then cool down after taking exercise.**

---

and worse. To help gain a better posture, get into the habit of performing the following simple stretch exercises.

1. Stand naked in front of a full-length mirror (if you can bear it), both frontally and sideways. Pull in your paunch until your stomach is as flat as possible. You have just performed a key abdominal stretching exercise. Remember the feel of it. The more times a day (fully clothed!) you do that single exercise, the better. Hold the position for as long as you can, remembering to keep breathing.

2. Stand on tiptoe and stretch your upper torso upwards as though you are trying to grow taller and 'touch the sky', but keep your arms relaxed by your sides. The 'love handles' of excess fat at your waist will appear to lessen, and, looking in a mirror, you will wish you were always so thin. Hold this position for as long as you can. Again, you can perform this stretch anywhere: on a train or plane trip, or in the office.

Victorian schoolteachers set great store by posture, and one of their favourite exercises was to make their pupils balance books on their heads as they walked slowly down a corridor. This remains an excellent way to train yourself to maintain the posture which will put the fewest strains and imbalances on your body structure. Consult the photograph on the next page and obey the instructional arrows.

Remember that slouching shortens the spine. Learn to use your muscles to correct your posture whether you are standing, running, sitting at your desk or driving your car.

The abdominal muscles are especially important in maintaining correct posture – especially for anyone carrying excess weight around their middle. In the absence of strong abdominal muscles, this extra weight causes forward pelvic tilt and pain and tension in the lower back. Moreover, the abdominals

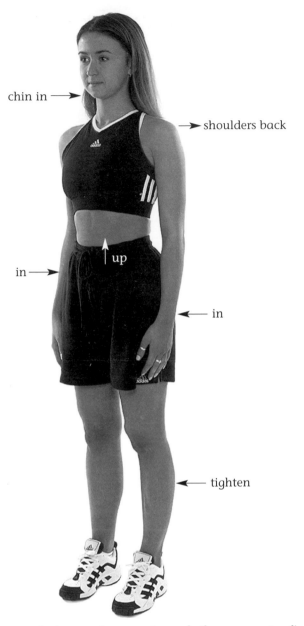

chin in ⟶

⟶ shoulders back

↑ up

in ⟶

⟵ in

⟵ tighten

Learn to use your muscles to correct your posture, whether you are standing, running, sitting at your desk or driving your car.

are the foundation on which your upper torso sits: if they are weak it is harder to keep your body upright and avoid slouching. When you walk you shouldn't rock from side to side, and your abdominals help prevent this. There is a chain of strength which runs from your legs to your hips, torso, stomach and back. Like any other chain, this is only as strong as

its weakest link, which in this case is generally the stomach.

The following simple stretch exercises are all easy to perform and unlikely to cause tissue trauma (unless you ignore the stretching rules given on page 54). Remember that stretching should be slightly uncomfortable but never painful.

Stretching Exercises

Lungs

Stand with your legs some 18 inches apart and your hands on your hips. Check your posture. Breathe in deeply through your nose and feel your upper stomach rise against your ribcage. Hold for four seconds, then breathe out through your mouth until all your breath has been expelled. Repeat five times.

Neck

Stand as before. Revolve your neck slowly through 90 degrees, first to the left, then to the right. Repeat each way three times.

Shoulders and Chest

1. For this exercise you should stand with your feet hip-width apart, knees and toes in alignment, and squeeze your shoulder blades together. Keep your knees slightly bent and your pelvis forward.

2. Lift your shoulders as high as possible and revolve them through 360 degrees in a forwards direction. Do this 15 times, and repeat, revolving your shoulders in the opposite direction.

Neck and Waist

Yoga Body Roll

1. Legs and feet together.

2. Hands grip waist. Push pelvis forwards a bit. Bend over from the waist, not the hips.

3. Slowly roll the top half of your body around to your left and hold for three seconds.

Neck and Waist

Yoga Body Roll

4. Now roll the top half of your body forwards and round to the right. Again hold for three seconds.

5. Slowly return your head to the front. This completes one rotation. Repeat this rotation twice more. Then relax like this.

6. Straighten up slowly. Now do three rotations round the other way.

Arms

Arm Roll (Windmill Roll)

Stand with your knees soft – that is, with your legs slightly bent rather than rigid with knees locked – and facing forwards so that your pelvis tilts forwards a little to take pressure off the lower back. Roll your arms windmill-wise 30 times forwards. Then 30 times backwards.

Arms, Shoulders and Chest

1. Stand as before. Bend arms horizontally at elbows, held at shoulder height. Piston the bent arms back twice.

2. Now, with arms fully straightened, repeat the back-piston movement twice.
3. Do both steps 30 times.

Triceps

1. Stand as before. Place your right hand behind your head and down the middle of your back as far as it will go. Hold for four seconds.

2. Now press your left hand against your right elbow to begin stretching your upper right arm towards your left.

3. Once you begin to feel uncomfortable, hold the position for four seconds. Repeat twice. Now switch sides and do three times with your left hand behind your head and stretching to your right.

Trunk

Do not do this exercise if your back is weak

Stand as before. Raise your left arm above your head and put your right hand on your hip. Bend to the right as far as you can go until you feel the stretch. Do not lean forward. Repeat to the left. Hold each stretch for four seconds. Repeat four times on each side.

Lower Back

I do this quick back and abdomen exercise every morning before dressing and every evening immediately before bed.

1. Lie on the carpet and raise your knees. Hug both knees to your chest quite hard and hold them there.
2. Holding your knees to your chest, concentrate on relaxing your lower back. Sometimes you will find there is no response; on other days, when your back is a touch out of alignment or strained, you will feel the soft tissues realign themselves. Hold the position for up to 10 seconds.

3. Lie straight and relax for a few seconds.

4. Still lying on your back, bend one knee at 90 degrees.
5. With your opposite hand, pull the bent leg up and over your other leg. Your head should remain relaxed on the floor. Repeat with the other leg.
6. Now lie straight, stretch and relax for a few seconds before carefully standing up.

Inner Thighs and Hips

Sit with your back straight, your legs bent at the knees and the soles of your feet touching. Keep your stomach in and allow your knees to fall as far towards the floor as they will go.

You should feel the stretch on the insides of your thighs. Hold at this point for five seconds, and repeat five times.

Hamstrings

The collective name for the muscles situated at the back of the thigh, three in all (biceps femoris, semitendinosus and semimembranosus), is the **hamstrings**. They run from the lowermost part of the hipbone down towards the knee.

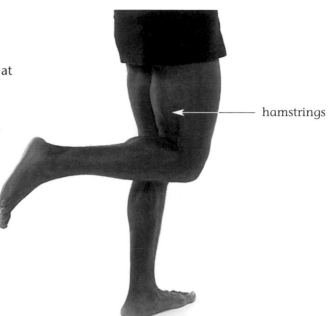

hamstrings

Hamstring Stretch

1. Sitting on the floor, straighten your right leg and allow the sole of your left foot to slightly touch the inside of your right thigh. Keep the right foot pointing upwards with the ankles and toes relaxed.

2. Slowly bend forwards from the hips towards the foot of the straight leg.
3. Hold the stretch for five seconds.
4. Do the exercise with your other leg and repeat five times with each.

Quadriceps

The quadriceps group, together with the sartorius, covers the whole of the front of the thigh. The quadriceps consists of four functionally linked muscles (rectus femoris, vastus medialis, vastus intermedius and vastus lateralis).

vastus intermedius, the deepest part of the quadriceps group

sartorius

vastus lateralis

rectus femoris

vastus medialis

Quad Stretch

1. Stand with one arm out, or one hand against a wall for balance.
2. Flex one leg and raise your foot up towards your bottom. Keep the knee of the supporting leg slightly soft.
3. Grasp your raised foot with one hand.
4. Push down with your foot and resist with your hand for five seconds. Repeat five times with each foot.

Knees and Achilles' Tendons

The Squat

1. From a standing position, squat down with your feet flat, heels between four and 12 inches apart and your toes pointing outwards. Keep your knees outside the width of your shoulders and above your big toes. Hold for 10 seconds.

2. Stand up to your full height. Repeat five times.

Calves

Calf Stretch

1. Stand as above with one leg stretched out behind you, both feet flat on the floor. Keep the knee of the stretched leg locked straight.

2. Placing your weight on the front leg, stretch forwards and downwards. Hold for four seconds and repeat six times with each leg.

To complete all these stretch exercises properly takes up to 15 minutes. How often you complete the full series is, of course, up to you but it will be time well spent. Even after years of running, calf, hamstring, groin and back muscles can become tight and sore. Daily stretching means the difference between enjoyment and discomfort.

Jane Fonda's famous maxim 'No pain, no gain' has been absorbed into the exercise lexicon but exercise therapists have discounted such a policy for over four decades now. There are, it is true, stretch exercises which use the point at which 'it begins to be uncomfortable' as a guide to when you should hold a movement, but the general rule of fitness is to avoid rather than invite bodily pain, because it is often the first sign of impending soreness and stiffness, if not an early symptom of an injury.

A warm bath, not too hot, is good for your soft tissues immediately after your stretching exercises.

Summary of Stretches

Body Part	Exercise	Duration of Holds	No. of Repeats
Lungs	Deep breaths	4 secs	5
Neck	Revolve neck	n/a	3 each way
Shoulders and Chest	Revolve shoulders	n/a	15 each way
Neck and Waist	Yoga body roll	3 secs	3 each way
Arms	Arm roll (windmill roll)	n/a	30 each way
Arms/Shoulders/Chest	Piston arms back	n/a	30
Triceps	Press hands down back	4 secs	3 each side
Trunk	Hand down side of leg	4 secs	4 each side
Lower Back	Hold knees to chest	up to 10 secs	None
Inner Thighs and Hips	Yoga semi-lotus	5 secs	5
Hamstrings	Grasp ankles, seated	5 secs	5 each leg
Quadriceps	Hold ankle behind bottom	5 secs	5 each leg
Knees and Achilles' Tendons	The squat	10 secs	5
Calves	Leaning forwards	4 secs	6 each leg

7

Equipment and Where to Train

Basic Equipment

Shoes

Good footwear is by far the most important single injury preventative. Pick a pair of shoes just for their price or their looks and you will almost certainly regret it. The sports footwear market is huge: you can buy running shoes designed for cross-country, trail, fell, marathon or track. There are up to 20 different models for marathon-running alone, depending on your weight, speed and gait.

So first of all you need to establish what you are going to use your shoes for. If you are going to concentrate on a single activity, invest in footwear specifically designed for your chosen sport. Most people who want to try a range of basic activities (walking, running, weights and circuits, for example) should consider cross-trainers, which are the descendants of the original 'trainers'. These are compromise shoes designed to meet the requirements of a variety of activities without necessarily excelling at any. Even the market for cross-trainers is now so vast that the do-everything training shoe no longer

exists, having been replaced by shoes designed for specific use, such as aerobic (running, aerobics and gym), court (tennis, squash and badminton) and strength activities (weights and gym).

Sports shoes have three basic components: the upper, which surrounds your foot; the outsole, which comes into contact with the ground; and the midsole, the thick layer of foam which separates the upper from the outsole and contains most of the cushioning and stability features within the shoe. How these three basic elements combine depends on the activity they are designed for. Running, for example, is a one-directional sport which puts great stress on your joints, so in a running shoe it is the midsole which attracts the design attention, whereas in tennis the need for lateral stability means the upper in combination with outsole grip is usually the main feature of tennis shoes.

In addition to the basic components there is a wide range of extra technical features often pitched as wonder solutions to particular problems in different activities. This technology is the battleground between companies operating in the market.

Technical sports shoes range in price from £30 up to £200 depending on the activity and the number of features they boast. The most expensive shoe is not necessarily the best, and could well be completely inappropriate for your foot or your level of proficiency. Here are some tips to help you negotiate the shoe-buying minefield.

Your Feet

Before you buy your shoes, ensure that you have a basic understanding of your own foot shape and your gait pattern, particularly if you are looking for running shoes.

- If you have a **normal** gait pattern the outside of your heel hits the ground first, and your foot rolls forwards and inwards before lifting off again from the forefoot.
- Your foot may roll too far inwards, putting strain and pressure on the inside of the ankle. This is known as **over-pronation** and, if unchecked, can lead to injury. If your shoe leans over to the inside when placed on a flat surface, you probably have an over-pronating foot.
- The opposite condition, **over-supination**, is much rarer. A sign of this is your shoe leaning noticeably to the outside.

Your foot shape will give you some guidance as to your gait pattern. You can determine your foot shape by performing a 'wet test': simply look at the shape of one of your footprints when you get out of the bath. It will fall into one of three general categories:

- The **normal foot** has a flare under the arch but one that connects the forefoot and the heel. You will need a semi-curved shoe with little added support or cushioning.
- The **high-arched foot** leaves a print with a narrow band, or no band at all, between the front

and back of the foot. Your gait is fairly rigid and your feet are not good natural shock-absorbers. You should opt for a curved shoe with plenty of cushioning. The high-arched foot is the one most likely to over-supinate.

- The **flat foot** leaves a print of the whole sole, and usually indicates over-pronation. It requires a straight or semi-curved shoe with added stability features built into the midsole or the upper on the inner side, or motion-control features.

Buying Footwear

- **Buy your shoes from a specialist sports retailer.**
- **You can find shoes in most categories within a wide price range, so set yourself a rough budget before you shop, and don't be talked out of it.**
- **Buy shoes later in the day when your feet will have swollen to their maximum size.**
- **Wear your exercise socks when trying on new shoes.**
- **Take with you an old pair of shoes you like to compare with the new ones. The shop's specialist may be able to 'read' the treads for signs of uneven gait.**
- **The ideal fit should give you about the width of a thumbnail between the end of your toes and the front of the shoe. Make sure you can wiggle your toes freely. The heel should be snug but comfortable.**

A word of warning: do not buy super-expensive running shoes and then forget all about your running technique in the mistaken belief that your new magic shoes have made you immune to injury. Exhaustive American surveys have proved that more runners are injured wearing expensive brands than wearing cheaper shoes. This is probably because people sporting top-of-the-range jobs put too much faith in their shoes and 'pound the ground' giving no thought to the jarring of their delicate feet, knees and spines. It certainly makes sense to wear a comfortable shoe with an impact-absorbing system of sorts, but there are plenty of these in the middle price range (under £50).

It is a good idea to buy two or more pairs of running shoes of similar or different brands and wear them alternately. They will all have a manufacturer's idiosyncrasy that strains one part of your feet or another. Wearing your shoes in rotation, as with car wheels, will help equalise the stresses. However small the stress to begin with, it can cause ever-worsening foot damage.

Do not put up with corns, bunions, ganglions or ingrown toenails: they will make you run awkwardly, whether you notice it or not, which may lead to strains. Visit a chiropodist, who will advise on the best course of remedial action. I have had trouble with frostbitten toes and gangrene stemming from pressure, often uneven, on my feet at very low temperatures. Towing a heavy sledge on the Arctic pack ice will quickly damage the feet, especially at the heels, toes and tendons, unless you use the very best socks and boots which carefully blend pliability and rigidity. I have my chosen ski-tour boots moulded to my feet at Snow & Rock in London. An equally custom-built effect can be achieved with moulded insoles which fit any running shoes. These are a boon to anyone who experiences trouble with all off-the-shelf trainers.

Before you start a fitness programme – or, if you have already started, then at any time – it is a good idea to undergo a **bio-mechanical screening** at a foot clinic, where a trained podiatrist will analyse your running technique, gait and foot shape and give you advice on correct footwear for your feet. Don't wait for a foot or back injury before you act. The point of the screening is to locate any existing muscular imbalance before it becomes a serious trauma. Podiatrists conducting foot clinics can be found through the recommendations of your local health club or gym.

Socks

Sock-manufacturers are developing new, high-tech socks all the time. Like shoes, you can buy socks custom-made for your chosen sport which offer the appropriate specific protection. For cyclists, for example, Dri-Stride Climate knits are available in four grades, each designed for a different temperature range. I find the Bridgedale range of socks unbeatable for both running and polar expeditions (see page 194).

Fox River Week-Dry Health socks for runners include an outer layer that absorbs moisture and an inner layer which repels it. A fully cushioned sole area helps to minimise 'concrete jar'.

Sweaty shoes, especially those which have been through puddles and worn wet, often become smelly. One tip for fighting shoe smells is to fill the toe areas of a pair of cotton socks with talcum powder and shove them into your shoes whenever they are not being used.

Reflective Clothing

Every year runners and cyclists die after being hit by cars. More often than not a car-driver cannot see a runner due to blinding sunlight in the daytime or oncoming vehicle lights at night. If possible do your running and cycling away from roads. If this is not feasible, at least be sure to wear a bandolier-type belt with reflectors front and rear. White or bright clothes are an additional common-sense measure. And never run on roads without verges.

Sunglasses

The widening hole in the ozone layer has given rise to concern about runners' eyes. Protect yours with a pair of sunglasses which block out UV-A and UV-B rays and stay firmly in place while you run.

Water Carriers

Keep a supply of water at hand to prevent dehydration. There are many well-designed water containers on the market, from camel-back bladders with suck-as-you-run tubes to easy-grip waist-carried bottles.

Sports Bras

Women who run need sports bras. Since breasts contain no muscle, high-impact exercise performed without a well-fitting bra can be traumatic. Any bra will reduce bounce by 30 per cent, but a sports-specific design will cut it by 60 per cent and lessen post-exercise tenderness and 'runner's nipple'.

The entire breast should be supported and your bra should have a broad band under your bust which is tight enough to prevent 'fall-out'. Adjustable straps should be fixed with Velcro so that they can't loosen. Underwear specialists Rigby & Peller (see page 194) estimate that 90 per cent of women wear the wrong-size bra when running. If the back strap rides up you need a smaller size; if the shoulder straps leave indentations, go up a cup size.

Check the fit carefully when trying on a bra in the shop and test it by bending down, running on the spot, etc. Bras made of materials which wick away sweat, such as Lycra, are better than cotton, which stays wet.

Smaller women can use compression-style sports bras which are more like one-piece tops. Larger breasts require separate cups. If you take a D-cup or bigger, ideally you should have your bra custom-made by a specialist like Rigby & Peller, if you can afford it. An alternative option is to wear a low-backed leotard over an off-the-peg sports bra.

Gym Wear

Whether you are exercising at home or at a health club, comfort and ease of movement are the prime considerations, so that you can concentrate on what you are doing – especially when using strength equipment. Since you will certainly sweat, choose clothes that are non-scratchy, cool and stretchable. For your first few sessions, just wear a simple T-shirt and shorts. When you are sure you are committed to the activity, you can think about investing in specialist gear.

At your fitness centre avoid wearing anything which makes you feel self-conscious. Lycra may seem the obvious answer, but you may not feel your body is yet ready for the surreptitious (or smug) glances, real or imagined, it may bring from your fellow gym-users. All-Lycra or semi-Lycra gym wear is also more expensive than cotton.

On the other hand, it is more efficient: it offers more support without limiting movement and keeps you dry throughout your work-outs. The downside of this property is that Lycra tends to hold body odour more than cotton does, so it needs more frequent washing.

When choosing undercarriage gear, think carefully of your legs: do they look like an elephant's thighs or like chicken bones? In either case opt for loose, lightweight tracksuit trousers. Is your bottom a touch flabby and pendulous? If so, tracksuit trousers are again a good idea, or, at least baggy cotton shorts (remember to wear underpants for modesty's sake). Most people have paunches, even gym-users, and you cannot hold yours in for a full half-hour. Instead hide it with a long-tailed vest or shirt. If your upper arms are a little puckered and loose, wear something with sleeves.

The knowledge that you are sensibly dressed will save any feelings of embarrassment until you are ready to reveal your newly taut and worked-out torso.

Do not use any headgear or neck-wrapper unless you are trying to lose weight through dehydration – which is, in any case, a thoroughly bad idea (see page 31).

Remember to use a towel or paper towel to wipe pools of sweat off the equipment when you have finished with it.

If you become a regular gym-user, and especially if you use weights and weight machines, it is a good idea to invest in shoes with a firm supporting base and not with the high midsole of, say, a running shoe.

All clothes and footwear should fit well to avoid skin-rub. If you are running in a race, keep your clothes dry if it rains while you are waiting to start by donning a plastic rubbish sack with holes cut out for your head and arms. Apply Vaseline to your crutch and armpits, and put plasters over your nipples.

Where to Train

Gyms

Many people find it impossible or impractical to go to a gym or health club. No problem: there are plenty of cardiovascular activities, such as running or cycling, to be enjoyed outdoors, and a wealth of exercises to do in any convenient space at home. But there are a great many undoubted advantages to be gained by joining a gym.

Individuals who go to the Alps, and decide to save money by teaching themselves to ski, nearly always end up with a host of dreadful habits, not to mention injuries, and any subsequent expert tuition is twice as difficult (and costly) because the instructor has double the work: he or she has to deprogramme *and* reprogramme the client.

So when you begin your fitness training you should take some expert instruction, or at least put yourself under the supervision of someone who knows what they are doing. Of course, you can read books and study diagrams and photographs of exercise movements, even watch expensive Jane Fonda or Mr Motivator-type videos. But you will inevitably develop wrong postures and faulty techniques if nobody in the know is able to keep at least a watching brief on your progress. Even simple activities,

like running, have basic rules. In a gym there will usually be someone to explain them to you.

The key to selecting the right gym or fitness centre lies in caution. Visit several alternative sites and have a good look at each. Time is valuable, and if you are going to stick to your new regime you will need a place which is within easy reach and which will be open at the times when you want to use it. A high percentage of people who sign up as members of gyms and health clubs drop out within the first six months, losing the balance of their joining fee (which usually ranges from about £100 to about £400), as well as the 'first year' fee (£300 to £1,000). It is sometimes possible to negotiate a fee for, say, two to six months only, but the majority of clubs stipulate the full 12-month fee up front and do not give refunds.

Think carefully about the practicalities. Perhaps you have a preference for somewhere with a swimming pool, but swimming is of little use as an exercise if you do not do non-stop lengths for at least 30 minutes, which can be difficult in a crowded pool.

And do you really wish to exercise in a machine room the size of a large bedroom with inadequate ventilation? Body odour permeates such places and tempers rise when several visitors want to use the only two running machines at the same time. They are fine if you are staying locally for a day or two, in which case almost any training site is better than none, but they are unlikely to fit the bill if you are going to pay good money and use them often.

If your bank balance is healthy there are clinics you can join in the Harley Street area of London where 30 sessions will set you back £1,600. For this you receive the attention of a personal trainer, personalised exercise programmes, nutritional advice and treatment by an in-house osteopath.

At the other end of the scale, the very worst gym I have ever used was on board a cruise ship sailing to Antarctica, which I joined as a lecturer. The purser, if you could find him, would sign the 'gym' key out to you with bad grace and a ritual muttering about 'your own risk'. The gym was about 13ft square and boasted two antique exercise machines and a set of ill-matched dumb-bells. The Southern Ocean is notorious for non-stop storms. The treadmill managed to tilt sideways and fall over with one violent roll of the ship's hull, and I ended up on the floor alongside a dozen loose and lethally rolling dumb-bells. I confined subsequent exercise sessions to games of poker in the saloon.

In London, working from nine to five in Victoria for eight years, I found that large, public leisure centres were usually a better bet than private clubs because their hours were longer and their facilities more extensive and able to cope with more clients. At off-peak hours I could be sure of completing my work-out and being able to swim without interruption or delay.

Finding somewhere where the instructors are professional, well trained and prepared to treat clients on a personal basis also makes a good deal of difference. Without such personal invigilation you are unlikely to learn correct use of the three types of equipment. **Cardiovascular** equipment includes stair-climbers, bikes, ski machines, rowing machines and treadmills. **Resistance** machines enhance specific muscles. **Free weights** (barbells and dumb-bells) do likewise but are more flexible and, of course, portable.

Aerobics Classes

Aerobics classes in gyms are an excellent way to achieve cardiovascular fitness. The range of classes and activities offered nowadays under the aerobics umbrella is impressive. Classes for beginners usually last for 45 minutes, including a 10-minute warm-up. The best aerobics instructors watch each class member with an eagle eye and correct small posture errors. *High-impact* aerobics involve both-feet-off-the-ground movements which you should avoid if you have knee or lower-back troubles.

Personal Trainers

If you have the money – in central London fees can be anything from £20 to £100 an hour – your very own personal trainer or specialist coach may well be a big boost in your fitness quest. To return to the skiing parallel, I skied for 26 years, becoming (in my own opinion, at least) reasonably fast and capable, though I was still utterly lacking in style and consistency. Then, at a French ski resort, I met a Yorkshireman with a Mohican hairstyle called Spike, who skied superbly and, when he was not off driving trucks in Florida, taught the odd Brit how to ski correctly. My wife and I had five sessions with Spike which dramatically improved our skiing, and we have never looked back. His secret was to study our style with great diligence and then to explain each tiny error over and over again until we understood exactly what we were doing wrong. Only then did he start correcting the problem. This is the function of any good specialist coach.

Personal fitness trainers are motivators who work with a range of people and structure a total-body programme around exercise. They will either come to your home or meet you at a gym, or sometimes they have their own 'clinics'. They will study your current training schedule, find out what you are aiming for and then explain what you should really be doing to make best use of your training time. For example, your personal trainer may find that you are lifting your weights wrongly, dieting foolishly, running with the wrong arm action, breathing out of sync with your exercise movements or committing any one of a host of other self-defeating errors. Pinpointing such faults in your system is not something you can do for yourself and staff at health clubs, however well trained and well intentioned, seldom have the time to focus on any single individual for long enough to spot such problems.

Creating Your Own Gym

Obviously you will need to have the space and the funds. You can place a treadmill in a corridor of your flat and call that a gymnasium, but you are trying to create training conditions which you will enjoy, so blocking up a passageway and sweating at home may be a stress-free option only if you live alone.

For years, when I worked in Palace Street near Victoria Station, my fellow polar expeditioners and I would go for a lunchtime run round the front of Buckingham Palace, down to Hyde Park Corner, through the underpasses, dodging the buskers, and twice round the Serpentine – a good 50-minute stint with a modicum of relatively fresh air in Hyde Park but a high dose of fumes en route. Better than nothing, given the circumstances, but not ideal.

During a particularly busy few months I did not have time for daily exercise around the Serpentine, so I took to running up and down the stairway of our 12-storey office block at the end of the day carrying a 30lb brick-crammed rucksack. One day a new cleaning firm took over at the office. At 5pm sharp, a small regiment of little, rotund cleaning ladies from Manila dispersed around the block with aerosols and sprayed every inch of the wooden banisters on all 12 floors with a noxious polish that lingered in the confines of the stairwell. I encountered this with my heart rate bashing 200 and my lungs gulping air, and the aerosol fumes had an effect on my brain very similar, I imagine, to that of raw glue on an amateur sniffer!

I finally decided to invest in my own exercise kit. In London this consisted of a bench with a cord-operated weight system bolted to the wall of a derelict garage. When we moved to Somerset I cleared and whitewashed a small generator shed (about 13ft by 16ft) and purchased second-hand exercise gear over a period of three years.

The secret in obtaining good second-hand gear is to be patient, know what you want and, above all, deal only with somebody known to your health-club staff or other cognoscenti.

You can expect to pay something in the region of the following prices for new gear, although the price range is quite wide. Always ask for a discount, especially if you are buying more than one machine from the same retailer.

Versaclimber machine:	£940 plus
On-the-spot running machine:	£200 plus
Concept II rowing machine:	£850 plus
Nordic Track ski machine:	£120 plus
Step-up machine:	£60 plus
Bicycle machine:	£120 plus
Two sets of dumb-bells:	£80

With this equipment you will be able to reach a high standard of strength and aerobic fitness so long as you also fresh-air train whenever your daily schedule and the weather allows.

There are a great many wonderful new exercise machines coming on to the market all the time which make extravagant promises of quick fitness results. Take the 'air-glider' machine, for example. This looks like a cross-country ski machine with suspended foot pads and claims to provide a full body work-out, burning up to 1,000 calories an hour without jarring your joints. In fact an air glider will provide only a weak aerobic work-out for any reasonably fit person. Running would be far more valuable. If you are too overweight to run or have joint troubles, a treadmill will be just as useful.

Once you have installed your equipment in your gym, ensure that the place is mouse-proof (mice enjoy eating electrical wires) and burglar-proof (there is a surprisingly large market in stolen gym gear) and that there is a good flow of air through the room when you are using it.

8
Choosing Your Sports

Now that you have assessed your fitness – or lack of it – familiarised yourself with warming up and stretching and considered the basic equipment and places to train, you need to decide upon the activity which will form your main exercise.

How do you choose which sport to take up? Are you too old for some sports? Many fitness gurus will advise running as the only real aerobic way to heaven; others promote swimming as the panacea for all ills on the grounds that it involves all the muscles in the body but no jarring movements. Next most popular with health-magazine pundits are bicycling, aerobics, cross-country skiing and walking. In the end you must go for something that you feel you will enjoy. If you have no strong preferences try various alternatives until you hit the jackpot. If you enjoy the exercise you take, you are more likely to stick at it for decades, not just years or even months, like the vast majority of people. I was training hard at the age of 16 and I am still at it at 54. There were large gaps of idleness en route, sometimes enforced, which I regret, but essentially exercise has remained a constant in my life. The fundamental principle of fitness is **once you have got it, hang on to it**. Becoming keen on an active sport, either a solo or a competitive one, will help you to do so.

Choosing a competitive activity will add an extra dimension to your training. As you get better at the sport, each forthcoming competitive event will become your reason for wanting to keep fit. Once this happens, motivating yourself to don your sports shoes, whatever the weather, will become much easier.

This chapter covers three basic categories of sport:

- Standard aerobic-activity sports.
- Burst-activity sports.
- Endurance sports.

There are areas where activities overlap, but not many. I have picked some examples of the most popular types of activity in each category and commented on their benefits and any drawbacks.

Standard Aerobic-Activity Sports

Treat the table below only as a comparison between the different sports. The precise number of calories you burn may vary from these estimates, depending on your body mass. The faster you exercise and the more effort you use, the more calories you will burn.

Walking

Next to running, walking is by far my favourite form of exercise: not strolling, but walking energetically. Aim for 4mph, the kind of pace you'd use if you were late for work, rather than 3.5mph, which is an average saunter.

I use 600 calories each time I run for an hour, or about 100 calories per mile, compared with only 400 calories during an hour's 4mph walk. But walking is better for your body because it is not as jarring as running. There is far less strain on joints and muscles.

With every step that we run a force equivalent to three times our body weight is transmitted to our feet and up through our legs to our lower backs. Fit people with years of running experience will absorb most of these shock forces due to the muscles they have gradually developed, but a deconditioned individual's musculo-skeletal system will often lack the shock-absorption capability to deal with triple body-weight jarring at every step.

So my advice to anyone starting out on the road to fitness, especially if you are overweight or have problems with knees, hips or back, is to begin a walking regime long before you try running. Anyone wishing to switch from non-weight-bearing activities, like cycling or swimming, to running should also spend a few interim months walking. There are over 60 million regular fitness-walkers in the USA alone, and every country has walking clubs, walk races of many distances and known cross-country walking routes, often of great beauty. There are over 140 recognised long-distance walks across Britain's most lovely countryside. The best known walk in Britain is probably the Pennine Way, which is remote, high and rugged. You need to commit yourself to some 25 miles a day for over a week in order to ensure that you always reach a village where you can stay overnight.

Average Calories Burned by Various Activities

	5 Mins	*10 Mins*	*20 Mins*	*30 Mins*
Running (6mph)	50	100	200	300
Cycling (13mph)	40	80	160	245
Rowing	40	80	160	240
Swimming (breaststroke)	45	90	180	280
Aerobics	35	70	140	220
Walking (3.5mph)	35	70	140	200

Note: The only safe rule of thumb is that you will burn *100 calories per mile* (whether you walk, run or sprint). There are variables such as your weight, the duration of long runs or walks and the intensity of effort, but these will not affect this rule significantly.

To burn more energy you need, of course, to increase your walking speed. Runners move forward partly with the assistance of their own momentum, so it is arguable that walking is more efficient at energy-burning than running, although runners burn more fat than walkers. West Virginia University conducted a test in which one group of women walked for 45 minutes four times a week and a second group went running according to the same schedule. After 12 weeks the runners had all experienced a significant reduction in body-fat percentage whereas there was no change in the walkers.

To increase your walking pace, do not 'stride out'. Instead take more steps and shorten your stride. If time is not on your side, go for shorter, faster walks to achieve a higher calorie-burn. To provide variety as well as to improve agility and balance, try walking backwards for one minute in every ten (outdoors, not on a treadmill).

If at all feasible keep away from roads and head for the country, or at least a park. You are less likely to be run over and there is less car exhaust about. During a 30-minute roadside walk, you will breathe in some 20 times per minute and subject your lungs, bloodstream and muscles to poisons equivalent to a full pack of cigarettes, so road-walking is a rare example of an exercise which is less beneficial than no exercise at all.

Another danger of walking in towns and parks is the risk of mugging. The experiences of mugged walkers suggests that the majority openly wore Walkman radios, Rolex watches and £160 Nike super-shoes, the envy of many an urban gang member. Whenever I train along the Thames towpath near Hammersmith or round the northern half of New York's Central Park, I slip off my watch and hold it in a clenched fist.

- Walking is a suitable exercise for millions of people who cannot run.

- You can go on walking well into your 90s.
- Although normal-stride walking may burn only 300 calories an hour, you can increase this rate easily by walking faster, carrying a load, adding gradients to your route or choosing an uneven surface across country.
- Even 3mph 30-minute walks will help lower bad-cholesterol levels and strengthen your bones against osteoporosis. Many people who suffer from knee problems when they run remain untroubled during brisk walks.

Walking Programme

When you begin your walking regime it will help to have time and distance goals in mind. My advice is to follow this three-step programme.

1. Make sure you can comfortably walk two miles in 35 minutes (3.5mph) and do so at least three times a week. Once you can do this (not before), start to increase your workload.
2. Next begin to check that you are maintaining about 70 per cent of your MHR throughout your walk (except in the warm-up and cool-down phases). Now aim to comfortably complete three miles in 36 minutes (5mph). At this rate you could realistically describe yourself as a power-walker. Step 2 may take six months to reach once Step 1 has been achieved.
3. You will need to walk at this rating three times a week for four-mile distances to maintain a reasonable level of fitness. When you feel ready for a change, you may wish to graduate to running.

Technique

To achieve a 5mph walking speed you will need to use your arms as well as your legs. Swing your arms forward with aggression. Keep them bent at right angles at the elbow and try to avoid swinging them across your body. This tendency will develop an unbalanced, side-to-side sway which will slow you down. Other points to watch:

- Breathe as normally and regularly as possible.
- Keep your back straight, chin level with the ground, shoulders relaxed and abdominals tightly pulled in.
- Swing your arms from the shoulders, raising them towards your chest.
- At each step, work your foot thrust from heel to toe.
- Wear loose, breathable clothing and lightweight, well-cushioned shoes with cotton socks.

Running

You will notice that the word 'jogging' is not used in this book. In the running community it has no definition to distinguish it from running, and furthermore it has acquired a pejorative sense, so it is best avoided.

Here we will deal with running for beginners and intermediates who are not involved in long-distance races but who just want to run to keep fit. For advanced training, including marathon-running, see pages 161–166.

Since running is a high-impact activity, do not use it as your path to fitness if you find it brings you a stream of nagging sprains and other soft-tissue injuries. Walk, swim or cycle instead. If these sports strengthen you and make you lose weight, perhaps you can give running another go later on.

Good stamina means that running for a bus will not make you gasp for breath. Exercise which makes you breathe more deeply builds stamina, training the body to be better at transporting and using oxygen. Running is an unbeatable method of doing this. Some people are fortunate enough to enjoy running from the outset. I did not enjoy it when I started as an Army cadet. I was part of a platoon of other trainees being barked at by a sergeant – not the best way to grow to love any activity.

Luckily for me, I then joined a regiment whose officers were nearly all horse-riding fanatics, so whenever an officer was needed to train the regimental team in canoeing, orienteering or cross-country running, I landed the job without a fight. In trying to kindle the enthusiasm of soldiers less fit than myself, I learned that anybody can come to love running, provided that they are not under constant pressure to improve their performance against others. It is purely a matter of perception. If you understand that running is the best thing for your health, that it costs nothing and can be done with minimal gear, and you know it is the key to enjoying a wide variety of stimulating activities, then you can persuade yourself to like doing it, and to do it regularly. There is no better way of losing calories. Remember, 600 calories are burned in a one-hour slow run and at least 2,000 calories in a slow marathon.

Teach Yourself to Like Running

- Start slowly, and increase your pace gradually to a steady lope. Keep this up until the finish. If I'm running for an hour I will probably not ease into the lope until halfway through the session. It is for the first few minutes of each run that you will feel the worst – sore in some areas and tight in others.
- Don't be too rigid over any programme if this means it will interfere with your social or business life. The pressures may build up and rob your runs of enjoyment. Instead keep your diary flexible to avoid developing hostilities with family, friends and business colleagues.
- My ultimate goal when running is competitive – but not in the sense of a short-term race. It is to be running well into my 90s, when all my running peers of today are in their bathchairs.

If you are unfit and have not run before, you can follow the 30-week programme below and progress gradually to relative fitness. Later chapters in the book will cover advanced running.

The 30-week programme involves straightforward runs at your own pace. To improve your stamina and ability, you may like to try different paces such as fartlek, hill running, long runs and resistance work.

From Beginner to Fit Runner

(30-week programme)

Week		1	2	3	4	5	6	7	8	9	10
Starting Out	Sessions Per Week	2	3	5	5	3	3	2	5	3	3
	Duration (mins)	–	15	14	12	12	11	10	16	16	14
	Distance (miles)	1	1	1	1	1	1	1	1.5	1.5	1.5
	and also:										
	Sessions Per Week	1	2	–	–	2	2	3	–	2	2
	Duration (mins)	–	–	–	–	–	18	18	–	22	21
	Distance (miles)	1.5	2	–	–	1.5	1.5	1.5	–	2	2
Getting Fit	Sessions Per Week	3	4	4	4	3	4	3	4	3	4
	Duration (mins)	18	18	24	23	17	22	–	22	17	21
	Distance (miles)	2	2	2.5	2.5	2	2.5	2	2.5	2	2.5
	and also:										
	Sessions Per Week	2	1	1	1	2	1	2	1	2	1
	Duration (mins)	–	–	–	40	–	50	45	60	36	65
	Distance (miles)	3	4	4	–	4	–	5	–	4	–
Fit	Sessions Per Week	3	5	3	4	4	4	4	3	3	1
	Duration (mins)	–	36	26	35	25	–	–	–	24	23
	Distance (miles)	3	4	3	4	3	4	4	5	3	3
	and also:										
	Sessions Per Week	2	–	2	1	2	1	1	2	2	4
	Duration (mins)	–	–	54	–	45	–	–	–	72	44
	Distance (miles)	4	–	6	8	5	10	8	8	8	5
	and also:										
	Sessions Per Week	–	–	–	–	–	–	–	–	–	1
	Duration (mins)	–	–	–	–	–	–	–	–	–	–
	Distance (miles)	–	–	–	–	–	–	–	–	–	12

Noakes' Law

There is a mass of conflicting 'rules for runners'. The best advice I have read for competitive-minded runners is contained in the 14 points of Noakes' Law, compiled by Professor Tim Noakes, a well-respected sports scientist from South Africa.

1. During any one year, train for 10 months and take a holiday from running for two.
2. Don't be ashamed to walk during any training run. Maximum benefit on any run is achieved by training at between 60 and 90 per cent of your MHR.
3. The important element of training is the amount of time you spend running each week, not the speed at which you run or the distance you cover.
4. All training schedules should be treated as guidelines, not concrete regulations. Learn to listen to your body so you can judge your own most effective schedule.
5. Always allow time for a hard run's micro-damage to your body to repair and for your energy stocks to replenish.
6. Find your happy training medium between the two adages 'No pain, no gain' and 'Train without strain'.
7. Don't race during training runs. Run races of over 10 miles only infrequently.
8. Running trains only the legs, not the upper body. Adding an activity such as swimming to your running programme is a good idea.
9. Never overtrain. Watch out for sluggishness and lethargy, loss of appetite and increased infection susceptibility.
10. Where possible work with a coach for encouragement and support.
11. Success in running involves training the mind as much or more than the body.
12. Rest before racing.
13. Keep a training logbook. It will allow you to check exactly what training you did before your best race results.
14. Everything you do, all day and every day, affects your running ability – nutrition, stress and sleep as well as exercise.

Fartlek

This ugly Swedish word means 'speed play'. Fartlek involves altering your speed from time to time with sudden short spurts of sprinting. You can sprint between two markers on your route, or just lengthen your stride for, say, 500 paces, counting them as you run.

One advantage of making yourself run faster than your normal speed is that it increases your VO2 max, the technical term for your maximum oxygen consumption limit. Beyond your VO2 max the heart can send no more oxygen out to your muscles. You can train your body to slightly raise this limit by running longer distances, but the best way to do it is to run faster from time to time. This will help your heart and muscles to learn how to use oxygen more efficiently.

Interval Training

Whereas fartlek runs are unstructured, interval

training involves varying your speed over set periods or distances, first running fast, then resting or walking, followed by another fast run. You might decide, for instance, to do six 1.5-mile circuits with three minutes' recovery between each circuit. If you do this once a month and record your overall time, you will be able to gauge the progress you are making in your training.

Hill Training

If you live in a hilly area or near sand dunes, you have the best possible training course to improve your general fitness and leg strength. No other form of running is as efficient at training your leg muscles to function at high levels for long periods without tiring. Running up hills is exhausting but the more

you do the less difficult it becomes. In a typical one-hour run I try to include at least 10 minutes of steep hill work, sometimes 15. In a city office, a fire escape stairway can be a good substitute.

Long Runs

Running for long periods (at least an hour) teaches your body to burn fat rather than glycogen and gives you the psychological ability to cope with longer distances. The downside is that regular long runs break down muscle fibres and deplete muscle glycogen, so you should always give yourself at least 36 hours' rest between sessions. The other days can be used for strength training and upper-body exercise.

Plodding away for two hours at a slow pace will

The author (centre), aged 32, with the Territorial SAS mountain race team in the Welsh 3000 race in 1975. John O'Callaghan

only train you to be a slow runner unless you inject some fast surges every so often. I run fast every 10 minutes for a count of 20 seconds. This is surprisingly tiring but it is well worth the extra effort.

Resistance Training

Wearing a weighted vest or carrying dumb-bells when running will slow you down and make you work harder, thereby increasing the number of calories you burn. But since resistance training also increases the risk of ankle injuries, it should not be undertaken more than twice a week to give the body time to recover.

A Sample One-Week Training Schedule

To maintain your fitness you need to run on a regular basis, whether or not you enter races. Everyone suffers from setbacks such as bad weather and feelings of lethargy which tempt them to skip their run sometimes. A weekly schedule helps self-motivation. It should include a sensible mix of strength as well as stamina training which won't be provided if you just endlessly repeat your favourite run.

The following sample schedule, designed to maintain fitness, is for use *only* once you have become fit.

Sunday

Your long run – at least six miles. Twelve to 13 miles is ideal. If you want to gradually increase the distance add a half-mile each week until you reach 20 miles and then revert to 13 again.

Monday

Use Monday for strength training and upper-body work. If you run at all, make it an easygoing three to six miles.

Tuesday

Find a hill or an area of soft sand, or use a treadmill.

After an easy warm-up of 15 minutes' slow running on the flat, complete six pretty tiring hill ascents, sand sprints or treadmill speed-bursts, each of three or four minutes' duration, with three-minute slow spells in between.

Wednesday

Do an undemanding run of about six miles followed by 30 minutes' strength work. Plyometrics (see pages 133–136), crunches, squats and stretches, etc. will help overall strength and flexibility.

Thursday

After a warm-up run, complete 45 minutes of interval training. Run at your best pace (but not a sprint) for four minutes using a circuit, or at least a known stretch of ground, to ensure that you extend yourself to your current fitness limit. Rest for three minutes by running gently. Then repeat the four-minute push. Do this five times, and finish with an easy 10-minute run.

Friday

Rest day.

Saturday

As Wednesday – a six-mile easy run plus 30 minutes of strength work.

Cycling

Cyclists, like swimmers, suffer fewer training injuries than runners. And if you cycle to and from work, you can skirt the traffic and actually save time as you exercise. Cycling will build your leg muscles, and since these large muscles generate quantities of the waste product lactic acid, you will increase your tolerance to its build-up.

The main muscles used in cycling are the glutes, quads, hamstrings and calves. Strength and power training are more effective on a bicycle than in the gym. Bodybuilders do not win cycle races! A strong lower back and abdominal muscles and hip flexors benefit cyclists, so exercises such as crunches and leg raises (see pages 140, 125 and 126) are worthwhile. A strong heart and lean body also contribute to cycling prowess. Male cyclists ideally show 10 to 12 per cent body fat and women between 15 and 18 per cent. Cycling is an excellent form of aerobic training but, strength-wise, your upper body does not receive much of a work-out.

Cycling does have disadvantages, most obviously a higher death rate than most other forms of fitness activity, due to road accidents caused by careless motorists or, sad to relate, by lack of thought on the part of cyclists themselves. It is also likely to be expensive initially, certainly compared with running and swimming. And there is car-exhaust pollution to consider. Pollution masks do not keep out noxious fumes, they merely block some physical particles in the air. So their usefulness is at best dubious.

A rough calorie-burning guide for cyclists is:

Cycle Speed (mph)	Calorie Burn Per Mile (flat)
10	26
15	31
20	38
25	47
30	59

Riding a good-quality, modern bicycle with hi-tech gears on flat surfaces, you are largely putting your effort into countering air resistance rather than into forward propulsion. Drag increases relative to wind speed, whether it is your own or that of the weather. Gradients will also provide hard work. To get an idea of your cycling fitness level, find yourself a three-mile flat course without too much traffic and preferably no potential hold-ups like traffic lights. After a warm-up, ride your three miles as fast as you can and record your time.

	Men	Women
Below average	>12 mins	>15 mins
Average fitness	8–12 mins	11–15 mins
Above average	<8 mins	<11 mins

Using the same circuit you can measure your ongoing improvement at later dates.

The trouble with cycling is the difficulty of knowing when you are training within your optimal training zone. On an exercise cycle in a gym there is, of course, no problem maintaining the rate on the monitor, but out in the big wide world there are pedestrian crossings and road junctions which hamper an uninterrupted work-out and useful heart-monitoring. Most beginners cycle at a cadence or pace of 60 to 80 revolutions per minute (rpm), a revolution being one complete turn of the pedal with one leg. Twenty-two revolutions every 15 seconds will give you about 90rpm, which is the optimal fitness training speed once you are cycling fit.

The skill of maintaining 90rpm, whatever the wind or gradient, involves knowing when to change to which gear, a skill which may take weeks or even months to acquire. Remember that the bicycle's gears are there both to make you go faster and save energy. Try to keep up a cadence of 85 to 95 on flat roads and 65 to 75 on hills. Maintain your momentum on short hills (up to 1,500ft long) by using more power with a slower cadence. On longer hills try to settle in and pace yourself to the top with a slower cadence.

Beginners often start in too high a gear (the higher the gear, the harder you have to pedal) and ride with their saddles too low. Your saddle should be level with the top of your hip when you are standing next to your bike. While you are cycling your legs should, when either foot is at the lowest point, be in the five to six position on an imaginary clock as shown in the photograph on page 86 to prevent over-extension of the knees.

Set your saddle height so that your legs are in the 'five to six' clockface position when the pedal is at its lowest point.

Before you begin the cycling programme on page 87 you will need to ensure that you have acquired a sound basic knowledge of cycling road skills and smooth gear-changing on all gradients, and that you are equipped with a bicycle to which you have grown accustomed, a helmet, shorts, gloves, shoes, drink bottles, reflective clothing and bandolier and repair kit. All these items should be bought from a specialist cyclists' shop.

It is difficult to be accurate about target times and distances due to wind speed and gradients, but try to gauge them as closely as possible. Above all, stick to your training programme as rigidly as you can. If you progress to the expert stage you will be cycling at 20mph like a veteran.

When you reach the intermediate level, you should introduce burst sprints into your training. Professionals advise one-minute bursts of speed twice during each 30-minute session – one in the middle and one near the end. When you have achieved the advanced level, increase this to four bursts of two minutes' duration each.

Mountain-Biking

Mountain-biking is one of the fastest-growing sports in the world.

I took it up because it was one of the endurance activities involved in the 1996 Eco-Challenge Race in which I participated. I found it extremely enjoyable and would recommend it, along with running and swimming, as one of the best ways of staying fit into your dotage. You can also do it anywhere, from the concrete jungles of the city to rugged mountain trails.

There are three main types of mountain bike: the entry-level bike, the enthusiast's bike and the full-suspension bike. The **entry-level** type is the most basic machine which can withstand fairly strenuous off-road riding without falling to bits. This costs around £250 to £300.

The **enthusiast**'s version is lighter and stronger and has a suspension fork that allows smoother, faster off-road progress. This costs about £600.

Full-suspension bikes are the best for any steep off-road work. They offer front and rear wheel suspension (making them a touch heavier), which gives a far smoother ride on steep, rough, downhill stretches. At between £1,000 and £4,000, they are, however, a serious investment.

Saddle Height

You can damage your knees if the saddle is set at the wrong height, so when buying a bike ensure that you follow the manufacturer's instructions in setting the height, and check that the frame of the bike is not too large or too small to allow correct saddle adjustment.

Riding Tips

• Bicycles are mainly steered by leaning rather than by turning the handlebars, and the faster you go the more this is true. Turning the handlebars too much off road on a loose surface will

Cycling Programme

	Week	1	2	3	4	5	6	7	8	9	10
Beginners	Sessions Per Week	3	3	3	3	3	3	3	3	3	3
	Duration (mins)	10	12	11	17	10	16	15	14	13	18
	Distance (miles)	–	2	2	3	2	3	3	3	3	4
	and also:										
	Sessions Per Week	2	2	2	2	2	2	2	2	2	1
	Duration (mins)	–	15	18	25	30	35	38	40	42	45
	Distance (miles)	–	3	–	5	–	6	–	7	–	–
Intermediate	Sessions Per Week	3	3	3	3	3	3	3	4	3	4
	Duration (mins)	20	16	20	24	15	28	18	26	14	22
	Distance (miles)	5	4	5	6	4	7	5	7	4	6
	and also:										
	Sessions Per Week	2	2	2	2	2	2	2	1	2	1
	Duration (mins)	55	40	50	–	48	58	45	–	53	–
	Distance (miles)	10	8	10	12	10	12	10	15	12	20
Advanced	Sessions Per Week	3	3	3	2	2	3	2	4	2	2
	Duration (mins)	21	25	30	17	13	19	22	26	25	32
	Distance (miles)	6	7	8	5	4	6	7	8	4	10
	and also:										
	Sessions Per Week	2	2	2	3	2	2	2	1	2	2
	Duration (mins)	50	–	–	40	58	–	54	–	52	70
	Distance (miles)	12	12	20	10	15	15	15	15	15	20
	and also:										
	Sessions Per Week	–	–	–	–	1	–	1	–	1	1
	Duration (mins)	–	–	–	–	–	–	115	–	–	110
	Distance (miles)	–	–	–	–	30	–	30	–	30	30
Expert	Sessions Per Week	3	3	3	3	4	3	2	4	2	2
	Duration (mins)	25	28	17	22	25	22	30	30	32	40
	Distance (miles)	7	8	5	7	8	8	9	9	10	12
	and also:										
	Sessions Per Week	2	2	2	2	2	2	2	1	2	2
	Duration (mins)	55	67	40	54	65	65	62	–	60	85
	Distance (miles)	12	20	10	15	20	20	20	25	20	25
	and also:										
	Sessions Per Week	–	–	–	1	1	–	1	–	1	1
	Duration (mins)	–	–	–	115	–	–	105	–	–	120
	Distance (miles)	–	–	–	30	35	–	30	–	40	40

David Smith, Steven Seaton and the author train in Wales for the mountain bike section of the 1998 Eco-Challenge Race in Morocco. Hélène Diamantides

often make the front wheel understeer. Practise leaning to turn your bike. Obviously, when travelling very slowly you will use the handlebars more – and you need good balance.

- Don't tug at the brakes – a mere finger-squeeze should be enough to lock them.
- Mountain bikes usually have 24 gears in three sets of eight. In average conditions use the middle set; when climbing very steep stuff use the low set, and choose the high-gear option for fast riding. Change gear while you are not pushing too hard on the pedals, except when a sudden climb forces you to change immediately.
- The technique of climbing on loose surfaces involves crouching down to get your upper body close to the handlebars to prevent front-wheel lift.

Use the gears actively, get your weight over the driving wheel and don't stand on the pedals.

- Going downhill, keep most of your weight back but make sure that you are still in full control of the handlebars and brakes.
- To avoid obstacles on a narrow track, lift the front wheel by transferring your weight quickly to the back wheel: push down hard on the pedals and throw your weight backwards. To clear large obstacles follow up with a 'bunny hop': simply jump in the air by pulling upwards on the pedals to lift the bike off the ground. (Pedal clips are of course necessary for bunny hops.)

Equipment

Mountain-bike crashes can be hard, so you need a

good, well-fitting helmet and proper bike gloves, with or without fingers, to protect the skin on your hands if you come off the bike. Bike glasses with plastic lenses (which should also keep out all UV light) will stop flying grit blinding you. You will need biking shoes. These have soles which allow you to pedal hard without hurting your feet.

Biking should not – except through constantly repeated pressure on the relevant artery – make men impotent, so ensure you use a comfortable saddle. You can choose from a wide variety of saddle shapes when you buy your bike, and you can get cushioning pads to slip over the saddle. Wear biking shorts with synthetic chamois padded inserts to cut down chafing and bruising between your legs. Even then you will feel some tenderness until you toughen up with practice.

Repairs

Make sure you know how to clean and oil the chain, remove the wheels and tyres and repair punctures. Otherwise, sooner or later, you will have a very long walk looking foolish.

Swimming

Swimming does not burn as much body fat or produce the same aerobic results as quickly as running or even cycling, but the water supports your weight, so there is very little pressure on your joints. This makes swimming ideal for anyone who wants to maintain their fitness but who is very overweight,

---

injured or pregnant. And it works more muscle groups than running or cycling. Swimming does not trigger exercise-induced asthma in asthmatics, unlike many other sports.

Obviously, if you cannot already swim it is not something you can learn from a book, and the same is true of technique improvements. If you decide to take it up at all seriously you must have lessons from a professional at your local club or pool, which are not expensive. Lessons will soon make you a great deal more efficient in terms of the distance

---

> ### *Swimming Tips*
> - **Anti-fog goggles are a must.**
> - **Do not swim within an hour of a meal.**
> - **Vary your stroke to work out different muscles.**

> ### *Sea Swimming*
> **The muscles of dedicated people who do a great deal of long-distance swimming often appear to be covered with fat. The body tends to store fat to allow better flotation and as insulation against the cold.**
>
> **Swimming in rough water is much harder work than swimming in a pool. It is harder to stay afloat and to find clear water for each propulsion stroke. Safety is an increased concern, so if you intend to swim in the sea, abide by these basic rules:**
>
> - **Study the beach alongside your proposed route at low tide to see where the deeper zones lie. You can then zigzag accordingly to stay in your depth.**
> - **Take local advice about the behaviour of the tide.**
> - **If there is nobody to ask, wade out to waist height and float for a few minutes watching a couple of fixed points on land to check which way the tide is taking you.**
> - **Always start your swim against the tide or current and return with it to your starting point.**
> - **Never swim deeper than waist height.**

Swimming Programme

	Week	1	2	3	4	5	6	7	8	9	10
Beginners	Sessions Per Week	2	2	2	3	3	5	3	5	3	5
	Duration (mins)										
	Distance (yds)	55	55	110	165	275	330	330	440	440	550
	and also:										
	Sessions Per Week	–	2	3	3	2	–	2	–	2	–
	Duration (mins)	–	–	–	–	15	–	–	–	–	–
	Distance (yds)	–	110	165	220	330	–	440	–	550	–
Intermediate	Sessions Per Week	4	3	5	3	5	2	3	5	3	5
	Duration (mins)	5	5	8	7	10	12	11	14	13	15
	Distance (yds)	220	220	330	330	440	550	550	660	660	770
	and also:										
	Sessions Per Week	–	2	–	2	–	3	2	–	2	–
	Duration (mins)	–	8	–	13	–	–	16	–	19	–
	Distance (yds)	–	330	–	550	–	440	770	–	880	–
Advanced	Sessions Per Week	2	2	2	2	2	2	2	2	2	2
	Duration (mins)	14	13	13	21	21	20	26	26	25	25
	Distance (yds)	550	550	550	880	880	880	110	110	110	110
	and also:										
	Sessions Per Week	3	3	3	3	2	2	2	3	3	3
	Duration (mins)	11	10	18	17	16	21	25	32	30	32
	Distance (yds)	550	550	880	880	880	110	1,210	1,320	1,540	2,595
	and also:										
	Sessions Per Week	–	–	–	–	–	1	1	–	–	–
	Duration (mins)										
	Distance (yds)	–	–	–	–	–	1,210	1,540	–	–	–
Expert	Sessions Per Week	2	2	2	2	3	2	2	2	2	3
	Duration (mins)	12	10	12	19	20	11	18	22	23	22
	Distance (yds)	550	550	550	880	880	880	1,100	1,320	1,100	1,100
	and also:										
	Sessions Per Week	3	3	3	3	2	2	2	3	3	3
	Duration (mins)	10	8	16	16	16	20	25	31	30	38
	Distance (yds)	550	550	880	880	880	1,100	1,210	1,540	1,540	1,980
	and also:										
	Sessions Per Week	–	–	–	–	–	1	1	–	1	–
	Duration (mins)										
	Distance (yds)	–	–	–	–	–	1,210	1,540	–	1,650	–

Note: 1 yard = 0.9144 metres

you cover for the energy expended. Additionally, you will avoid developing or continuing bad habits, such as swimming with your neck craning out of the water, which can lead to back problems. As a general rule, remember that with breaststroke it is your leg kicks, assisted by the arm strokes, that are your powerhouse. With crawl, backstroke and butterfly your arms provide the most propulsion. Breathing technique is critical.

When swimming it is easy to slow down to below your optimal training zone, thereby largely wasting your time and effort. The swimming programme given here offers a structured regime which will prevent this from happening. The distances in the programme are all in yards, so if measurements are not given at your pool you will need to ask an attendant or pace out the length of the pool (a rough guide is that one adult stride equals one yard or roughly a metre). The advantages of avoiding the confined nature of a pool are considerable, so if you are able to use a lake or the sea it is well worth working out the distances on an Ordnance Survey map (make sure you follow the safety precautions on page 89).

Swimming Programme

If you can already swim the crawl or backstroke non-stop for 110 yards you should skip the beginner stage. Vary your stroke between crawl and breaststroke with the occasional backstroke thrown in, and by the end of the programme you will be swimming a mile in 25 minutes.

- Before each session plan how many lengths (or how far along the beachside) you are aiming to swim.
- Swim a few leisurely lengths to warm up and stretch your limbs before you start each session (if the water is cold, leisurely may not be an apt description).

- Be sure to complete all the sessions each week. If only a time is given, swim for that time, no matter how far you go. Likewise, if only a distance is given, swim that distance for however long it takes.

Rowing

Rowing uses a number of large muscle groups and provides good aerobic training. The vast majority of oarsmen or women join clubs and use club boats – there are more than 200 open rowing clubs in Britain. Rowing in a team boat or sculling solo (useful for days when the rest of the team cannot make it) requires access to a river or lake and two or three weeks of instruction. You can start at almost any age, depending upon your fitness. To locate your nearest club, contact the Amateur Rowing Association (see page 193).

Thousands of oarsmen and women do the majority of their training on rowing machines, usually indoors. Many individuals who have never rowed on a river, nor wished to, are addicted to competitive machine-rowing. Undoubtedly the best-known machine is made by Concept II, which runs a series of worldwide ongoing competitions for both sexes in every grade of age and body weight. They publish annual lists, so in theory you can work your way up, in your own home, to become the best in your grade in Britain, if not in the world. In terms of an incentive to help self-motivation, this is certainly a winner.

Early in 1998, not having rowed since I was 17, I started training at home for 15 minutes twice a week on a Concept II Indoor Rower. Some seven weeks later I used the rowing machine in an hotel where I was staying for a conference. The in-house health-club manager suggested I try my luck at the 2,000-metres timing. He set the monitor and I sweated away until he told me my time was up.

'Not bad!' he exclaimed. 'Seven minutes twenty seconds.' I checked this in the Concept II ratings for 1997 and discovered that I was the 15th fastest in Britain for my grade (over 11 stone 11lbs and between 50 and 59 years of age). If I added the lighter entrants of the same age group, I dropped to 22nd. I would need to lose only a mere 20 seconds to reach the top 10, so the incentive for me personally is excellent. My problem, and that of many would-be rowers, is that there are few sports worse for aggravating lower-back problems.

Instructors will tell you there is nothing to worry about if you keep your back flat and your abdominals pulled in and avoid jerky strokes. My London back surgeon, once the long-distance canoeing champion of England, disagrees. However, for the majority of people, who are not susceptible to lower-back weakness, rowing is definitely a good fitness training option, indoors or on the river, whatever your age.

Rowing Programme

The training programme on page 93 is applicable for river work and you should stick to the times given, whatever the wind conditions. For indoor rowing machines, you need to know which readings on the monitor are best for you to aim at, and that will depend on your current ability. Each machine has a resistance-setting lever. This should be set at the halfway position and then forgotten.

The monitor gives you your stroke rate per minute (spm). You need to watch this and keep it at whatever rating puts you into your personal cardio-vascular training zone (see pages 43 and 45–46). If, on a given day of the programme, you are to row for 20 minutes, you may choose to vary your stroke rate with two-minute speed bursts alternating with slower stretches.

Row slowly and concentrate on correct posture as well as rhythm with each stroke for five minutes before beginning each session. Do not do the longer session on consecutive days if you can avoid it. Remember to cool down with slower strokes for two or three minutes at the end of each session.

Aerobics

'Aerobics' has become a general umbrella term to describe a variety of different group-fitness classes, all of which share the common goal of carrying the group through an extended exercise period to develop their basic aerobic fitness. The instructor sets the pace and tone for you to follow. Classes usually last for 30 minutes to an hour.

Although aerobics classes are open to anyone, they tend to be more popular among women, and are a good starting point for women who want to take up an exercise regime for the first time. The integration of music into the routines makes them fun and blurs the distinction between exercise and dance.

Custom-designed footwear with a low-profile, well-cushioned midsole and ankle support is important for many of the high-impact forms of aerobics, such as step classes. Overuse injuries such as shin splints are common problems for regular participants.

If you are overweight or have weak knees, you should start with the low-impact movement classes rather than high-impact ones. As an alternative to a dance class, step classes feature plastic steps which add an extra muscle work-out to plain dance-type movements. This is especially successful in firming up hips, thighs and buttocks.

New classes are introduced constantly. The names they are given vary, but the following examples show the kind of sessions generally on offer:

Orientation: An introductory course covering various types of studio activity, such as step, aerobics and body-conditioning.

Rowing Programme

	Week	1	2	3	4	5	6	7	8	9	10
Beginners	Sessions Per Week	1	1	1	1	1	1	1	3	1	1
	Duration (mins)	5	6	8	9	11	13	15	17	17	19
	and also:										
	Sessions Per Week	–	2	2	2	2	2	2	–	2	2
	Duration (mins)	–	7	9	10	12	14	16	–	18	20
Intermediate	Sessions Per Week	1	1	1	1	3	1	1	1	1	1
	Duration (mins)	14	15	16	17	18	19	21	22	23	25
	and also:										
	Sessions Per Week	2	3	2	2	–	1	2	2	1	2
	Duration (mins)	15	16	17	18	–	20	22	23	24	26
	and also:										
	Sessions Per Week	–	–	–	–	–	1	–	–	2	–
	Duration (mins)	–	–	–	–	–	21	–	–	25	–
Advanced	Sessions Per Week	2	1	2	4	3	1	14	3	1	–
	Duration (mins)	23	24	26	27	28	29	30	32	33	34
	and also:										
	Sessions Per Week	2	3	3	1	2	4	3	1	2	4
	Duration (mins)	24	25	27	28	29	30	31	33	34	35
Expert	Sessions Per Week	1	3	1	3	2	4	3	5	3	2
	Duration (mins)	31	32	33	32	34	35	36	38	39	43
	and also:										
	Session Per Week	3	2	4	2	3	1	2	–	1	3
	Duration (mins)	31	32	32	33	35	36	37	–	40	45
	and also:										
	Sessions Per Week	–	–	–	–	–	–	–	–	1	–
	Duration (mins)	–	–	–	–	–	–	–	–	42	–

Aerobics: A combination of high- and low-impact movements designed to condition the heart and lungs.

Low-Impact Blast: Low-impact, low-intensity aerobics – a good class for fat-burning.

Body-Conditioning/Body-Sculpting: An all-over, easy-to-follow exercise which tones specific muscles, with or without hand weights.

Aerobic Conditioning: A combination of aerobics and body-conditioning.

Stretch and Tone: Increases flexibility, muscular strength and endurance.

Contours: A slow, intense class concentrating on deep stretching and tightening of the major muscle groups.

Lower-Body Blitz : A body-conditioning work-out for the muscle groups of the lower body.

Aqua: A total-body work-out in water.

Aqua Natal: A work-out in water particularly suitable for ante- or post-natal exercise or for women who are new to exercise.

Boxercise: Boxing/martial-arts-style training without the fighting.

Triple Challenge: A cross-training class combining step, aerobics and body-conditioning.

Step: An aerobic work-out using choreographed moves on a step to promote cardiovascular fitness and strength.

Hydrotherapy

Hydrotherapy is water exercise and treatment – an ideal activity if you are injured. It provides the same benefits as other aerobic exercise but with the cushioning safety of a weight-bearing environment.

The secret to a good cardiovascular work-out is maintaining a straight posture in the water by aligning the head, shoulders and hips. Even when you move forward to move faster you should keep this posture. If you are not used to water, wearing a flotation belt will help. Beginners often find it difficult to control their posture and co-ordination in the pool. You can increase the intensity of a work-out by cupping your hands as you move them through the water.

After only a few sessions a quality 30-minute work-out will provide fitness benefits comparable to 30 minutes of running. The added resistance of the water also develops muscular strength.

Whatever type of aerobics activity you favour, you may not wish to feel obliged to keep up with the rest of a group, preferring instead to work to your own level. However, if you want to exercise solo at home with a video you should combine this with instruction sessions so that you don't form bad habits.

If you decide on private exercise at home, you will benefit from a situation of no competition, no intimidation, just you and your mirror reflection, the television and your work-out videotape. When buying tapes do not be influenced by the appeal of the well-muscled person on the cover. Your personal ability must be the yardstick for your choice of the most suitable tape – are you a beginner, intermediate or advanced at aerobic exercises? Why not borrow some videos from a friend or rent them to find out what is on offer before spending good money on the wrong tape? Whatever you go for, make sure it includes adequate warm-up and cool-down stretch data.

Three 30-minute sessions weekly should be your minimum programme. Sort out your aerobic room so there is plenty of space, make sure temperature is OK and wear comfortable clothes and shoes. Never rush a session.

Skipping

Skipping is hard work but excellent for aerobic fitness, calorie-burning and low-impact landings, since your feet only just leave the floor. Choose a skipping rope with swivel handles. To check that the rope is the correct length for you, stand with both feet on the centre of the rope. The handles should reach your armpits.

Start with 30 skips, and rest for 30 seconds. Repeat twice more. At your next session, reduce the rests by five seconds and thereafter knock off five seconds each time until you have eliminated the rest periods altogether. Once you have the knack of leading with the same foot, try alternating with the other foot.

Keep your feet within an inch of the floor. Bend your knees slightly to absorb impact, relax your shoulders and keep your upper arms close to the body. Turn the rope with your wrists, at hip height. Hold your back straight, abdominals in and head up. Try jumping with both feet.

Buy a skipping video.

Skipping Programme

	Week	1	2	3	4	5	6	7	8	9	10
Beginners	*Sessions Per Week*	1	2	2	3	3	2	2	3	3	3
	Duration (mins)	3	4	5	7	8	9	11	14	17	20
	and also:										
	Sessions Per Week	–	–	–	–	–	1	–	–	–	
	Duration (mins)	–	–	–	–	–	13	–	–	–	
Advanced	*Sessions Per Week*	3	3	3	3	4	3	2	4	5	5
	Duration (mins)	12	14	16	18	21	24	27	33	36	40
	and also:										
	Sessions Per Week	–	–	–	–	–	1	–	–	–	–
	Duration (mins)	–	–	–	–	–	26	–	–	–	–

Cross-Country Skiing

In suitable countries with relevant climates, cross-country skiing, or langlauf, makes more sense than running, at least in winter.

The British, of course, are somewhat disadvantaged by a lack of snow-covered terrain, but there are a number of excellent cross-country ski machines on the market which are easily portable and will fit into a space not much larger than a typical treadmill would require. Exercising on a ski machine requires a good deal more effort than using a standard runner's treadmill because you are working your upper and lower body simultaneously. However, some statistics indicate that ski machines are apt to fall into disuse more quickly than most other exercise machines, which is presumably a reflection of the innately idle nature of most of us.

For five years in the early 1960s, I taught Scottish soldiers in the British Army how to langlauf in the Bavarian mountains. I gained third prize in the British Army 20-kilometre langlauf/shooting biathlon race in 1967–8 and spent three months every winter training hard. When racing you need to be extremely fit and capable of many intermittent sharp accelerations along with an overall unrelenting pace. You must develop style and technique because a skilled skier can easily cover twice the distance using half the energy of a skier as fit but less skilled.

Considerable upper- and lower-body strength allied to agility, flexibility, balance and endurance make langlauf racing a superb low-impact sport for all-round strength and aerobic fitness, but the majority of cross-country skiers, who enjoy the sport without racing, use rather less energy than the average runner because they glide along with maximum help from momentum.

The author, aged 19, temporarily leading the field in the 20km Biathlon Championships (British Army on the Rhine). Melville Jamieson

Burst-Activity Sports

In contrast to aerobic sports, in which movement is for the most part continuous, burst-activity sports involve participants in bursts of spasmodic, explosive energy with interim periods of lower-level activity or rest. These sports include golf, soccer, rugby, tennis, martial arts and hockey. A different emphasis on training is necessary for 'burst' sports, muscular strength being more important, along with flexibility and agility. Short-term endurance is also needed. A lot of these sports burn calories more

effectively than many aerobic sports. For instance, in a single basketball game, a player will use up, on average, more calories than someone doing a 30-minute continuous run.

Of the three main categories of sport I would least recommend burst-activity sports if you are selecting an activity merely as a good way to keep fit. Either they require very specific muscular training, which will involve you in a great deal of additional time on top of your basic aerobic work, or they carry a high risk of injury which will interrupt your fitness maintenance.

Contact sports such as soccer and judo are not a choice I would advise from a long-term fitness point of view because of the likelihood of injury.

Once you are injured, your chances of maintaining your fitness plummet. Rugby has the worst record as far as injuries are concerned. Most rugby injuries are fractures, and most of them will radically interfere with your ongoing ability to keep fit.

If, however, you already play one of these sports, I would recommend that you add aerobic training to your strength and flexibility repertoire if you have not yet done so. This will make you less prone to injury.

Golf is a burst-activity sport which is popular with both sexes and a wide age range. If you decide to take it up as your route to fitness, you will need to concentrate on certain specific training to get the best out of your body and you will also have to add an aerobic activity, such as running, unless you can include enough continuous brisk walking in your round of golf to satisfy minimal aerobic needs (see pages 8–9).

Take Tiger Woods as an example of superlative golfing ability. He does not look especially beefy, but he is both strong and flexible due to a weightlifting programme and can generate a faster club-head speed than any other professional on the international circuit.

The faster the club head hits the ball, the further the ball will go. Strong and flexible muscles produce greater force and move faster than weak, inflexible ones. Because Tiger Woods is very flexible, especially in the rotational muscles of his torso, he can achieve a huge shoulder turn at the top of his backswing, and this comes from the specific nature of his muscular training. This principle of specificity of training applies to all burst-activity sports, and the more professional your instructor, the better your chances of achievement through the right training regime.

Sports Injuries

Violent sports like rugby can cripple players for life, but the majority of contact sport injuries are fractures which are unlikely to result in permanent disablement. After splinting and rest, the fractured bone simply 'resets' and exercise can be resumed.

Equally common are strains and sprains. A strain is an injury to a tendon (which connects a muscle to a bone). A sprain is an injury to a ligament (which connects one bone to another).

When a weapon like Will Carling's knee strikes and traumatises your thigh muscle, the resulting bruised area may well bleed internally and form a haematoma. This will make itself felt as a localised pain when you try to take further exercise. The best method of dealing with injuries of the haematoma type, or painful swollen joints, is RICE (Rest, Ice, Compression and Elevation).

Rest is needed to avoid further trauma to the injury. Ice lessens the bleeding and should be applied every three hours for periods of 20 minutes. Compression (by bandage) limits the area of swelling and thus helps the healing process. Elevation of the damaged area to above the level of the heart uses gravity to help drain excess fluids.

If you see your GP, he may add further treatment, or even arrange an X-ray just to check that the damage is not worse than you think.

Endurance Sports

The third and last activity category is endurance sports. Rock-climbing, marathons, orienteering, cross-country running, steeplechasing and, since 1993, high-altitude sky-running are but a few of the challenges you could enjoy. You may wish to move on to these once you have reached a high level of fitness and need an added incentive to help you maintain it. For this reason, I have covered endurance sports later on, in Chapter 13. By planning to participate in an endurance race of some sort once every year, I have managed to keep very fit, largely through the fear of making a fool of myself on the day of the race if I don't.

Endurance racing is becoming more and more popular and new varieties are springing up annually to add to the many long established events all over the world. Marathon-running requires you to keep fit all year round for a specific goal, which is by far the best way to avoid recidivism.

Once you join a running club you will hear on the grapevine of a welter of competitive opportunities. Every type of race, over just about any distance, will be happening somewhere. You can run as a team member or as an individual, and there are even family races. You never hear about these happenings until you start joining in, but then they can become as much of an obsession as you want them to be.

9

Keeping It Up

Whatever type of exercise you favour, you should gradually increase the duration of your sessions. If you have opted for running, for instance, but have not used the programme on page 81, then after a month or two of regular 10-minute running sessions, you should graduate from 110-calorie to 350-calorie work-outs (30 minutes), and once they become well within your grasp, move on to 35 minutes, increasing to 60 minutes. At 60 minutes (600-plus calories) and more, depending on your speed, your rate of aerobic fitness improvement will level out.

A good way of deciding how to balance your intensity and frequency needs is to aim to expend around 2,000 calories a week to stay reasonably fit. You must choose the best way of achieving this goal.

Your options (assuming a 6mph speed) include:

- Running for 30 minutes (300 calories) daily for seven days a week.
- Running for 40 minutes (400 calories) daily for five days a week.
- Running for 50 minutes (500 calories) daily for four days a week.

- Running for 60 minutes (600 calories) daily for three days a week.

Training effects are reversible if your work-outs stop or become inadequate in intensity or frequency. There will be on average a 50 per cent loss of achieved fitness status after about 10 weeks' inactivity and a 100 per cent loss after about 30 weeks.

Remember:

The Intensity, duration and frequency of your training should be above your training threshold and below your overload point but, as you grow fitter, both of these should increase.

If you are training hard you will only stay healthy if you can rest adequately between your work-outs. Fitness comes through the recovery process after training as much as through the training itself.

After each intense training session, the body's

99

tissues are slightly damaged with micro-trauma (tiny tears) to muscles. The repair process takes 36 hours, and if new trauma occurs prior to repair, scar tissues can develop, leading to ongoing damage. The nervous, the immune and the hormonal-release systems also need time to recover after high-stress activities. You should *feel* recovered after one training session before starting another. By alternating long runs with gym-training days, muscles and the other stressed body systems can be given an adequate rest and overtraining trauma avoided.

Overtraining is as harmful as under-recovering: extreme levels of exercise can cut the body's glutamine (an amino acid) levels, which affect the immune system. A symptom of this may be frequent colds and illnesses. Overtraining is more of a risk for non-professional athletes because they may exercise five or six times weekly in tandem with a highly stressful schedule of long office hours and late nights.

Ninety per cent of those who make an initial decision to take regular exercise fall by the wayside because they lack motivation. Staying fit is like staying married: you have to work at it – if you do not, you will fall out. Two in five marriages end in divorce. Like many others, my marriage went through difficult patches for the first three or four years of settling down, but we weathered the storms and now, 28 years later, I thank God that we did, because things could not be better and we have learned to deal with the occasional bad days.

Even after 30 years of taking exercise, you will still have off days when the temptation to be lazy is especially strong. Having an overall, long-term aim – such as simply to stay healthy – is important, but the key to sticking with regular exercise is to maintain a series of short-term goals. Your conscience must revolt powerfully each time your willpower starts to wilt at the thought of exercise (maybe the weather is horrible or your partner needs more attention. You are too busy or you feel tired). You must sort out a mental drill that helps you to fight these voices of temptation. The biblical response 'Get thee behind me, Satan' is fine if it works for you, but I find I need something much more positive and personal. I must know exactly why I am training and why I need to keep exercising regularly rather than merely when the mood takes me. So I give myself a specific annual, or sometimes biannual, goal, such as entering a team endurance event scheduled for a year's time. Then I have the incentive of meeting up with the other team members for weekends every now and again to compete in minor races or to participate in some joint testing activity. In between these weekends, it is up to each of us to keep fit or risk letting down ourselves and the rest of the team. This is the principle used by Alcoholics Anonymous – a sort of group therapy which fights temptation – except that in our case the temptation is idleness rather than alcohol.

This section offers some basic tips on making things easy for yourself both mentally and physically, especially when things go wrong or at times in your life when your normal routine is broken.

Most people who try to keep fit have to squeeze their training into a tight schedule – and at the same time keep the boss and the family from becoming grumpy. You must therefore make every training moment count. Be aware, too, of other factors which may work against your fitness efforts. These include:

Sleep

Lack of sufficient sleep impairs concentration, causes stress and lowers the body's defences against illness. Most people under 60 need an average of eight hours a night at least. After that age, the nocturnal sleep quota begins to diminish and is partly replaced by daytime naps.

Light

Lack of fresh air and sunlight lowers the morale. If you have to work indoors, perhaps without windows, from first light to sundown, do what you can to enjoy as much daylight as possible. Use your lunch hour and weekends for open-air exercise if you can, and sleep with at least one window and the curtain open. Go for a stroll before bed, even if it is only for five minutes.

Temperature and Skin Care

Always aim for moderate temperatures whether you are running a bath, having a sauna or setting the thermostat at home. Try to have your office temperature reasonably regulated. Unfortunately, the climate in many office blocks is centrally controlled with sealed windows and standard heat settings. All the office germs are piped around for general consumption. After a day at work you hop on the bus, tube or train and catch any virulent strains of flu which you have failed to pick up in the office. If a small office pressure group (ideally chaired by a friend, not by you, so your file is not labelled 'troublemaker') makes a strong point to the powers that be, you can often succeed in greatly improving your quota of fresh air or at least making your environment less stifling by arguing that healthy working staff make more economic sense than high heating bills.

Avoid draughts, especially constant ones that can affect you day after day. Dress to keep comfortable all day, so that you are never too cold or too hot – layered clothing you can take off and put back on is the answer, whether you are commuting, hill-hiking or running (a tracksuit top ties easily around your waist during a run). The most effective clothing thermostat is a soft cap for your head that fits in a pocket when not in use.

Temperature moderation is, of course, also important at night. It is generally best to sleep under a light duvet which keeps you slightly on the cool side of warm.

Your body temperature is regulated by your skin's pores, so skin care is important for both sexes. My facial skin began to wrinkle and crack in my early 30s due to too much exposure to extreme conditions. When I found that my wife's day and night creams from Clarins kept post-polar skin troubles at bay better than the cortisone cream prescribed for me, I carried on using them, and now, 20 years later, I still apply them morning and night. My face is still as unwrinkled as it was 20 years ago, despite the annual battering it receives from blizzards, extreme cold and dangerously high UV levels. (See also pages 167–168 on skin cancer.)

Weak Links

Many serious fitness disciples suffer some forced time off from training every year due to troubles with 'weak links'. Perhaps in time human evolution will put these basic design faults right, but for now it is advisable to take precautionary measures before a weak-link injury occurs. The main problem areas are the ankles and lower back.

Ankles

The Achilles' tendon must be treated with respect or it may cause ongoing difficulties. Your Achilles' is easily identifiable, unlike most tendons, since it is clearly visible at the back of your ankle.

The trouble usually starts with gradual tendon deterioration over many runs or country rambles. Overweight people, especially the over-40s, are well advised to keep clear of steep climbs and uneven ground. Sports, like football, that involve jumping are not a good idea for anyone with Achilles' problems.

Footwear which inhibits the full play of the tendon during exercise is bound to spark off trouble.

The tearing of the tendon as a result of a sudden inappropriate overload will leave you in no doubt as to what has happened, for the pain is usually acute. You will be unable to walk on your toes and the area around the tear will swell, often dramatically. Surgery may be necessary. Either way, the tendon will need an immobilising plaster cast for at least eight weeks. Thereafter, and in close consultation with your GP, you should progress to an airbag splint or at least elasticised ankle supports.

Rehabilitation has to be planned with great care to avoid undue strain to the tendon before it has properly healed. Even stretching exercises should be treated with caution. Ice and heat applications are often a help. There are plenty of upper body and 'other leg' aerobic and strength exercises to do while the tendon recovers.

Other common runners' injuries include blood blisters under the toenails, accompanied by painful swellings. You should see a doctor to have the blisters lanced and, when you are ready to run again, be sure you have properly fitted footwear. Normal blisters on your feet respond to the same treatment. They can be prevented by wearing modern anti-blister two-layer socks, which cut down friction.

Ankles, and to a lesser extent heels, have to put up with a great deal of load stress and torque, as well as sudden unexpected linear twistings. The many delicate foot bones and tendons do their best, but matters are made worse if your poor ankles do nothing for 23 hours a day but sit under a desk, lay in bed or pump the clutch and then suddenly find themselves involved in a violent work-out and under great stress.

For years I suffered ankle pains, especially first thing in the morning and for the first 10 minutes of any exercise. I limped along to see doctors, used Ralgex and elastic bandages, but nothing worked for long. If anything my ankles seemed to be getting slowly worse. Then, in 1996, Jonathan Beevers, my fitness adviser, taught me a series of simple ankle-strengthening and stretching exercises (see opposite). Since I started to do these exercises, touch wood, my ankles have been pain-free. For the first three months of the regime I did all four exercises, with three repetitions each, three times a week. Now, to keep my ankles in good condition, I just complete each directional stretch twice, which takes only one minute.

Lower Back

My back has been subjected to the rigours of parachuting, and mountain-racing with backpacks, followed by 25 years of hauling heavy sledgeloads over broken ice with a 'cold' body. The result has been a loss of elasticity of the ligament tissue around the base of my spine. You can experience the same problem with your lower back after just a few months of far more gentle forms of exercise. It's a question of luck and genetics.

My GP directed me to a specialist he knew in London, whose own back problems had interfered with his sporting career and prompted his determination to help others likewise afflicted. Dr Bernard Watkin of Wimpole Street was the British long-distance canoe champion for a number of years and official doctor to the British Olympic canoeing team in 1972. He is an expert at easing back pains by deep injections of a dextrose/glycerine/phenol solution into the ligaments of the lower back on either side of the spine. After my first two sessions with Dr Watkin I felt rejuvenated and suffered no further pains for at least two more years of intense pre-expedition training and hauling 500lb sledgeloads for thousands of miles.

When additional years of violent exercise undid the effects of the sugar solution and the spasms returned, I simply returned to Dr Watkin and a further injection instantly put things right in time for the next expedition. If I was to stop the rough treatment of my back I would probably need no further visits to Wimpole Street.

Ankle Stretches

Arrows denote the approximate area you should *feel* stretching

Lie down flat and move your feet as follows. Heels move as little as possible.

1. Move ankles as far as possible in a downwards direction. Hold for three seconds. Return to normal position. Repeat six times.

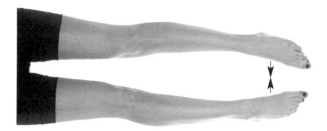

3. Start with feet at least 24 inches apart. Move ankles inwards as far as possible. Repeat six times.

2. Move ankles as far as possible in an upwards direction. Hold for three seconds. Return to normal. Repeat six times.

4. Move ankles outwards as far as possible. Repeat six times.

For the many thousands of us who suffer from recurring lower-back twinges (varying from localised aches to several days of immobilisation), there are thousands of others currently unaffected, but whose running and other training work will sooner or later have a bad effect on their lumbar regions. There are a dozen general guidelines to help you avoid this – do not use rowing machines, do not do push-ups, do not run on hard surfaces, etc. – all good advice, but lower backs will still give trouble.

I have learned never to try to carry on when my back goes wrong. If you do it can lead to lasting lumbar damage. I am not prescribing any preventative measures that will put things right for ever: I have suffered spine-jolting falls on to iron-hard ice blocks and come away without a single twinge, whereas at other times I have turned over in a warm bed at home and, bingo, my back has managed to slip out of place. What I am recommending is a few basic rules that I have followed for ten years, since my lower back began increasingly to give trouble when I was 44. They have improved the problem enormously, even though there has been no change in my expedition and exercise workload.

- Always be aware of your posture – especially when you are sitting at a desk, watching TV or driving (see pages 55–56).
- Use back cushions (obtainable by post – see page 195) on any chair or car seat which you use regularly.
- Do a floor exercise to strengthen your abdominals every morning and evening of your life (for example, the crunch exercise on page 140). This will not produce a washboard stomach, but it will greatly relieve your lower back from unnecessary stress.
- Avoid running on hard surfaces and wear shoes with cushioned soles. Avoid running downhill. If this is unavoidable, follow the rules on page 160.
- Swimming is the best exercise for the lower back (but not breaststroke or butterfly). The next best is walking. Running, however, involves a forward lumbar tilt which can stress the discs in your spine.
- Lift things and put them down in the correct way. Bend at the knees, not at the waist, and ensure that no part of your body is twisted when you are lifting or lowering anything heavy.
- When you want to carry a backpack, use a rucksack with a well-designed frame and adjustable straps. Both Berghaus and Karrimor offer excellent types which can be found at most specialist retailers. If you go for long hikes with quite heavy loads, it is good practice to intermittently alter the rucksack strap settings to ensure that the weight borne by your back and shoulders is evenly distributed.
- My back specialist finds that the majority of his patients are middle-aged business people who spend most of their day at a desk and then try to get fit on a haphazard basis. Try to find a good back specialist so that when things do go wrong, you can quickly get medical help and avoid permanent damage. Information on back care is available from the Back Pain Association (see page 195).

Fitting Your Training into a Busy Day

If you have a full-time job, on a working day you have only three chances to train: before work, during your lunch break and after work.

In the interests of domestic harmony, lunchtime is the most diplomatic choice for those of us with partners and families. And there are other advantages, not least daylight, especially if you are training outdoors in wintertime. If you are concerned about weight control, lunchtime work-outs have the added bonus of lessening your appetite during the period of maximum temptation. After a run or visit to the gym, develop the habit of having a healthy snack, say a bottle of water or juice with a wholemeal salad sandwich and nuts. If this sounds disgustingly inadequate to you, as once it did to me, I can only ask you to give it a try for a week. After a few days you will find such a meal can be tasty and filling without the addition of a bar of chocolate or doughnut.

If you are working hard and feel tempted to skip a lunchtime work-out, remember that training now will actually make you work better during the afternoon. It breaks up the stresses of the day and accelerates the metabolic rate of your body, including your brain, in readiness for the next batch of tasks. Go to the gym and complete a mix of aerobic and strength exercises for at least 30 minutes (not including warm-up and cool-down/stretch time). When you return to the office after showering and changing, you will feel much better for the rest of the day.

If you are self-employed and can choose which time of the day to train, pick the time which suits you best and when you enjoy it most. Morning exercise may burn more fat but it does not use more calories, so if you are trying to lose weight any time of the day will do equally well. However, it is worth considering that most heart-attacks occur in the morning.

If you do not work in an office, but in a factory, hospital or school, for example, you will need to try to adapt this advice to your own circumstances. An overload of work, no free time in your lunch break, young children, unsympathetic partners and night-shift work can all conspire to wreck your exercise regime.

It may prove difficult to avoid social friction if you stick rigidly to a pre-set training schedule. Be prepared to be flexible, but do not use this as an excuse for weakening. Accept that keeping fit may infringe on other activities and keep focused on your priorities.

Tips for Travellers

If your job involves a lot of travelling, and therefore lacks routine, it can be difficult to stay fit and healthy. Problems include lack of training facilities, and, especially if you travel overseas, lack of sleep, food poisoning and infections.

Exercise Facilities

One obvious solution for travellers is to always choose hotels with swimming pools and gym facilities. Indeed, if you can do this, with everything on site it may be much easier to fit your training into your working day than it is at home.

If your company's budget doesn't run to such hotels, many cities have excellent, centrally located parks with minimal pollution where, at least by day, there are safe areas for runners. Central Park in New York, Hyde Park in London and the lake front in

Chicago are fine examples. However, when seeking out suitable green spaces, ask someone with local knowledge rather than just picking out a likely-looking area on the city map. In Seoul I once pre-selected a hotel which my map showed as being adjacent to a spacious park. When I arrived in the South Korean capital and ran up the hill to the centre of the park, the thick miasma of diesel pollution soon had me coughing and spluttering.

Of course there are many people whose work involves travel, such as sales reps or lorry-drivers, who do not always have either the budget for posh hotels nor the time or facilities to run or swim on work days. They need to be especially adaptable if they are to train at all regularly. If you are a lorry-driver, you could keep a set of dumb-bells in your cab, for example. Where there's a will, there's a way.

Lack of Sleep

When you are going abroad and crossing time zones, sleeplessness begins on the flight out, especially on long-haul trips when you are travelling against the Earth's rotation and your body clock (i.e., westwards). To counteract this:

- Always take your shoes off as soon as you are seated on an aircraft.
- Do not converse with your neighbours.
- Use the headset to counter the snoring of others and the eyeshade 'blindfolds' against intrusive lights.
- Drink lots of water and avoid alcohol.
- Eat as little as possible.
- Do not succumb to the temptation to watch videos.
- Take a sleeping tablet or two if you are travelling Economy, and therefore in a seat which renders unassisted sleep almost impossible. (This is a rare example of a situation where taking a sleeping tablet is worthwhile.)

Food Poisoning

Hundreds of thousands of cases of food poisoning occur annually in Great Britain at home as well as from eating out. But the most dangerous bugs are those to which we have never been exposed and against which we therefore have no immunity, so travelling abroad increases the risk of food poisoning. Cats, dogs, chickens, mice and rats all carry the salmonella bacteria which cause anything from mild to lethal intestinal infections in humans. E-coli bacteria are yet more virulent. The world-famous US parasitologist Michael Kliks wrote that humans have only to travel outside their normal environment and dietary range to substantially increase their habitual dose of potentially deadly bugs.

Water-borne parasites cause jaundice, cholera, amoebic dysentery and many other nasties. In much of south-east Asia and Africa, people work in warm, wet fields often fertilised with human manure and seething with parasites. So only drink bottled water from known safe sources. Avoid ice in your drinks and don't eat salads. Peel all vegetables and raw fruits. Make sure you clean your teeth using only bottled water.

Tips for the Pregnant

Most research indicates that exercise has no adverse effect on pregnancy or birth. Indeed, it reduces complications during pregnancy and delivery and can shorten labour by as much as a third. So women who are fit when they become pregnant will benefit from continuing their training schedule with only one or two minor adjustments. However, you should not start a fitness regime when you are pregnant unless there are extreme circumstances necessitating this, in which case you should seek medical advice. As long as they are healthy, pregnant women will find that their bodies are more than able to cope with the dual stresses of pregnancy and exercise. In fact, athletes have often improved their overall peak performances when pregnant, while non-pregnant colleagues on the same training programme have not.

Exercise can minimise many of the annoying and debilitating symptoms that often accompany pregnancy; what is more, pregnant women who have reduced their exercise regimes have reported an increase in such symptoms. If you become pregnant, check with your gynaecologist before continuing any exercise programme. Once you have the all-clear, you should ensure that you exercise regularly, not intermittently, and avoid all jerky or bouncy movements. Note also the following advice offered by a top Paris clinic:

- Drink lots of water to help cut down fluid retention.
- Eat plenty of fibre to ward off constipation.
- Wear a well-padded bra to support and protect enlarging and tender breasts (see pages 73 and 194).
- Take additional naps to combat pregnancy fatigue.
- Eat small meals and healthy snacks often, not big meals, to minimise nausea.
- Never smoke, drink alcohol or continue any low-calorie diet.

Exercise Advice

If your pregnancy is normal you can exercise with minimal limitations and without fear of harming your baby or your body. Walking, swimming and low-impact aerobics are far better than running. Machine-wise, the best options are stair-climbers, treadmills and, in early pregnancy, rowing machines.

Activities to avoid are those which involve lying on your back, cause dehydration, require good balance, risk buffeting the abdomen or involve a change in atmospheric pressure (such as scuba-diving).

There are some excellent videos on the market

giving clear, concise instructions and demonstrations of how to work out during all stages of pregnancy (an especially good one is available from Virgin Vision).

Avoid weightlifting, unless you are practised at it, in which case limit your work to weights light enough to allow you to complete a dozen repetitions easily, and adhere strictly to the following list of 'don'ts' for the duration of your pregnancy.

- Do not use any leg-resistance machines.
- Do not do squats, lunges of any type or leg curls.
- Do not do hip-abductor exercises, or indeed, any back or hip exercises.
- Do not lift weights on consecutive days and never strain, hold your breath or wear a tight belt.
- Never lift weights when you are alone.
- Never exercise in any way if any of the following conditions apply to you:
    A history of pre-term labour.
    Persistent bleeding.
    Incompetent cervix.
    Pregnancy-induced hypertension.
    Pre-term rupturing of membranes.

If you feel tired or have unusual symptoms, check again with your doctor before continuing with your regime.

Tips For the Menopause

Twenty per cent of women experience no menopausal problems at all. Others may suffer from loss of sexual desire, hot flushes, thinning hair, dry skin, breast changes, dry vagina, weight troubles, mood changes and memory lapses, usually between the ages of 45 and 55. Loss of the hormone oestrogen after menopause can lead to strokes and osteoporosis, but this can be reduced by Hormone Replacement Therapy (HRT). (See chart on page 108.)

Like puberty, the menopause is an inevitable fact of life, but observing the following points will help the associated symptoms:

- Take regular exercise. This will reduce hot flushes as well as diminish the risk of heart disease and osteoporosis.
- Take vitamin E. This will reduce sweating and flushes some three to four weeks after you start a course.
- Eat fewer fatty foods and more fruit and vegetables.
- Reduce caffeine and alcohol intake.
- Cut down on cigarettes. Better still, cut out cigarettes altogether.
- Sleep on a towel to absorb night sweats and have warm showers rather than hot baths.

Tips For the Elderly

The natural tendency for all flesh is to decay slowly but surely. It is largely up to you how you speed up or slow down your own decay rate. As you grow older you will become fatter, slower and hunched if you let things go. Your heart will be able to cope with less and less exertion unless you keep it exercised, and your arteries free of 'bad' cholesterol, through aerobic activity.

Of course, athletes who keep fit, eat and drink sensibly and do not smoke will find their performance deteriorating slowly with age, but they will enjoy vastly improved health compared with people who take less trouble about body maintenance. The more you exercise, the slower you decline. The greatest fall in fitness is due to sitting around. Exercise at a reasonably high level and you should stay in fine shape well into your 90s.

Heart-attacks can be brought on by exertion. Many people die in their 50s in everyday situations like mowing the lawn, climbing a ladder, travelling on an aeroplane or working in the garden. Most of them could have avoided a heart-attack by taking

HRT: The Pros and Cons

Millions of menopausal and post-menopausal women already use HRT (hormone replacement therapy) but it can have serious side-effects. Each woman must weigh up all these factors and make the HRT decision based on her own circumstances. Someone with osteoporosis in the family may decide it is sensible to go for HRT whereas someone with a genetic history of breast cancer would perhaps be best advised not to take it.

Advantages

• The oestrogen in HRT keeps skin smooth, nails strong and hair thick. Women past their menopause often find that fat tends to accumulate at their midriffs, and oestrogen reduces this tendency. It also cuts down harmful fats and clotting substances in the blood, thereby helping to stave off heart disease and arteriosclerosis.

• Oestrogen is thought to enhance bloodflow to the brain, thus delaying senility and dementia.

• The main reason many women use HRT is for relief from unpredictable hot flushes and night sweats, to avoid osteoporosis, if they believe they are vulnerable to it, and to maintain their sex lives.

Dangers

• The downside of HRT is the increased risk of breast cancer, asthma, increased blood pressure and depression. Other less serious side-effects could include renewed menstrual bleeding, headaches and unwanted body hair.

more aerobic exercise, not smoking and controlling their diets.

As you grow older, the rules of exercise and food-control become more and more important. By the time you are 80 your output of digestive juices will have dropped by 25 per cent, so easy-to-digest foods become increasingly necessary. You will find it more difficult to lose weight as you age because your output of those hormones which encourage muscle growth and lean body mass will decline. The only way to actively raise growth-hormone production is to take exercise.

From the age of 20 your muscles will only maintain their integrity if you keep exercising them. If you give them no exercise at all, perhaps because you are immobilised in a hospital bed, your muscles will atrophy and waste away in a matter of weeks. You need to exercise all muscles as you age to counter their naturally declining strength. Any muscle that you gain through exercise will be a handsome and precious bonus in providing extra bodily protection and support against injury. Likewise, regular muscle-flexing or stretching will improve your day-to-day comfort and minimise your chances of injury.

Bones become more fragile and less dense with age. Bone mass can be kept dense and less susceptible to fracture by taking plenty of exercise. Research has shown that men and women over 70 can significantly increase their strength, co-ordination, balance, cardio-fitness and flexibility by gym exercising. There are hundreds of examples of elderly individuals leading healthy, happy lives after deciding to spend time on work-outs of one sort or another.

One such is Jessie Welsh from Kent, who underwent double hip-replacement surgery in 1994 at the age of 72. To help her rehabilitation she took up indoor rowing on a Concept II machine, since this was less likely to worry her new hips than walking or running. Soon she was putting in up to an hour a day on her machine. She decided to enter her age class in the international Concept II rowing competition. Within three months she had set a world record for 2,500 metres which she still holds today. Her husband Harry, 71, also had a double hip operation and he is now ranked sixth in the world for his age at 2,000 metres. There are literally hundreds of people who have taken up running in their 60s and later. Many are completing marathons in their 80s. It is never too late to start.

As you age you will find it more difficult to sleep at night. This is partly caused by the diminishing production of melatonin, the hormone associated with sleep. This can develop into progressively worsening insomnia. The only known way of maximising your body's melatonin production is to take plenty of exercise. Melatonin supplements may have side-effects, so I would advise against them.

If you go to bed early or take a nap during the day, you can expect to wake up well before dawn. A whole day spent away from daylight will not help sleep either. I have spent five months living in non-stop daylight and five months in permanent darkness on different polar journeys, and it always took me a while to acclimatise. The saving grace was that I was very active, which made for sound sleeping.

Research into closed communities like Roseto in Pennsylvania, where Italian immigrants lived in a mutually caring society, have shown how strong human bonds help health and longevity, fulfilment and happiness. We need to communicate for many reasons and one is the relief of anxieties. The isolated lives many people lead are known to increase susceptibility to heart disease and cancer.

Few of us have any more reason to accept loneliness than, say, the inevitability of ill health. Having just one good friend will help. Phone calls are a lot better than nothing. Feeding wild birds or sharing your home with a pet will give you an aim and a relationship. If you are lonely, why not find somebody older, less healthy or more lonely than yourself in your community and visit them? Join a local community organisation, try to make friends and do not give up on everybody if you face a few rebuffs from some. Run errands for someone bedridden or help a charity. The opportunities are endless, but you have to make the effort to search them out. There are few things more therapeutic than doing something for others.

Happiness really is all in your mind. You can try to see that every glass is half full or you can go through life determined that they are all half empty.

10

Strength Training

Once you have established your exercise programme and reinforced your overall resolve, it is important to identify your principal aims. If you intend to run a marathon, aerobic fitness will be paramount. If you wish to look macho for your holiday next summer, you will want to lift weights. If you are worried about the effects of getting older, you may be keen to mix aerobic work with stretching and strength training to keep the ageing process at bay.

Having decided upon your training goals, fix for yourself a programme which, week by week, includes suitable activities. If you have chosen a regime of aerobics exercise, stick to the training regimes featured in Chapter 8. If you would like to progress to strength training, read on . . .

For years muscular fitness was considered unnecessary to general health and was viewed as a mere indulgence for the conceited. Athletes, it was agreed, should develop muscles specific to their sports, but the general public could safely ignore their muscles and concentrate on their heart and lungs.

Now, however, medical research has concluded that muscular fitness *is* essential to our health, although such fitness does not necessarily involve any visible growth of our muscles. Muscle growth is crucial in helping to avoid general back problems; it can and does help stave off the crippling bone wastage of osteoporosis. In humans strength declines slowly after our early 20s and rapidly from the early to mid-50s. This deterioration can be decelerated by strength training.

The strength-training exercises in this chapter will give muscular endurance, flexibility, speed, power, agility, balance and co-ordination. They will increase the force you are able to muster when pushing, pulling or lifting. This is relevant to all of us in everyday life, whether we are carrying shopping, unscrewing jar lids or wielding a spade in the garden. Strength also helps protect against sprains, strains and bad posture.

No matter how far you run or swim, you will always contract your muscles against the same amount of resistance. As you become more aerobically fit, you will therefore increase your endurance, but not your strength. When any muscle is repeatedly exposed to loads that exceed its normal level of contractile activity, that muscle will exhibit an increase in the size of certain of its components. The most common method to achieve this is by performing progressive resistance exercises, i.e., weight training.

Machines Versus Free Weights

To mix your weight training between the machines available at the gym and free weights (dumb-bells or barbells) helps prevent boredom and allows every muscle to be worked on. It is a mistake to rely solely on machines, because they create a forced or guided two-dimensional movement pattern which you have to follow, unlike free weights, which permit three-dimensional movement.

Machines cannot mimic the specific movements which you may need to make to train your muscles for certain sports. Also, machines provide resistance only at a single joint, whereas free weights offer full-force resistance to your muscles throughout the entire range of each given contraction and extension.

An Introduction to Training With Equipment and Weights

If you want to weight-train to look good, you will need a specialised bodybuilder's programme. There is a myth that merely working with weights will bulk out your muscles. Sadly, this is just not true. My exercises *will* make you stronger, depending on how much work you put in, but you will not suddenly be transformed into a Mr Universe. If you have never trained with weights before, you will gain considerable advantage from spending at least a couple of sessions learning the basics on stance, lifting techniques, safety and effectiveness from a professional at your club or gym. Irrespective of your aerobic

---

Drugs

There are athletes in all sports who use drugs such as steroids or stimulants to enhance their chances of beating rivals. Drug checks often fail to catch abusers and they become addicted to these substances to maintain their optimal performance. As a result many superb athletes have died young due to drug abuse.

The most commonly used drugs include amphetamines, anabolic steroids, cocaine, iso-proteronal and ephedrine. Use of such substances leads to the reduction of good cholesterol, the promotion of bad cholesterol, inflammation of the liver and an increased tendency of the blood to form clots. The older the abuser, the worse the risks. Irreversible damage is done to the arteries, the heart and the tendons. Skin becomes prematurely aged.

Other downsides include sterility, testicular atrophy, high blood pressure, liver cancer and uncontrollable mood swings.

Anabolic steroids are synthetic derivatives of the male sex hormone testosterone which, when taken combined with weight training, enhances the tissue-building process. A great many bodybuilders achieve their 'Incredible Hulk' appearances with help from steroids because muscle-building without them can be an incredibly time-consuming, difficult process.

The temptation to become a superman or superwoman by taking such substances is undeniably great for many athletes and muscle-builders, but the associated risks are a heavy penalty to pay.

Important Note for All Weightlifting Exercises

The weights I have suggested for dumb-bells and barbells should be treated as an approximate guide only. You must find the weight that suits you best for each exercise – not too light and not too heavy.

You should be able to complete 10 lifts correctly, but your muscles should be feeling the strain and the last lift of each set should be a bit of a struggle to achieve.

---

training schedule, you should weight-train at least twice a week, and ideally three times, working on alternate, not consecutive days.

The terms *repetitions* and *sets* will by now be familiar to those of you visiting the gym. Repetitions are the number of times you repeat a given movement with a given load. Research has shown that maximum benefit is derived by performing between eight and 12 repetitions before you have a short (30-second) rest. Those eight to 12 repetitions make up one set. When you become strong enough to complete the first set, you need to follow the 30-second rest by doing a second set of the same number of repetitions.

Many experts favour high-volume weight training, which involves 12 to 40 sets of exercises per muscle group per week. But low-volume experts, who go for between three and six sets per week, argue that more sets are unnecessary. They reason that, once a muscle has been forced to contract to the point of failure for a couple of consecutive sets, this is sufficient for muscle growth to occur, and any additional lifting only stresses the muscle beyond its immediate recuperative potential. They dismiss the success of many high-volume performers – such as the musclemen seen between magazine covers – on the grounds that such people are genetically dis-

posed to large musculature, and in any case usually use steroids. Any volume of weightlifting would therefore give them large muscles.

The answer for mere mortals with standard or pigeon chests and scrawny or flabby limbs is to ensure regular weightlifting on the basis of a minimum of three sets per muscle group per week. To prevent boredom, you can change the number of repetitions and/or sets you complete on successive training days or weeks. Likewise, you can take longer over each weightlifting movement every now and again. For instance, try contracting an exercise movement for 10 seconds and then extending it for 10 seconds. Do this for as many repetitions as you are comfortable with. (The Pilates and Super Slow weightlifting systems recommend long, slow lifts and releases as the main recipe for strength.)

General Guidelines

- Run on the spot for a minute or two to get warm, then do gentle stretch exercises relevant to the limbs you intend to work out.
- Balance your work-out between upper and lower body, as well as between large and small muscle groups. Ensure that you work your opposing muscles. For instance, if you do a triceps exercise, follow it with some biceps work. Similarly, pair lower back with abdominals, hamstrings with quadriceps, and so on.
- Every exercise should be performed with a slow, controlled movement, not a jerk, whether you are contracting or extending the muscle. I usually contract for two or three seconds, then extend for two or three.
- Do not assume that you will be able to keep up with the progress of a friend if he or she has a shorter, more muscular build. Taller people must exert force over a greater distance and so have to work harder to achieve the same performance in weightlifting.

When Using Dumb-Bells or Barbell

- Keep your back straight and your knees slightly bent.
- Concentrate hard on the actual muscle that you are working. Try to *feel* the effect of the exercise on that muscle.
- Never 'lock' a joint, especially the elbow. To avoid this, keep the elbow slightly bent so that the arm is never completely stretched out flat.

Use of Barbell

A moderately wide grip achieves the best results. The easiest way to specify this is to lie on the floor or on a bench holding the bar above your chest, keeping your elbows on the floor. Your ideal grip position is when your forearms are at 90 degrees to the floor. If this is uncomfortable for you, move your grip inwards a little.

Some Specific Weightlifting Exercises

Fingers

Hold the handle of a small sledgehammer between your fingertips. Try to 'walk' your fingers up, then down, the handle. You'll feel the bases of your fingers 'burn'. If they don't, use a heavier hammer or weight your hammer.

'Walk' your fingers for 15 seconds. After one minute, rest and repeat. Do this three times, and repeat the exercise after a two- or three-day gap.

Wrists

Wrist Curl

Barbell or dumb-bells
Try this exercise with a 50lb (22.5kg) barbell as a maximum weight and reduce if this is too heavy.

1. Sitting on a bench, hold the weight with your palms facing upwards.

2. Curl the weight upwards.

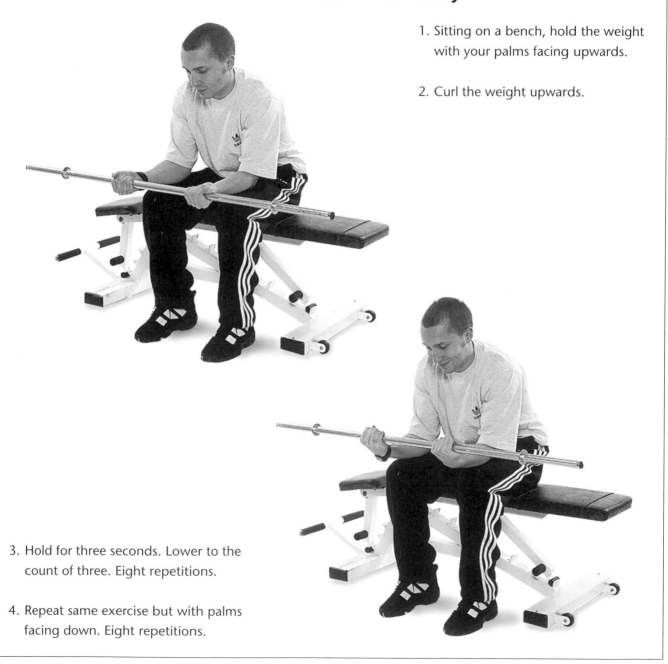

3. Hold for three seconds. Lower to the count of three. Eight repetitions.

4. Repeat same exercise but with palms facing down. Eight repetitions.

Biceps

Shoulder Press

Standing or seated, 10–15lbs (5–7.5kg) each dumb-bell
Do 10 to 12 repetitions

1. Hold dumb-bells at shoulder height, palms facing forwards.

2. Push arms upwards slowly to the count of three. Lower to the count of three.

Triceps

Triceps Extension

Standing or sitting, 10–15lbs (4.5–7kg) each dumb-bell
Eight repetitions with each arm

1. Clench dumb-bell, palm forwards.

2. Move arm to the point where it is pointing
   upwards. The movement is slow, to the count
   of three. Return to position with bent arm to
   the count of three.

Upper and Lower Arm

Dumb-Bell Curl (Biceps Curl)

Standing, each dumb-bell 10–15lbs (5–7.5kg)
Alternatively, you can use a 30–45lb (15–20kg) barbell. Ensure that
you breathe out with each move up and each move down
Do 10 to 12 repetitions

1. Grasp dumb-bells, palms forwards. Do not allow your body to move, only your arms.

2. Bring dumb-bells from lowest position slowly, to the count of three, to uppermost position. Lower to the count of three.

Shoulders

Lateral Shoulder Raise

Standing, each dumb-bell 10lbs (5kg)
Take care to breathe out explosively as you lift, taking
one or two seconds to lift, likewise to lower
10 repetitions

1. Place your feet shoulder-width apart. Clench dumb-bells, palms facing inwards.

2. Keep arms almost straight, with a *very* slight bend at the elbows and none at the wrists. Raise hands out to the sides until they reach shoulder height, then return to your sides. Keep a strong, upright position.

Chest

Dumb-Bell Bench Press (see also page 131, with barbell)

Lying, each dumb-bell 15–20lbs (7.5–10kg)
You can use an 80–120lb (35–55kg) barbell. If you do, complete
the first set of repetitions with a reasonably light weight. Then
progressively increase the weights for the second and third sets.
Make them as heavy as you feel you can manage
Do 10 repetitions

1. Lie back on a bench with your feet flat on the floor. Hold dumb-bells straight overhead, palms facing inwards.

2. Slowly lower the dumb-bells till they are level with the bench. Take three seconds to raise and three seconds to lower each time.

Breathing Pullover

Lying, using only one dumb-bell of 20–30lbs (10–15kg)
Do 10 to 12 repetitions

1. Hold the dumb-bell loosely with both hands, allowing it to hang directly downwards throughout the exercise. Keep your arms as straight as possible throughout (an exception to the normal rule!).

2. Move the dumb-bell from directly above your face, lowering to the count of three, to let it hang behind your head.

3. Lower to the count of three, then raise to the count of three. You should feel a stretch of your chest each time you raise. *Force* your arms out.

Back

Single-Arm Dumb-Bell Row

Bending plus bench, one dumb-bell only, 20–30lbs (10–15kg)
Do 10 to 12 repetitions on each arm

Right knee on bench, left foot on floor, palm inwards, back kept straight. Lift dumb-bell to the count of three right up to the chest. Lower as far as possible, extending through the whole shoulder to the count of three. Change to the right arm.

Bent-Over Row

Standing, barbell with 25–60lbs (12.5–25kg) or
dumb-bells approximately 16lbs (7.5kg)each
Do eight to 10 repetitions

1 Keep legs shoulder-width apart. Bend knees, grasp bar with overhand grip. Keep upper body parallel to floor. Lift bar off floor, but keep upper body as before.

2. Now, to the count of three, lift bar using arms only until It touches the stomach. Lower to the count of three. Do not straighten up or let bar touch the floor between repetitions.

Abdominals

I do not recommend using weights for abdominal muscle-building. However, to ensure that you work opposing muscles, after exercising your back muscles, it is important to balance any improvement with abdominal work. So, at this point, fit in two sets of 12 to 20 abdominal crunches (see page 140).

Waist

Side Bend

Standing, each dumb-bell 15–20lbs (7.5–10kg)
Do 10 to 12 repetitions on each side

1. Legs apart, dumb-bell in each hand, palms inwards. Keep a good, upward posture.

2. Bend sideways. Do not tilt forwards or backwards. Reach down as far as is comfortable on outside of leg, then slowly return upright, always to the count of three. Keep knees 'soft'.

3. Repeat movement on the other side.

Quadriceps and Hamstrings

Leg Extension

Using bench with leg extension
with 80–100lbs (35–45kg) on bar
Do 10 repetitions

1. Sit on bench with feet under foot bar. Grip sides of bench firmly. Sit with good posture.

2. Straighten your legs as far as you can by pushing up against the bar. Alter the weights on this bar until it is demanding.

3. Push the bar up to the count of three, then lower to the count of three.

Leg Curl

As for extension, but forcing the bar downwards
Do 10 repetitions

1. Using the leg curl machine, sit with a good posture and your calves resting on the pad as shown.

2. Push the pad downwards as far as it will go. Count to three, then control the pad's return to its original position.

Remember: Keep Checking Yourself

- **Always concentrate your mind on the muscles you are working. Try to feel them working.**

- **Always aim for a controlled, fluid movement in both directions.**
- **Breathe out as you take the strain.**

Quadriceps (Buttocks/Gluteals)

The Squat 1

Each dumb-bell 15–20lbs (7.5–10kg)
Do eight to 10 repetitions

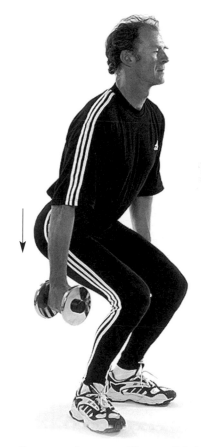

1. Hold dumb-bells at shoulder height. Palms face inwards.

2. Place your feet about 18 inches apart. Keep your head up and back straight and squat by bending your knees until your thighs are nearly parallel to the floor. Be sure your knees always point ahead, like your feet, and keep your arms to the sides. Lower in this manner to the count of three. Then raise to the count of three.

3. Alternate squats with dumb-bells held up and squats with arms to your sides.

The Squat 2 (Plié Squat)

One dumb-bell, 20lbs (10kg) minimum
Do 15 repetitions twice a week

1. Begin with feet turned out and placed wider than shoulder-width apart.

2. Grasp the dumb-bell with both hands, as shown, with arms fully extended downwards.

3. Keep your back straight and head up (ensure that your abdominals are firm).

4. Lower yourself into the squat position, as shown in the photograph, by bending your knees slowly. Lower until your thighs are parallel with the floor. Pause for four to five seconds, then rise slowly back to the upright position.

Calves

Calf Raise with Barbell

Barbell with 20lb (10kg)
Do 10 to 12 repetitions

1. Ensure that the barbell is comfortable on your back and shoulders.

2. Keeping your balance, raise your heels until only the balls of your feet are on the ground. Hold for the count of three. Lower to the count of three.

Women and Weightlifting

Women are inclined to steer clear of weightlifting and 'strength' machines because they think such exercise will make them big, not slim. This is wrong. Women with normal female hormones will not build bulky muscles, so weightlifting will merely streamline their figures (at the same time toning their muscles and helping to prevent osteoporosis).

Additional benefits, especially for chest and shoulder exercises, include:

- Firmer tone.
- Flatter stomach.
- Stronger upper body.
- Less vulnerability to lifting injury.

Chest

Dumb-Bell Fly

Lying on bench or floor, each dumb-bell 10–15lbs (5–7.5kg)
Do 10 repetitions

1. Grip dumb-bells with palms facing inwards.

2. Flex your legs at 90 degrees with your feet flat on the bench or floor.

3. Keeping your arms slightly flexed, slowly lower the dumb-bells, ensuring that your elbows remain perpendicular to your body. Breathe in while lowering the weights.

4. Slowly raise dumb-bells to starting position, breathing out during this movement.

Flat Bench Press

Barbell or dumb-bells. Start at 40lbs (18kg) and
increase to whatever weight suits you
Do eight to 12 repetitions

1. Lie on your back, feet flat on the floor or bench and hip-width apart. Keep your lower back as flat as possible and pull in your abdominals.

2. Take overhand grip of the barbell, hands about one and a half times shoulder-width apart. Keep your wrists straight and knuckles up. Breathe in.

3. Breathe out while pressing the barbell to arm's length. Keep elbows soft.

4. Hold briefly and breathe in as you lower the barbell to the midline of your chest, leading with the elbows.

Shoulders

Upright Row

Standing, each dumb-bell 10lbs (5kg) minimum
Do eight to 12 repetitions

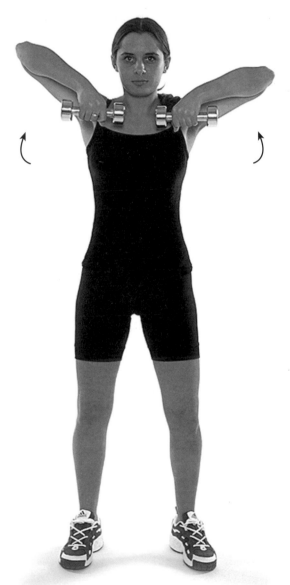

1. Hang your arms down in front of you with your hands around the dumb-bells, palms facing back and knuckles facing downwards.

2. Leading with your elbows, raise arms up as shown until elbows are higher than shoulders. Raise and lower to the count of three.

11

Plyometrics and Circuit Training

Plyometrics

Plyometrics can be defined as any exercise that enables muscle to reach maximum strength in as short a time as possible. This speed–strength combination can be described as power. Plyometrics can be beneficial in trying to boost explosive power but carries a high risk of injuries such as tendonitis. Such training should therefore be attempted only when you have a solid base of weight training and should never be undertaken more than twice a week. Don't be overambitious when deciding how many repetitions of an exercise to do. Start with a few and build up gradually.

Circuit Training

In any gym you will notice a number of clients who complete set work-out circuits which have been designed, usually by the gym supervisor, according to the personal aims of the client. If you prefer to make up your own circuit, you will need to bear in mind certain factors.

- The benefits of circuit training in a busy gym are often minimised by the constant interruptions of other equipment-users. So do your circuits only in venues and at times when you know interruptions will be minimal.
- Earlier I dismissed the doctrine 'No pain, no gain' as out of date. A slight qualification applies to hard circuit training, especially the plyometric parts, because pushing your circuits to squeeze out each last exhausting repetition is a sound practice to obtain maximum fitness and strength benefits.
- Deciding when to rest and for how long is an integral part of circuit planning. The key is to make your rests short enough for you to be able at least to complete all of the planned work-out, but not so long that your muscles fully recover between exercises. I find 30 seconds ideal.
- To design your circuit, concentrate first on working the muscles you need most for the sport or sports in your exercise programme. If you are a beginner to circuits, choose a maximum of 12 assorted exercises covering your main muscle groups (arms, legs, back and stomach).

The Effects of Sex on Fitness

This is a subject riven with myth and old wives' tales. Psychoanalysts are currently greatly in favour of sexual activity; some even recommend that an orgasm a day keeps the doctor away. Advantages resulting from this particular form of physical exercise include cholesterol control, prostate protection and stress reduction.

If you have sex three times a week in a fairly non-strenuous way you will burn 7,500 calories a year, which is the equivalent of running 75 miles. With calorie-burning every little helps and many people find sex more enjoyable than running!

There is no proof for the widely held belief that sex lowers your performance at sport. On the contrary, regular sex increases testosterone levels in men, which makes it easier to build muscle. Some individuals do lose some of their natural aggression for a few hours after orgasm, but this has only a marginal effect.

The French describe the orgasm as *le petit mort*, the little death, but this could not be further from the truth since the risk of getting prostate cancer is lessened by regular sex.

- A typical circuit involves performing one exercise (say push-ups) only once. On your second tour of the circuit (i.e., when you are doing your second set of each exercise) you will repeat the exercises of the first circuit. To work certain muscle groups harder and more effectively, you can repeat the same exercise immediately after a short (30-second) rest. For example, complete 12 squats, take 30 seconds' rest, then do 12 more squats.

- Once any part of a circuit becomes easy, increase the difficulty a touch by adding a repetition or two, doing an extra set or cutting down the rest periods. If you don't do this, the benefits that you have already gained will stagnate. You should keep your heartbeat within your optimal training zone (see pages 45–46), you should sweat and you should feel your muscles strain.

Good Exercises for Circuits

Plyometric Exercises

Tuck Jump

1. Jump up so that you bring both knees up towards your chest. Try to keep your chin high. Swing both your arms up to assist.

2. Use your landing to help propel you into the next immediate jump. No resting at all between jumps.

Star Jump

1. Jump up, flinging your arms and legs outwards.
2. While still off the ground, your feet and arms must return to the vertical (i.e., arms by sides and feet together). This is how you should land, keeping your knees soft.
3. Immediately upon landing, jump up again into the next star jump.

Sprint

1. Place your palms on the floor, as shown, and take up a position as if you were about to start a sprint race.

2. Fling one leg back, and bring the other forward, thus swapping the position of your legs. You are effectively 'sprinting' on the spot, bringing alternate knees up to your chest.

Squat Thrust

1. Take up a position as for Sprints above, but this time both your knees should be under your chest.

2. Fling back both your legs as far as you can, landing them on the balls of your feet and with your feet together.

3. Immediately pull your legs back again to the first position and fling them back again.

Burpee

A burpee is a combination of a squat thrust followed straight away – with no pause – by a star jump. Make sure you throw yourself as high as possible with each star jump and that your legs are fully extended with each squat thrust.

Non-Plyometric Exercises

Triceps, Shoulders and Chest

Push-Up

Do not do push-ups if you suffer from a weak back

1. Lie outstretched on your front. Place hands beside shoulders. Slowly push yourself up from the floor, straightening your arms slowly so that only your hands and toes touch the ground. Keep your back straight. Note the optional variation for women on page 50.

2. Now slowly lower yourself until your chest is just off the ground. Repeat until you cannot hold the correct position. (See also page 50.)

Variations include:

Speed Push-Ups

Simply perform as many standard push-ups as fast as you can.

Clapping Push-Ups

Only for the strong and supple. As your arms lift you upwards, use the momentum to briefly lift your hands from the floor and, if possible, clap them together before you commence the downwards movement.

Hands Variations

By varying the position of your hands or, if you are a super-strong show-off, by using only one hand, you can change the emphasis between the muscle groups you are working. For example, if your hands are closer together there will be more involvement of your triceps.

Against a wall

Stand with your feet three feet from a wall. Put the palms of your hands on the wall, shoulder width apart. Keeping your back straight, do standard push-ups.

Triceps, Shoulders and Upper Arms

Bench Dip (Reverse Dip)

By placing your legs on a chair, you can make bench dips
more difficult for the triceps and shoulders

1. Place your hands behind you, palms down, as an exercise bench (or any solid fixture higher than your knees). Lower your bottom towards the floor, taking most of your body weight on your arms and as little as possible on your thighs. Hold for four seconds.

2. Briefly return to the upper position and repeat 20 times.

Arms and Stomach

Chin-Up

1. Use a heavy bench or table strong enough to support your weight without tilting. Sit on the floor under the table with your feet out in front of you and under the table.

2. Place your hands on the table, shoulder-width apart, and pull yourself up until your chest touches the edge of the bench. The straighter your legs, the more difficult the exercise.

Abdominal Muscles

Crunch

You can buy a light alloy frame (ab-trainer) to help you do your crunches. Some folk swear by them, but although I have one I find it unnecessary

1. Lie on your back with your knees bent and your heels quite close to your buttocks. Your hands should be gently touching your ears (not propped behind your head), or you can cross them over your chest. Do not use your hands to lift your head off the ground.

2. Thinking of your stomach muscles, slowly lift and curl your chest off the ground. Hold this position for three seconds. Then slowly lower your shoulders (but not your head) back to the ground. You should feel strain on your abdominal muscles.

Variations

A. To train the oblique muscles at the sides of your abdominals, you must complete crunches exactly as above, but as you curl up, rotate your right shoulder towards your left knee. This will slightly twist your trunk (crunch with twist). Repeat this twist to the opposite side.

B. To emphasise work on the lower abdominals, as you curl up your chest you should simultaneously lift your (bent) legs in the air. Leg lifts done one leg at a time involve your abdominal muscles only minimally, so lift both at once.

General Points on Abdominals (For Men)

The best exercise for your abdominals, other than daily crunches, is rowing a boat or using a rowing machine.

All men who aspire to fitness (and who are honest) would love to have macho-looking abdominals, colloquially known as six-packs, but very few ever achieve them. Those who do have a good income from being photographed for magazines or appearing on *Neighbours*. Since the resulting images appear just about everywhere, this tends to give the impression that every second university-age student has a flat stomach. Nothing could be further from the truth.

In fact the human male's mid-section is the most difficult area of the body to perfect. Unlike most other muscle groups it is not enough to simply blitz the stomach muscles with exercise. Watching your weight is equally important, since fat tends to accumulate around this region and it takes only a thin covering of fat to hide even a firm strong set of abdominals as soon as you relax. So it takes great effort and discipline to obtain visually aesthetic abdominals.

If you despair of ever acquiring abdominals that look like a washboard even when you relax, don't worry too much. As long as you have managed to develop strong if 'invisible' abdominals, they will stop your paunch wobbling so much, reduce lower-back troubles and give your whole body a sound balance of strength for all aerobic and weightlifting activities.

Nine out of every 10 males in the West are genetically predisposed to a pot belly. It is a sad fact of life that as you get older your waist thickens. Researchers at the Berkeley National Laboratory in California studied 7,000 habitual runners and found that the average 6ft runner gained 3.3lbs and three quarters of an inch round his waist for every decade, regardless of how much mileage he did. The only way to counter this trend is for each individual to increase his exercise (including abdominal work) and food-control activities as he ages, which is the opposite to what normally happens.

Back

Back Extensions

Lie face down with your hands together behind your back. Lift your head and shoulders while stretching your arms backwards. Look down moving only your eyes to help prevent straining your neck. Ensure that your feet do not leave the ground. Hold for three seconds, then lower. Staying on your front, gently lift one leg, keeping it straight. Lower, then repeat with the other leg.

Summary of Planning Circuit Training Exercises

- Choose a selection of the exercises covered so far, using a suitable mix of machines, free weights and plyometrics, depending upon the availability of equipment. Exercises you can include:
  Plyometrics
  Strength exercises with machines
  Strength exercises with free weights (barbell or dumb-bell)
  Free exercises (or with skipping rope).
- Change your selection from time to time to avoid boredom and muscle-improvement stagnation.
- Maintain exercises that work out the different muscle groups and which help both aerobically and strength-wise and, if your sport demands (if you are a sprinter, say), then anaerobically, too.
- Plan numbers of repetitions, sets and rest periods with advice from a professional.

Make yourself a circuit-training sheet specifying a different programme for each day of the week you train. Make copies of each blank sheet to fill in after each work-out so that you can keep track of your development. The chart below is an example of what a typical day's circuit-training session might look like. Only 11 exercises are used, assuming that you are a beginner as far as circuits are concerned. Add more exercises as you improve your fitness and strength.

Daily Circuit Programme

Date:

Run on the spot or skip until warm.

Type	Exercise	•	Reps	Sets
Dumb-bells	Bicep curl	A		
Dumb-bells	Triceps extension	A		
Plyometrics	Sprint	L		
Free Ex.	Bent-over row	B		
Free Ex.	Abdominal crunch	AB		
Bench	Bench press	C		
Bench	Breathing pullover	C		
Plyometrics	Star jump	L		
Dumb-bells	Side bend	W		
Bench + Ext.	Leg extension	L		
Bench + Ext.	Leg curl	L		

Cool down with stretch exercises.

(Abbreviations have been used as follows: A – arms; B – back; AB – abdominals; C – chest; W – waist; L – legs.)

Training with Special Devices

You will almost certainly have noticed, and you may already have bought, various 'miracle' devices which, it is claimed, will somehow make you fit and bulging with muscle or reduce your unwanted fat in no time at all. There are cylinders, elastic ropes and stretching wires which, after a daily five minutes of 'almost effortless' work, will give you a 'body to be proud of'.

Many of these gadgets do provide resistance for strength or muscular-endurance training, but they are far less adaptable for aerobic-fitness training or weight control. The vast majority of such quack equipment ends up being thrown out. Then there are electrical exercise-simulators which you strap to your waist and which, it is said, exercise various parts of your body while you read a book or do the ironing. Medical research has warned against any device which sends out electrical currents, since these can interfere with the normal activity of the heart.

And we have all seen advertisements for cure-alls for the obese, for people with bad backs or small breasts, for under-endowed men, bad complexions, etc. These potions are often accompanied by impressive testimonials from past users or minor celebrities who may well have been paid for their snap opinions even though they have never used the product. My advice is to steer well clear of all such offers unless you first check them out with a fitness professional you trust.

12

Moving into the Top 2 Per Cent

If you have followed the previous chapters and spent at least four months practising the various points on food control and exercise, you will now be fitter than 80 per cent of the population (assuming, of course, that you are an average person, not somebody with an advanced illness or over 90 years old).

With a little additional effort and knowledge, you can move into the top 2 per cent of the population in terms of fitness, even if you are over 60 years of age. To take this extra step will involve three key points on food control, further work on cutting out the insidious effects of stress and a simple alteration to your aerobic programme.

Free Radicals

Free radicals are powerful chemicals that are produced in the body in a number of ways, for example when oxygen reacts with healthy tissues or certain types of fat. These chemicals can damage tissues and it is thought they may lead to the development of cancer. The oxidisation process that causes free radicals is exactly the same as that causing metal to rust and fruit to go rotten. The damage occurs

slowly; it is a chemical disintegration, much of which, in terms of human body cells, is reversible by sensible food control.

Many triggers can spark off an overproduction of free radicals and some are known to medical science. Pollution, radiation and certain foods are proven irritants. There is little we can do to eliminate unseen sources of pollution and radiation, but a good deal that we can alter diet-wise, both in cutting out known bad foods and in increasing our intake of foods containing antioxidants, substances that boost our body's own defence mechanisms in the fight against free radicals.

Some foods contain bad fats such as polyunsaturates that easily oxidise and create free radicals, whereas others (like fish and garlic) contain antioxidants that counteract the free radicals. Since one in every five of us is likely to die of cancer, you will appreciate the importance of knowing what to eat and what not to eat. And long before free radicals lead to our deaths, they have a profound effect on the level of our general health and fitness capacity.

One little-known producer of free radicals is,

unfortunately and ironically, the very act of taking exercise. Sporadic bouts of exercise increase our free-radical production and cause cellular damage. So a little sporadic exercise can be a dangerous thing. The same is true for people with weak hearts. The answer is obvious and scientifically proven: regular exercise (the minimal three-times-a-week, 30-minute sessions we've already discussed) renders our bodies adept at producing antioxidant substances which counter the corresponding rise in free radicals. Simple blood tests on fit and unfit people, after they have taken arduous exercise, have shown significant cellular damage only in the unfit subjects.

For years medical scientists agreed that a standard diet provided enough free radical-fighting material to counter much of the damage, but modern life has tipped the balance against our health by increasing the risk factors. Pesticides, nuclear radiation, car-exhaust fumes, smog, processed and irradiated foods are but a few examples of the new age of pollution feeding the age of cancers. Further measures are called for in the form of antioxidant minerals and vitamins to boost our body defences and our chances of good health, not to mention survival. As a result we cannot be certain, even if we exercise a good deal, that the mere consumption of five helpings of vegetables and fruit a day will give us sufficient ammunition to cope with today's cancer-inducing environment.

The British government, after exhaustive research, published in 1993 a set of Reference Nutrient Intakes (RNIs) recommending optimum daily amounts of vitamins and minerals. (These were previously known as Recommended Daily Amounts, or RDAs.) However, the Institute of Optimum Nutrition in London, and other such bodies, advise higher levels for safety. After cross-checking the charts from ten such official bodies, I have given a safe average of their recommendations in the chart on page 146. The recommendations assume that you are an average person with no special needs.

The main functions of each key vitamin and mineral are as follows.

Vitamins

Vitamin A
Can reduce the incidence of cancers of the lung, kidney, bladder and breast. Vitamin A can actually reverse a pre-cancerous state of the cervix, the stomach and the throat. Essential for cell growth, vision and function of the immune system.

- Comes from: **oily fish, betacarotene (carrots** and other **orange, yellow and red vegetables), egg yolks, butter, cheese** and **green, leafy vegetables**.

Vitamin B
There are more than a dozen different B-complex vitamins, including:

Vitamin B1 (thiamine). Needed to obtain energy from carbohydrates and fats and to fight potentially lethal toxic build-ups. Keeps the nervous system, muscles and heart functioning normally.

- Comes from: **fortified breakfast cereals, potatoes, nuts, pulses, liver** and **pork**.

Vitamin B2 (riboflavin). Needed to release energy from food. Promotes healthy skin and hair.

- Comes from: **fortified breakfast cereals, yoghurt, fish, meat** and **eggs**.

Vitamin B6 (pyridoxine). Releases energy from proteins. Very important to avoid neurological problems, also for the immune system and to form red blood cells. Older people need progressively more vitamin B6 (up to 20 per cent more) than the under-40s.

Vitamin and Mineral Chart

VITAMIN/ MINERAL	AMOUNT FOR MALES	AMOUNT FOR FEMALES	MY VITAMIN AND MINERAL TABLET RECOMMENDATION if you exercise food control as advised in this book	ADVICE
A	700mcg	700mcg	–	
B1 (Thiamine)	1mg	1mg	–	
B2 (Riboflavin)	1.3mg	1.3mg	–	Vegans
B3 (Niacin)	17mg	17mg	–	
B6 (Pyridoxine)	1.4mg	1.4mg	3mg	
Biotin	10–200mcg	10–200mcg	–	
B12	1.5mcg	1.5mcg	See pages 24, 147	Over-50s, vegans, pregnant women
Folic Acid (Folate)	200–400mcg	200–400mcg	–	Important for women planning to conceive and during the first three months of pregnancy
C	60mg	60mg	1,000mg, see page 161	Take with water (not with ginseng). Do not take with chlorine or ferrous sulphate
D	From sunlight	From sunlight	10mcg, see page 190	Osteoporosis sufferers
E	4mg	4mg	400mg	
Calcium (Carbonate or Citrate)	700mg	700mg	1,000mg	
Phosphorus	550mg	550mg	–	
Magnesium	300mg	270mg	–	Take with water after a meal
Potassium	3,500mg	3,500mg	–	
Chloride	2,500mg	2,500mg	–	
Iron	8.7mg	14.5mg	–	
Zinc	9.5mg	7mg	–	Take 2 hours separately from calcium supplements, milk, bread or cereals
Copper	1.2mg	1.2mg	–	
Selenium	75mcg	60mcg	–	
Iodine	140mcg	140mcg	–	
Multivite/ Mineral	To include 100% of RNI for most of the above		One per day	Take with a meal

Note: milligrams – mg; micrograms – mcg

- Comes from: the **same sources as vitamin B2** and from **wholewheat bread, bananas, yeast extract** and **soya beans**.

Vitamin B12. Key vitamin for cell formation – for making DNA and the myelin sheath which surrounds nerve fibres. Huge numbers of individuals over the age of 60 suffer from atrophic gastritis, which causes vitamin B12 deficiency and mimics dementia or Alzheimer's Disease. Vitamin B12 supplements often stabilise or even improve this condition. Vegetarians, and others not eating enough meat, are especially at risk since meat, fish, chicken and dairy products are the main source. Fortified cereals are luckily an exception. Anybody over 50 who suspects slight but increasing memory loss should take vitamin B12 tablets (between 6 and 500mcg daily) – check with your doctor.

- Comes from: **meat, fish, poultry, dairy products** and **fortified cereals**.

Folic acid (folate). Folic acid is vital for women who are planning to have children, even before conception. Certainly during the first three months of pregnancy they need a 400mg tablet daily to supplement their normal dietary intake and it is preferable to take this supplement for three months before conceiving. Deficiency is linked with babies suffering from spina bifida and other congenital abnormalities. Folic acid is needed for cell division and DNA formation.

- Comes from: **broccoli, wheatgerm, fortified cereals, wholemeal bread** and **green, leafy vegetables**.

Vitamin C (Ascorbic Acid)

This is adequately provided for in a standard diet, but smokers, women using oral contraceptives and certain other groups often need supplements.

Vitamin C makes collagen, which is needed for gums, bones, teeth, cartilage and skin. It promotes the absorption of iron, fights many illnesses, including colds, and, being a key antioxidant, reduces the risk of certain cancers. To help protect against cancer, take a daily supplement of 1,000mg. However, your main source should remain lots of fruit and vegetables. Vitamin C also promotes the formulation of good cholesterol, helps clear arteries and rejuvenates white blood cells. It is water-soluble and is not stored in the body, so we need a constant supply.

- Comes from: **fruit, especially citrus fruit**, and from **vegetables**, including **potatoes** and **peas**.

Vitamin D

Needed for healthy bones.

- Comes from: **fish-liver oils, tuna, salmon, sardines** and **eggs**.

Vitamin E

Vitamin E is lacking in the diet of a great many people today, and it is key to the prevention of oxidisation of fatty acids in the tissues leading to the production of free radicals. Because this vitamin is so important and yet is not easy to take in sufficient quantity in a standard diet, I recommend a daily supplement of 400mg to be taken with a meal. Doses above this amount can, like an aspirin, have a mild anti-clotting effect on the blood.

- Comes from: **extra-virgin olive oil, wheatgerm, nuts** and **seeds**.

Do We Need to Take Supplements?

For anyone consuming their statutory five helpings of fruit and vegetables daily, it may be unnecessary to take any supplements, but there are many occasions when people cannot or do not manage to meet the minimal intake of a particular key vitamin.

There are also many situations when above-average intakes of certain vitamins are advisable but are not taken (such as smokers needing extra vitamin C and pregnant women needing extra folic acid). This need definitely increases over the age of 40. One Canadian government health trial recently proved a halving of the risk of a variety of common infections in people over 50 who took daily multivitamin/mineral supplements.

People with a high osteoporosis risk need extra vitamin D and calcium supplements. Children under three years (especially those who were or are still being breastfed) may need vitamins A, C and D.

Middle-aged and elderly people can benefit from vitamins D, C and B12, folic acid and iron supplements. Vegans and people on diets may well need supplements of vitamins B12, D and riboflavin, plus zinc, calcium, iodine and iron.

Make the Most of Vitamins From Food

- **Wash but don't soak vegetables, to retain water-soluble vitamins B and C.**
- **Don't make salads long before you will eat them. Fruit and vegetables left around after cutting up lose their vitamins.**
- **Don't thaw frozen vegetables before cooking.**
- **Fresh-frozen fruit and vegetables are better than fresh items bought but then stored for three or four days before being eaten. So the vitamin content of frozen peas will be higher than that of fresh peas left in your fridge for a week.**
- **Boil or bake potatoes in their skins.**
- **Don't cook vegetables using baking soda, or you'll lose vitamins B2 and C.**
- **Frozen foods are preferable to canned ones.**
- **Cook in steel pots. Metal from copper or aluminium pots may leach into the food.**

Warnings

- **Most vitamin supplements are best taken with an evening meal, except for the B vitamins, which should be taken before noon since they commonly promote vivid dreams and fitful sleep.**
- **An overdose of some vitamins or minerals may lead to side-effects or illness, even death in extreme cases. Mixing certain vitamins and minerals can cause additional problems or deficiencies. To avoid such risks, seek advice from your doctor or pharmacist.**
- **Excessive iron supplements have caused fatal poisoning in children. Always consult your doctor if you think your child needs more iron.**

Before embarking on any supplements programme, it is a good idea to check with your doctor (not, of course, for a mere daily multivitamin tablet).

Minerals

Like vitamins, most minerals come to us daily in acceptable amounts through our normal diet. They are essential for our normal cellular functions, account for 4 per cent of our body weight and diffuse through our bones, cells and fluids. It will help to know a little about the more important ones.

Calcium

All **green leafy vegetables**, most **fruit**, **raw nuts** and **sesame seeds** contain calcium, so it is not necessary to drink milk to 'beef up' on calcium. Our bodies were designed to take some 3,000mg of calcium a day and our Stone Age ancestors, through plant forage, achieved that rate. Today's average intake is closer to 500mg and decreases as we become older because the body begins to absorb less calcium.

Calcium is essential for normal muscle function. Osteoporosis is not the only danger: rectal and colon cancer can also be caused by calcium deficiency. To improve absorption of your calcium intake through food and drink, ensure you are not short on vitamin D and those fats found in **olive oil** and the salmon/tuna type of **oily fish**.

Phosphorus

Eighty per cent of our bodily phosphorus content is combined with calcium to help provide strength to our bones. It is also key to energy transfer, and so of special importance to anyone taking lots of exercise. Phosphorus is found in all plant and animal protein.

Potassium

Along with sodium and chloride, potassium enables nerve impulses to control muscle activity, balance and water distribution, as well as to regulate our cardiac rhythm.

A single gym work-out can lose you 800mg through sweating. Cramps can result. Eating a **banana** (contains 450mg potassium) will help. Other potassium values include:

Jacket potato:	840mg
Cup of raw spinach:	820mg
Glass of orange juice:	500mg

Selenium

Countries with high selenium levels in their soil traditionally show low cancer rates. Europeans whose diets in the pre-European Community years included selenium-rich wheat from the USA have been found recently to have lower levels of the mineral.

Like vitamin E and the other antioxidants, selenium neutralises potentially dangerous free radicals. Good natural sources include **whole cereals, brewers' yeast, eggs** and **Brazil nuts**.

Iron

Iron deficiency causes anaemia and is more common in women due to iron loss during menstruation and pregnancy. Iron aids growth and prevents fatigue.

Nobody should take iron supplements unless they have been found to be deficient in iron by a medical test. Good natural sources include **dried fruit, baked beans, wholemeal bread, fortified cereals** and **kidneys**.

Magnesium

Magnesium helps transfer brain messages to the muscles and increases oxygen delivery. Eat plenty of **nuts** to help ensure enough daily magnesium, also **green, leafy vegetables, wholegrain cereals** and **dried figs**.

Chromium

The USA's RNI is 200mcg daily, and many US dieticians recommend 400mcg. Experiments on rats

---

- **If you take mineral, vitamin or fibre supplements (or athletes' proteins), be doubly sure to drink plenty of water daily. This helps protect the kidneys.**
- **Steer clear of the vast field of DUPES (Dressed-Up Placebo Energisers) which are marketed in various bottles, tins, bags and canisters and seldom, if ever, live up to their advertising hype. Clichés to beware of include:**

Helps fight disease
Helps you live longer
Boosts your sex drive
Helps you sleep with no side-effects
Helps improve memory
Makes you feel good

indicate that chromium helps to lengthen life expectancy. It is associated with the glucose metabolism which is critical to diabetics. It is found in **brewers' yeast, wholegrain cereals, molasses, cheese** and **eggs**.

Zinc

Zinc contributes to the immune system and is essential for tissue growth. **Lean red meat, oysters** and **wholegrain foods** all contain zinc. Too much can cause iron loss.

The Ran Fiennes Food-Control System

In addition to the points mentioned previously, there are three basic elements to the way I eat and drink to keep healthy:

1. **Fruit**
2. **Water**
3. **Food-mixing**

We looked at the importance of water to the body and the benefits of fruit in Chapter 3. If you want to take your fitness a stage further you need to add a third element: food-mixing, or which types of food to eat with which and when.

Fruit. For 30 years I ate fatty foods whenever I felt like it and I grew podgy. Every time I trained for an expedition the exercise reduced my spare tyre, and each time I reverted to the desk-bound months I put on between 20 and 30lbs of excess weight. Any attempt to cut down on chocolate, cakes and ice-cream was defeated by my overpoweringly sweet tooth. I was well into my late 40s when I started to eat more fruit in the mornings and benefited from an immediate reduction of my craving for sugar. This was because the fructose in the fruit was

supplying some of my sugar needs. At that stage of my life, my body-fat ratio hovered around 22 per cent: an improvement on the 26 per cent of my pre-fruit days.

It was not until 1995 that I was told by the health nutritionist advising my polar work that eating

---

Fruit

- **The more slowly you eat fruit (or any food), the better it will be for your digestion and the greater the effect the fructose in your bloodstream will have on your hypothalamus, the part of the brain which controls your appetite.**
- **Fresh fruit juice has the same benefits as fruit itself. In fact, due to the easier digestion of juice, it has advantages: juice contains as much roughage, or fibre, since it is merely a liquidised form of the same components.**
- **All fruits combine well with one another and with nuts and seeds.**
- **Fruit can soften tooth enamel and allow tooth decay, so cleaning your teeth first thing in the morning and last thing at night is important. Chewing sugar-free gum and/or drinking water after fruit or juice, and drinking juice through a straw, all help to minimise tooth trouble.**

---

plenty of fruit was only two thirds of the battle: the other key factor was *when* to eat fruit and *with* what other foods. I adopted my 'fruit only before midday' policy to simplify my fruit intake, so that I wasn't constantly having to remember not to mix fruit with other foods.

Since I started this system, I have felt better and fitter and keep a stable body-fat ratio of 15 per cent, despite the intermittent occasions when events like parties, foreign travel, Christmas and other holidays disrupt the system altogether. As soon as life returns to normal I revert to the system. A bonus has been that, having previously been prone to catching every cold germ anywhere in the vicinity, for the first time in my life I have found that as people around me succumb to coughs and sneezes, I remain resistant.

Water. The second element of my system, water, has also been a great help in solving my weight problems. Because I have to put on a lot of excess bulk prior to polar man-haul journeys, I have fluctuated between my ideal weight of 13 stone (182lbs) and 15.5 stone (217lbs) on a seesaw basis throughout my 40s and early 50s. When I come home after an expedition, my body, having experienced starvation for a few months, wants to compensate and lay down a store of fat in readiness for the next nasty shock. Drinking plenty of water has proved by far the easiest way of keeping my weight down to 13 stone without dieting.

During any given day when I am in training my weight will fluctuate beween 13 stone after exercise and 13 stone 9lbs after eating my main meal with a complex-carbohydrate side dish.

I have an extra glass of water (over my daily eight glasses) if I feel peckish in between meals, and as often as not, about half an hour later the hunger pangs disappear.

In countries where tapwater is delivered via filtered, central systems, there should be hardly any chance of contamination. If you pay water rates it will cost you very little to have a professional test on your water supply. You may find a high chlorine reading: chlorine destroys vitamin E. If you do, take a supplement to replace this key gap in your nutrients. Yoghurt also helps to replace the intestinal good bacteria which the chlorine may have destroyed.

Some homes still have lead pipes; others have lead-soldered joints in copper pipes. Lead dissolves more easily in soft water. If your tapwater shows too high a lead level or – unlikely but possible – too much aluminium, fluoride or nitrates, you can have a water filter fitted. You can find a local supplier in the Yellow Pages or *Which?* magazine. Be sure to change your filter regularly as advised by the supplier.

In countries where water supplies are suspect, drink bottled water, but remember to check that the bottle top is sealed. Buy recognised brands if they are available – scams in which tapwater has been bottled and sold as mineral water have been exposed in many countries. Remember, too, to check the bottle's sodium content.

Why You Should Not Mix Certain Foods

Certain chemicals, when mixed, create poisons which can kill. The same is true of different foods, even if the effects are much more gradual. So it is important to ensure that you do not mix types of food which react adversely with each other in the stomach.

In 1915, a 40-year-old New York doctor, William Hay, was diagnosed as obese and found to have lethally high blood pressure. He avoided imminent death by devising a food-control system which cured him in months. Indeed, he lived on in good health until he was killed in an accident at the age of 74. Scientists later pronounced some of Hay's theories wrong, but his basic thinking remains sound nonetheless. Now that we can adjust it according to more recent nutritional research findings, we can benefit greatly by following some of his food-combination rules.

Dr Hay's main premise, in his day a revolutionary one, was that proteins and carbohydrates should not be eaten together. This theory falls down at once because many foods contain both proteins and carbohydrates, but the basic principle that there are some foods which go better together than others is eminently sensible. There are hundreds of thousands of Hay disciples alive today who saved themselves from killer diseases by following his food-mix rules, and countless others who have avoided contracting such diseases (especially cancers, arthritis and heart disease) by eating the Hay way.

The chemical results of mixing the wrong foods lead, after digestion, to an accumulation of acids which the body cannot get rid of. This toxic waste is a fertile base for many diseases. Fruit and vegetables eaten by themselves are readily digested and well suited to our systems because, as we have seen, humans were designed to cope with them. All other foods make hard work for our digestive systems, and if they are mixed badly our systems cannot cope well enough to digest everything. Fermented excess carbohydrate cannot be used by healthy tissue, nor can putrefied protein, so they remain in our bodies as toxic acids. The following chart shows which foods do and do not mix well.

Notes on Food-Mixing

- Any oil-based salad dressing improves the digestibility of vegetables.
- Sadly, you should not eat fruit or puddings on a full stomach, i.e., at the end of a meal, even though tradition dictates otherwise.
- Abominably, the worst mix of incompatible foods present in a single delicious dish is muesli eaten

Food-Mix Chart

You can mix A with B. You can mix C with B. You should not mix A with C

A	B	C
All fruits including tomatoes but **excluding** avocados, bananas, dates, grapes, figs, raisins, sultanas, currants, very sweet pears and papayas	All vegetables **except** potatoes	All cereals, bread, flour, oatmeal, rice, pasta
All meats, fish, milk, yoghurt, cheese	Nuts and seeds	Bananas, dates, grapes, figs, raisins, sultanas, currants, very sweet pears and papayas
Legumes, lentils, butter beans	Avocados	Potatoes
Soya, tofu	Butter, margarine, egg yolks, cream	Beers and lagers
All salad dressings and mayonnaises	Herbs	
Wines and cider	Honey and syrups	
Diluted frozen orange juice, concentrated apple juice	Vegetable oils (including olive oil)	
	Spirits	

with milk and sugar. Muesli contains fruit, nuts, oatflakes, raisins, honey and milk. And the worst time to eat it is first thing in the morning when the digestive juices are least active. In the privacy of my own home I eat cereal for lunch or tea. It tastes just as good then, and I do not attract sidelong glances from shocked traditionalists because they can't see me doing it.

I do not have the heart to advise you to steer clear of muesli altogether. After all, it is brimful of goodness if its contents are eaten separately. The best way round the problem is to stick to oatflakes mixed only with items found in columns B and C, not A, in the food-mix chart.

The more you study the chart, the more appalled you will be, and you will probably throw down this book in disgust. All I can do is to beg you to have a good look at the various delicious options which do mix well together and experiment with them. Abandoning the bad mixes we all love – bread and cheese, meat and spuds, chicken and rice and so on – is as difficult as giving up smoking, with the additional disadvantage that you are not immediately aware of any benefits. But they are very real for your long-term health, so the system has to be worth a try.

Quantity

However successful you are at food-mixing, you need also to guard against stuffing yourself with too much, too fast. The digestive system will fail to process all protein and starch residues if you overload it, and toxic waste will still accumulate even if the mix is sensible.

As food passes into the stomach it first hits the stomach wall, where digestive juices make contact. Food pushed to the centre of the stomach by more incoming food before it has been digested by the juices will sit around undigested and ferment. So too much food arriving too quickly can lead to big problems.

The end goal of food-mixing is to digest foods thoroughly before they arrive in the large intestine (colon). Biopsies of colon-cancer victims in countries with rich, unhealthy diets show the terrible damage bad food-mixing and thus inadequate digestion can wreak on the large intestine. Indeed, specialists in cancer clinics often refer to it as the 'organ where death lurks'.

Appetite and Control

If you are overweight, you are in a health danger zone because your body will be storing excess fat. Ideally a man's body-fat percentage should be between 10 per cent and 15 per cent and a woman's between 20 per cent and 25 per cent (see pages 46–49 for notes on measuring your body-fat percentage).

Food habits affect death rates. For proof of this you need only compare the numbers of deaths from heart-attacks (per 100,000 people) a year in Scotland, where a typical diet includes a lot of fat, and Japan, where it does not:

	Men	Women
Japan	49	20
Scotland	535	218

Most diets are based on weight loss through eating fewer calories. This process works well in the short term but is nearly always a long-term failure because the human body is pre-programmed to store up fat for periods of drought. The body notices when we cut down on calories and automatically cuts its metabolic rate in order to preserve fat and energy. Cravings increase and, almost invariably, the would-be dieter gives in and regains all the lost weight. Constant attempts to diet have a bad effect on the health, and especially on the heart.

When we take exercise we burn **carbohydrates**

(in the form of glycogen) and **fat**. Sadly, it is far easier to lose the glycogen, which we need, than the excess fat, which we do not. This is because fat is dense: a great many calories are packed into every ounce of fat. So, to lose 1lb of weight in glycogen takes 18 miles of running, compared with 35 miles to lose 1lb of weight in fat. One calorie of fat weighs one ninth of a gram, but a calorie of glycogen weighs one quarter of a gram. The body can quickly be persuaded to lose glycogen weight but is reluctant to part with fat mass, which is its insurance against starvation.

Thus, when we start to try to lose weight through dieting and/or exercise, we quickly use up glycogen, not fat. The lost glycogen, the form in which glucose is stored by the body, gives us an apparently satisfactory reading on the scales. However, our bodies demand that glycogen back again, come hell or high water, and the weight soon returns.

The only dependable, healthy way to lose fat weight is to keep your glycogen level and to follow a lifestyle that burns more calories than are eaten. If you maintain your glycogen by eating enough carbohydrate, the calorie deficiency will come from your fat store. This is a slow but sure process; give it time, and the fat will go.

If you make no change to your current diet but run a mere three extra miles every week, you will lose 4lbs of excess fat per year.

The message is exercise and sensible eating. Both can be difficult to enthuse over. So how can we make things easier when our appetites are constantly making it difficult, if not virtually impossible, for those of us who do not possess wills of iron? One avenue of potential is to study the workings of the appetite, since it is sensible to know your enemy.

The appetite is controlled by the appestat, the part of the brain which gauges hunger and then tells the appetite to start pestering you. The smell or even the mere thought of food can spark the appetite. Saliva is quickly produced. Ten thousand

---

Tips to Help Weight Loss Through Exercise

- **If you are already in good shape but wish to lose a few more pounds, you will find it difficult. One answer lies in mixing your training at each session.**

- **Remember that anaerobics and strength training do not do much for body fat unless they are combined with aerobics.**

- **Forget the myth that walking burns as much body fat as running. The reality is that fast exercise burns more fat than slow exercise as long as you keep your heart rate in your optimal training zone. However, *fast* walking is an underrated form of exercise. Besides being particularly suitable for beginners, it is a good option for anyone having trouble with running or other high-impact activities.**

- **Outdoor exercises like running and cycling, or indoor machines such as the treadmill and the stair-stepper, keep your heart rate going at an uninterrupted level, but stop–start activities like tennis are not truly aerobic. Bicycles and bicycle machines are also less effective because they carry part of your body weight for you.**

---

tastebuds situated in various regions of the tongue get ready to discern flavours and the gallbladder empties its contents of bile into the small intestine in minutes in preparation to process the anticipated intake of food. This is all quite impressive and acts powerfully to persuade the body to devour food. If your body thinks you are about to fall off a cliff it will send out messages to try to dissuade you from doing so. If an alluring member of the opposite sex attracts you, your body will instruct you accordingly. None of these three instinctive reactions are easy to deny, however hell-bent you may be on dieting, suicide or chastity.

The appetite can be affected by factors other than instinctive food cravings. Mood, stress, depression and boredom can lead to overeating, as can social customs or mere food availability in the form of a tempting buffet. A great help in controlling sudden sugar cravings is to recognise that you are being attacked by them, and to tell yourself to wait 30 minutes before grabbing that goodie. Drink water, eat fruit or even chew sugar-free gum, and wait for the craving to pass. The appestat works on messages from the bloodstream. It can take half an hour or so for many foods to enter the bloodstream and tell the appestat to shut up, so you may carry on reaching for doughnuts unaware that in a short while the craving will be switched off.

Bearing in mind that you are trying to achieve a calorie balance by burning off fat through energy expenditure, it is salutary to remember the nasty fact that:

One half-pint of beer	= 1.4 miles of running.
Fifteen potato chips	= 1.5 miles of running.
Two teaspoonfuls of jam	= 2.5 miles of running.

Nine out of every 10 calorie-counting dieters revert to their initial weight within 12 months. Be aware of the calorific value of foods and avoid the worst offenders, but forget calorie counts unless you are very strong-willed, persistent and fully aware of the dangers of missing out on an overall balanced diet.

Does Exercise Reduce Appetite?

In general, active people eat more and weigh less, whereas inactive people eat less and weigh more. Regular exercise and the sort of low-fat, high-carbohydrate regime suggested in this book enable you to eat lots of nutritious food – and to binge occasionally – while maintaining your ideal body weight and body-fat percentage.

Another factor I have noticed is the difference that temperature makes to the appetite after exercise. After training in the polar regions I feel far hungrier than I do after training in Arabia. Even at home I am aware of this: a two-hour sweating run results in little or no increased appetite, whereas an hour's swim in the sea makes me voracious.

Does Unused Muscle Turn to Fat?

Many heavyweight athletes and weightlifters need to work hard to avoid becoming overweight when they stop practising their sport. William Perry of the Chicago Bears American football team plays at 320lbs and, out of season, averages 375lbs. He will need to watch out when he retires that he does not emulate the US Olympic wrestler Chris Taylor, who competed at 450lbs (32 stone) and died in his sleep, aged 29, from an obesity-related illness. Unused muscles do not turn to fat, they merely atrophy (shrink) and lie dormant until you start working afresh on them. If you eat too much, excess fat may well appear alongside muscle, but the two remain separated.

Can You Reduce Specific Areas of Fat?

The answer is no. When you run, fat is used up from all over your body, not just from the legs. Right-handed professional tennis players have as much fat on their right arms as on their left. And people who have spent long hours working on abdominal exercises have failed to produce visually impressive stomach muscles, or even flat stomachs, unless they have worked equally hard at overall food control.

Fat-Control Devices

Sauna belts and body wraps may temporarily compress fatty tissue and make you think you are slimmer, but any benefit will always be short-term and illusory. Fat can only disperse if it is used up as a source of energy via active muscle. Cellulite is fat and will also disappear only through exercise and weight control. It usually appears, especially in women, on the hips and thighs, which are natural fat-storage areas and therefore the most difficult from which to shift blubber. No machine or cream has ever been proven to remove cellulite or body fat. The healthiest man in the world may be moon-faced, and the fittest, most beautiful woman may be blessed with puckered hips.

I would advise against taking slimming pills (appetite suppressants) since these drugs have never been proved to be completely clear of dangerous side-effects.

Stress Management

Stress is caused only by events you cannot control. Modern life brings with it many stress factors such as worries about relationships, financial fears and ongoing, nebulous concerns which contrive to raise our blood pressure. As a result, we live constantly with a high tension level which leads to a great many ailments including the obvious killers: heart-attacks and strokes.

Conversely, conditions such as those I encounter on polar expeditions (confrontations with bears, crevasses and so on), which might on the face of it seem very stressful, seldom cause any stress build-up because they involve clear-cut hazards which call for immediate action. These are situations which are controlled quickly (if they are not you are dead, and very unstressed). Your blood pressure rises as adrenaline, glucose and fatty acids are pumped into the bloodstream to deal with the problem. The instinctive fight-or-flight mechanism comes into play, the physical exertion it involves burns off the chemicals generated and the blood pressure then returns to normal.

Ongoing stress, on the other hand, is a slow, silent killer, like hypothermia. So we need to try to diagnose ourselves from time to time to see if we are becoming victims. Stress symptoms include: lower back and neck pain, headaches, various nervous tics, irregular heart-fluttering, imagined throat lumps, fast pulse, sweating, dry throat and mouth, lethargy, insomnia, stomach ulcers, fidgeting, tearfulness, irritability and inability to concentrate.

If you think you recognise a number of these symptoms in yourself at any time, you should examine your personal situation to identify the events causing this stress. The *Reader's Digest* stress list is an established indicator:

Highest Stress: Death of partner, divorce or separation, prison sentence, death of close relative, personal injury or illness, marriage, job loss, moving house.

High Stress: Reconciliation with partner, retirement, grave ill health in family, pregnancy, sexual problems, new baby, change of job, financial worries, death of close friend.

Moderate Stress: Family arguments, large mortgage, legal action, new work responsibilities, child starts or finishes school, child leaves home, in-law problems, change in living conditions, problems with boss.

Low Stress: Change in working conditions, change of school, holidays, change in contact with relatives, minor law violation, joining or leaving a social group, Christmas, small mortgage or loan.

The list tallies with many medical research findings but is by no means exhaustive. There is no mention, for instance, of commuting, yet I have often found that to be the most stressful factor in my life. Driving under stress leads to road rage. I know I have felt extremely angry with the actions of other drivers even though, when I think about it, I'm well aware that I have been guilty of the same conduct.

Two aspects of stress. At the PR desk at Occidental Oil in 1987 (left), *trying to cope with the energy press – an example of ongoing stress caused by my not being in control of a situation for which I was technically responsible.* Damart

*Cautiously checking a mine for booby-traps during the Dhofar anti-terrorist campaign in 1968 (*right*). Situations like this, which call for immediate action, rarely lead to a build-up of stress.* Salim Khaleefa

Such an irrational and unbalanced response is a sign of stress. If I am late for an important appointment, each time I overtake another car I can physically feel a tightening of my chest unless I consciously fight to relax. Before I begin the act of overtaking I say to myself aloud, 'Calm down'. Once past the vehicle, I check that my body *is* physically relaxed.

Another item not listed is boredom, often caused by life being too regimented and routine. This can make us lethargic and creates a sense that there is nothing to look forward to. You have been doing the same thing for too long and nothing stimulates you any more. If the situation seems to be beyond your control, it can lead to mounting stress, increasing irritability and even nervous breakdowns.

Tips on Stress-Avoidance

If, one Monday, you find yourself worrying about some domestic niggle or about a business rival working a flanker on you, your worries will be causing you stress. This is unhealthy; it is also unnecessary. For if, on the Tuesday, your doctor tells you that you have cancer, Monday's worries are immediately put into their true perspective and you will completely forget about them. Try to apply this perspective to all your day-to-day worries and force yourself to realise they are not worth stewing about. Jesus, who was unarguably a sensible bloke, asked, 'Which of you by taking thought will add one inch to his height?' Meaning, of course, that there is no point in worrying about something if you cannot do anything about it.

Domestic arguments often repeat endlessly, like the seasons. Self-perpetuating marital rows help nobody and lead nowhere. When you find quarrels becoming so familiar that you can predict the next accusation, and your own response, it is surely time to make a vigorous attempt to reach a compromise agreement. Start by:

- Forcing yourself to compromise.
- Attempting to repair damage rather than increasing it during quarrels.
- Remaining as calm as possible and not raising your voice. If you do reach boiling point, go outside and, if you must, hit something inanimate with something that cost nothing and which you will not miss tomorrow.

Stress-Reducing Foods

Beans

Blackcurrants

Broccoli

Oranges

Potatoes

Steaks

Walnuts

Lots of water

Plenty of wholemeal bread

When you stop quarrelling you will be amazed by what an improvement it will make to your life. You will wish you had made the effort to confront the problem years earlier.

Many people live with somebody they love but who annoys them, an elderly parent, perhaps, or a difficult child. The secret to coping is to plan your week, ensuring that you allow yourself a period of at least an hour every day when you can completely relax by yourself or with friends. And book at least one evening a week to do something you really enjoy, and to which you can look forward. You may find it hard to hold on to these sacred periods due to other calls on your time, but be firm and you will be thankful. Long-term diary-planning should include your annual holiday, too.

Because stress comes only from events you cannot control, try to control your environment in as many small ways as you can. The more carefully you plan your future, in both the short and long term – from allowing enough time to make a particular journey to completing your will so that you do not create family chaos by dying intestate – the less scope you leave for outside forces to take over.

Make lists prioritising tasks for the next day and tick them off as you go along. Do not let small jobs keep deflecting you from more important ones with fast-approaching deadlines. And if you can clearly predict that you will not make a given deadline, it is far better to bite the bullet and ask well in advance for an extension.

Talk over your problems with a friend or relative you can trust. Even if he or she is unable to help you find a solution, you will feel better for having let off steam.

The best stress-reliever I know is exercise, especially out in the country. It is also a tonic for those who suffer from depression or women with premenstrual tension. As you run or cycle, you have time to think things out with nothing to interrupt or distract you. Aerobic exercise reduces stress hormones and helps the body to relax. Taking up yoga, and learning contemplation and breathing techniques, interwoven with flexibility exercises, is an excellent alternative, especially if you are unable to exercise outdoors. Hot baths sprinkled with lavender aromatherapy oil, especially when taken after exercising, help most people relax. If you are feeling wealthy, throw in a professional all-body massage for good measure.

Stress and caffeine are often deadly partners in a downward spiral. When you are feeling stressed you should steer clear of coffee, tea and cola, and resist the temptation to reach for a cigarette and a shot of alcohol. Instead try a glass of milk laced with a small amount of honey. This prompts the body to release the chemical serotonin, which will help you to relax.

Keep on Running

Once you have taken on the food-control and fitness regimes described in this book, you will, barring exceptional personal problems, join that top 2 per cent of the population, as promised at the start of this chapter, whether you are 20 or 65. Ongoing attention to such details as food-mixing, vitamins and stress will help to ensure that you stay there. The secret to remaining fit is keeping at it. If you are a runner – and in nine cases out of ten, you will be – you must keep on running. If you are not, this advice applies, of course, to whatever other main form of exercise you do.

You will need to run for a certain number of hours and miles without periods between runs that are so long you lose the benefit of previous runs. How long or how far you run, and whether you do so six days a week or every other day, is up to you. Whether you stick to a firm routine or keep changing your programme should be guided by whatever keeps you enjoying the process of keeping fit. Olympic gold-medal cross-country skiers run for three hours every morning and cross-train for an hour with another sport every afternoon, six days a week. Many African long-distance runners training for the 'big' marathons, and ultimately for Olympic marathon medals, do 20-mile sessions at altitude twice a day, six days a week, all year round. Running becomes their very existence, and they need this level of training if they are to stand any chance of achieving prominence in an intensely competitive sport. But I doubt they actually enjoy such a programme.

My own training schedule during periods when I am ticking over and maintaining a basic level of reasonable fitness, as opposed to during the run-up to an expedition or an endurance race, is a mixture of running and indoor circuits. I do not stick to a hard-and-fast programme because my business life is too unpredictable. However, a typical week would involve one hilly run of one and a half hours and one of two hours (12 miles), alternating with days when I do an 80-minute gym circuit along the lines of the following:

Warm up	5 minutes
Weightlifting with dumb-bells	22 minutes
Step-up machine, or Versaclimber (1,200 steps), plyometrics	15 minutes

Treadmill		
480 steps walk @ 4.2mph	3 minutes
800 steps run @ 5.5mph	4.5 minutes
200 steps run @ 6mph	1.5 minutes
1,000 steps run @ 6.5mph	6.5 minutes
1,000 steps run @ 7mph	6 minutes
1,000 steps run @ 8mph	5.5 minutes
480 steps walk @ 4.2mph	3 minutes
Stretch	10 minutes
	(Total: 82 minutes)

Heart-rate maximum: 144.

Whenever feasible, include uphill work in your runs. However, what goes up comes down, so take care when running downhill again: it is tougher on

---

Aspirin

Many runners take aspirin, the worldwide wonder drug which helps prevent heart disease, to ease the pain of aching joints. I would advise against aspirin use before exercise because it is only the ability to feel slight pain twinges that warns you of problem areas and enables you to prevent further damage by resting or checking an ill-fitting shoe. You need your pain sensors to remain keen, not deadened, when you take exercise. Aspirins can also cause inflammation of the stomach's lining, leading to ulcers.

your body because gravity makes for greater impact. When each foot lands, the leg has to absorb the downward momentum at the same time as it is trying to go in the opposite direction towards push-off. This can lead to aching calves and sore thighs unless you remember the rules of downhill running:

- Relax your neck. Do not look up at the sky.
- Keep your chest high and lean slightly forward in relation to the gradient.
- Pump your arms in tandem with your legs, but do not flail them around in the air. All four limbs will move a touch faster than when you run on flat ground.
- Do not overstride, but make your stride slightly longer than it is on the flat.
- Land as softly as you can – on your heels, not your toes, as a general rule. Sometimes, on steep or uneven areas, you may land on your heels and the balls of your feet simultaneously.

To give your body the best chance of feeling good during and after runs (and thereby giving yourself the best chance of enjoying them), be sure to drink more water than you think you need some 30 minutes before you set out (two standard tumblers in my case). If you run for two hours or more, consider en-route drinks as well.

After a long, tiring run, your body usually wants to eat more, drink more and sleep more. Let it – enjoy the excesses you have earned. You need to reload with carbohydrates as soon as possible to replenish your glycogen store. And remember that your legs will need to recover after a long run. Medical research indicates that after a marathon, legs take at least three days, sometimes up to 10, to recover fully. Forget this and you may find mere soreness turning into injury.

These rules have helped me to keep exercising for over 30 years, on a relatively regular basis, without ever becoming stale.

If you have not yet thought about competing in endurance events, this might be the time to consider committing to a race to add that extra incentive to your fitness training. Once you start enjoying endurance races, the sky really is the limit. My first was the Welsh 3,000 race.

Back in the 1970s, I needed to find two men to join me, unpaid, to complete the first journey around the Earth on its polar axis. Physical endurance, mental balance and a good many other special personal qualities would be essential. I searched within the ranks of the Territorial SAS Regiment and, over a period of four years, put more than 100 volunteers through their paces in the Welsh 3,000, a mountain race. Each winter, over nine weekends and in all weathers, I ran the men over the 24-mile course, which included Snowdon and 12 other peaks over 3,000ft. The two men eventually selected then joined me on separate trials in Greenland and on Arctic Ocean sea ice before they were finally chosen for the three-year polar circumnavigation of the Earth. By the beginning of the main expedition, and thanks to the Welsh 3,000, we were fit for whatever tribulations the Arctic, the Antarctic, the North-West Passage and the rest of the 30,000-mile route might throw at us. We became the first people in history to reach both poles the hard way – and all our basic fitness training had been completed at weekends on the Welsh 3,000, which, at 24 miles, was very similar to a marathon.

If you become fit enough to run a half-marathon and then a real marathon, you may next aim at improving your marathon time to less than four hours, or even three hours. I ran my first-ever half-marathon in Exeter in April 1998, clocking up one hour and 37 minutes and coming in 266th out of 1,200 runners. In 1999 I hope to be among the top 250. It's all a question of setting yourself small, progressive goals to help with self-motivation.

Marathons

The marathon is a great challenge and a gateway to ultra-endurance events. The total distance is 26 miles, 285 yards. A big-city race like the London Marathon, with over 27,000 competitors, has atmosphere, crowds and a great sense of theatre about it. Smaller marathons may not have the same prestige, but they do not entail as much dodging around all the other competing bodies. You can get full data on most scheduled marathons from *Runners' World* several months in advance (the London event is always oversubscribed).

I entered my first marathon, the New Forest Marathon, when I was about 43, without any preparation. My time was a tortoise-like four hours 45 minutes. In 1998, aged 54, I completed the same marathon fairly comfortably in under four hours after a four-month build-up of two-hours-plus runs on hilly terrain three times a week. Many three-and-a-half-hour marathon-runners are well into their 60s and a happy sprinkling of 80-year-olds still complete marathons in respectable times. Whether you manage to finish one marathon and start planning for the next, or are put off for ever by the first, will be determined by how you train. The type of training you do depends largely on what level you run at and what your expectations are. Other sports may help, but marathon fitness really only comes from running. Before even contemplating a marathon you will need to have run fairly regularly for a year or so. Some naturally fit types might find that a mere month suffices, but sadly, this does not apply to the majority of us.

Twelve to 16 weeks, according to your level of fitness, is usually long enough for a fit person to train specifically for a marathon. To stay healthy during the heavy training you must eat and sleep more. You will require an extra 100 calories for every additional mile you run, so if you can increase your weekly distance from, say, 30 to 50 miles, you'll

Finishing my first marathon in 1988 at the age of 43.
New Forest Marathon

need to consume another 2,000 calories a week. Eat this supplementary food within two hours of exercise (but not last thing at night), so that the calories will be stored as carbohydrate, not fat.

Training hard makes you susceptible to viral infections, so take 500mg of vitamin C tablets a day. Increase your fluid intake, ideally to a glass of water every waking hour.

The most important training run is the long run, which accustoms your body to being on the move for two hours and more, and if you don't already run to a structured weekly schedule, it will be a great help if you do so now. But treat it as flexible, and as usual don't run if you have a sprain, inflammation or a virus. Help and advice from more experienced runners will prove encouraging too.

The following three schedules were designed by *Runners' World* to train three grades of runner (novice, experience, elite) for marathons. The terms they use to specify running speed are explained as follows:

Easy: A slow run.
Slow: Slower than your expected marathon pace.
Steady: Roughly your marathon pace.
Brisk: Your half-marathon pace.
Fast: Your six-mile race speed.

The Novice Schedule

Suitable for those who do not run a great deal and whose ambition is simply to finish the course. It involves running for four days each week, including a long run at the weekend. You can take rest days between each running day, but obviously you will have to run on two consecutive days at least once a week. Where 'race' is mentioned, and if you can't find a suitable local event, simply use 'fast' pace.

Week 1
Day 1: 20 minutes easy
Day 2: 20 minutes easy
Day 3: 20 minutes easy
Day 4: One-hour walk/run (e.g., 10 minutes' run, five minutes' walk)

Week 2
Day 1: 20 minutes easy
Day 2: 25 minutes easy
Day 3: 20–25 minutes easy
Day 4: One-hour walk/run with more emphasis on running

Week 3
Day 1: 25 minutes easy
Day 2: 25 minutes easy
Day 3: 25 minutes easy
Day 4: 80–90 minutes' walk/run

Week 4
Day 1: 25 minutes easy
Day 2: 20 minutes, including six faster bursts of 50 yards
Day 3: 25 minutes easy
Day 4: six–12 miles race, with 10-minute run before

Week 5
Day 1: 25 minutes easy
Day 2: 20 minutes, including five minutes at faster pace
Day 3: 25 minutes easy
Day 4: 90–100 minutes' run/walk

Week 6
Day 1: 25 minutes easy
Day 2: 30 minutes, including six one-minute surges
Day 3: 25 minutes steady
Day 4: 100 minutes' run/walk

Week 7
Day 1: 25 minutes easy
Day 2: Five minutes easy, including some short bursts
Day 3: 35 minutes, including two five-minute runs at faster pace
Day 4: One hour's running – try not to walk at all

Week 8
Day 1: 25 minutes steady
Day 2: 25 minutes, including five one-minute fast bursts with slow-run recoveries
Day 3: 35 minutes easy
Day 4: Two-hour run, walking the last five minutes of the first hour and the first five minutes of the second hour.

Week 9
Day 1: 25 minutes easy
Day 2: 30 minutes, including six faster one-minute fast bursts with slow-run recoveries
Day 3: 35 minutes steady
Day 4: 80–90 minute run, or half-marathon

Week 10
Day 1: 25 minutes easy
Day 2: 20 minutes, including two one-minute fast bursts, two minutes slow, then five fast
Day 3: 25 minutes steady, including five one-minute fast bursts
Day 4: 150-minute run/walk – take it very easy

Week 11
Day 1: 20 minutes easy
Day 2: 20 minutes, including six one-minute fast bursts, one minute slow
Day 3: 20 minutes, including three minutes fast
Day 4: 150-minute run/walk – take it very easy

Week 12
Day 1: 20 minutes easy
Day 2: 20–30 minutes, including eight one-minute fast bursts, one minute slow
Day 3: 25 minutes easy
Day 4: Half-marathon with one-mile slow run before and afterwards

Week 13
Day 1: 20 minutes, including six one-minute fast runs, one minute slow
Day 2: 20 minutes steady
Day 3: 20 minutes, including three two-minute fast bursts, two minutes slow
Day 4: One-hour run

Week 14 – race week
Day 1: 20 minutes easy
Day 2: 20 minutes easy
Day 3: 15 minutes easy, in race kit
Day 4: Race day

The Experienced Schedule

The experienced runner should devote four to six hours a week to training. Depending on your speed and the terrain, this will mean somewhere between 35 and 55 miles per week. One rest day is allowed.

Week 1
Day 1: 35 minutes easy
Day 2: 40–50 minutes, including 10 one-minute fast bursts, two minutes slow
Day 3: 40–45 minutes steady
Day 4: 45–50 minutes, including two five-minute fast bursts, five minutes slow
Day 5: Rest
Day 6: 35–45 minutes off road
Day 7: 60–70 minutes steady. No pressure

Week 2
Day 1: 35 minutes easy
Day 2: 40–45 minutes, including six to eight fast bursts of 30 seconds each
Day 3: 40–45 minutes steady, with a brisk finish
Day 4: 20 minutes easy, 15 minutes brisk, 10 minutes easy
Day 5: Rest
Day 6: 30 minutes easy (racing tomorrow!) or 10 minutes slow
Day 7: six- or 10-mile race or 75–85 minutes. No pressure

Week 3
Day 1: 35 minutes easy
Day 2: 40–45 minutes, including 10 one-minute fast bursts, two minutes slow
Day 3: 40–45 minutes steady
Day 4: 40–45 minutes, including eight one-minute fast bursts, 90 seconds slow
Day 5: Rest
Day 6: 15 minutes easy, then timed two miles at planned marathon pace, then 10 minutes slow
Day 7: 80–100 minutes slow

Week 4
Day 1: 35 minutes easy, off road if possible
Day 2: Warm up, then three to four five-minute fast bursts (with three-minute recovery runs), then cool down
Day 3: 35–45 minutes steady
Day 4: 10 to 15 400-yard stretches fast, with 60–90 second recovery runs

Day 5: Rest
Day 6: 20–40 minutes easy
Day 7: 10 miles or a half-marathon, or 70–90 minutes, including five minutes brisk

Week 5
Day 1: 30–40 minutes easy
Day 2: Hills. Warm up, then six to eight 90-second runs uphill with slow recoveries
Day 3: 35–45 minutes steady
Day 4: Six to eight 800-yard stretches fast, with two-minute recovery runs
Day 5: Rest
Day 6: 20 minutes easy, including six 100-yard fast runs
Day 7: 90–105 minutes slow

Week 6
Day 1: 30–40 minutes easy
Day 2: 35–45 minutes, including six bursts of 150–200 yards fast
Day 3: 40–50 minutes steady
Day 4: 10 minutes easy, 15–20 minutes fast, five minutes easy
Day 5: 30 minutes easy, including a few bursts at speed
Day 6: Rest
Day 7: Half-marathon race

Week 7
Day 1: 30–40 minutes easy, off road if possible
Day 2: 35–40 minutes easy fartlek
Day 3: Hills. Warm up, then 10 to 15 30–40-second uphill runs with slow recovery
Day 4: 35–40 minutes steady
Day 5: Rest
Day 6: Two to three 10-minute fast runs with five-minute recoveries, plus five minutes fast
Day 7: 120 minutes easy. Practise drinking on the run.

Week 8
Day 1: 30 minutes easy

Day 2: 10 to 15 40-yard fast runs, with 60–90-second recoveries
Day 3: 40–50 minutes steady
Day 4: Five to eight three-minute fast runs, two minutes slow
Day 5: Rest
Day 6: 20–40 minutes, depending if race tomorrow
Day 7: Six-mile or half-marathon race, or 75–90 minutes steady

Week 9
Day 1: 30–40 minutes, off road if possible
Day 2: 40–50 minutes fartlek
Day 3: 40–50 minutes, including 20–30 minutes of threshold pace in middle
Day 4: 30–45 minutes easy
Day 5: Rest
Day 6: 30–40 minutes steady
Day 7: 120–135 minutes slow

Week 10
Day 1: 20–30 minutes easy
Day 2: 40–50 minutes steady
Day 3: Hills. Six 80–90-second uphill runs with slow recoveries
Day 4: 40–50 minutes fartlek
Day 5: Rest
Day 6: 20–30 minutes slow with one mile at race pace
Day 7: Half-marathon race

Week 11
Day 1: 30–40 minutes easy
Day 2: 30–45 minutes steady
Day 3: Warm up, then three 10-minute fast runs with five-minute recoveries
Day 4: 40–50 minutes steady
Day 5: Rest
Day 6: Five to 10 minutes easy, then 20 minutes brisk, five minutes slow
Day 7: 135–150 minutes. Should take you to more than 20 miles, depending on the terrain. Take drinks

Week 12
Day 1: Rest

Day 2: 30–45 minutes, start slowly, finish faster

Day 3: Warm up, then four five-minute fast runs with three-minute slow recoveries

Day 4: 40–50 minutes fartlek

Day 5: Rest

Day 6: 30 minutes easy, including a few bursts

Day 7: Half-marathon race

Week 13

Day 1: 30–40 minutes easy

Day 2: 40–60 minutes brisk

Day 3: 20–30 minutes steady

Day 4: Hills. 12–16 30- to 40-second uphill runs (long warm-up and cool-down)

Day 5: Rest

Day 6: Warm up, two miles steady, cool down

Day 7: 60–80 minutes at faster than marathon pace

Week 14 – race week

Day 1: 30 minutes easy

Day 2: 25–35 minutes, including 15–20 fast bursts

Day 3: 30 minutes easy, including six 200-yard bursts

Day 4: Rest or 20 minutes easy

Day 5: Rest or 20 minutes slow in racing kit

Day 6: Warm up. one mile at race pace. Cool down

Day 7: Race day

The Elite Schedule

This schedule is for runners who really want to commit to a serious marathon preparation. It includes some twice-a-day training, and more runs of around two hours than the previous schedule. The hard sessions should be hard, but you have to decide how hard to push yourself in the steady runs. Again, the aim is to avoid getting ill or injured, so if in doubt ease off.

Week 1

Day 1: a.m. 30 minutes easy
　　　p.m. 30 minutes steady

Day 2: Warm up, then four one-mile reps with three-minute recoveries

Day 3: a.m. 30 minutes easy
　　　p.m. 30 minutes steady

Day 4: Hills. Warm up, then 10–12 40-second uphill runs. Cool down

Day 5: 30 minutes easy

Day 6: 45 minutes easy

Day 7: 80–90 minutes slow

Week 2

Day 1: a.m. 30 minutes easy
　　　p.m. 45 minutes steady

Day 2: Warm up, then eight 1,000-yard runs at six-mile pace, with two-minute recoveries

Day 3: a.m. 30 minutes easy
　　　p.m. 45 minutes easy

Day 4: Timed fartlek: six two-minute fast runs, one minute slow, six one-minute fast runs, one minute slow

Day 5: 30 minutes easy

Day 6: 30 minutes easy

Day 7: Six-mile or 10-mile race, with long warm-up and cool-down

Week 3

Day 1: a.m. 30 minutes easy
　　　p.m. 40 minutes steady

Day 2: 50–60 minutes fartlek

Day 3: Warm up, then 15, 10 and five minutes fast with five-minute recoveries

Day 4: 40 minutes easy, with eight 100-yard strides on grass

Day 5: 30 minutes easy

Day 6: 30 minutes easy

Day 7: 120 minutes easy

Week 4

Day 1: a.m. 30 minutes easy
　　　p.m. 40 minutes easy

Day 2: 16–20 400-yard runs, or 20–24 one-minute fast runs, with one-minute slow recoveries

Day 3: a.m. 30 minutes easy
　　　p.m. 45 minutes steady

Day 4: Warm up, then six two-minute uphill runs. Cool down

Day 5: 30 minutes easy

Day 6: 30–50 minutes, depending on tomorrow

Day 7: 10-mile race, or 90 minutes steady

Week 5

Day 1: a.m. 30 minutes easy
　　　p.m. 30 minutes easy

Day 2: Warm up, then five one-mile runs with three-minute recoveries. Cool down

Day 3: a.m. 30 minutes easy
　　　p.m. 40–50 minutes easy

Day 4: 60–70 minutes steady

Day 5: 30 minutes easy

Day 6: 30–40 minutes easy

Day 7: 120–140 minutes slow

Week 6

Day 1: a.m. 30 minutes easy
　　　p.m. 30 minutes easy

Day 2: a.m. 30 minutes easy (optional)
　　　p.m. 60–70 minutes; start slowly, finish faster

Day 3: a.m. 30 minutes easy
　　　p.m. 40–50 minutes steady, including eight 100-yard strides

Day 4: Warm up, then eight 800-yard runs with two-minute recoveries, then cool down

Day 5: 30 minutes easy

Day 6: 30–50 minutes easy, depending on tomorrow

Day 7: Half-marathon race, or 90 minutes steady

Week 7

Day 1: a.m. 30 minutes easy
　　　p.m. 45–55 minutes steady

Day 2: a.m. 30 minutes easy (optional)
　　　p.m. 50–60 minutes fartlek

Day 3: a.m. 30 minutes easy
　　　p.m. 40–50 minutes steady, including eight 100-yard strides

Day 4: Warm up, then 15, 10, five

minutes fast, with five-minute recoveries

Day 5: 30 minutes easy

Day 6: 40–60 minutes steady

Day 7: 120–165 minutes. Practise taking drinks

Week 8

Day 1: 30–40 minutes easy, off road if possible

Day 2: 40–50 minutes steady

Day 3: Warm up, then 12 600-yard runs, with 90-second slow recoveries

Day 4: 60 minutes steady

Day 5: 30 minutes easy

Day 6: 40–50 minutes easy fartlek

Day 7: Half-marathon race, or 90 minutes steady

Week 9

Day 1: a.m. 30 minutes easy

p.m. 40–55 minutes steady

Day 2: Eight 90-second runs, two minutes uphill. Slow run down to recover

Day 3: a.m. 30 minutes easy

p.m. 45–60 minutes steady

Day 4: 60–70 minutes steady

Day 5: 30 minutes easy

Day 6: 10 minutes easy, then 15–20 minutes brisk, then 10 minutes easy

Day 7: 120–150 minutes. Take drinks

Week 10

Day 1: a.m. 30 minutes easy

p.m. 30–40 minutes easy

Day 2: a.m. 30 minutes easy

p.m. 50–60 minutes steady, including some faster surges

Day 3: a.m. 30 minutes easy

p.m. five one-mile runs, with three-minute recoveries

Day 4: 50–60 minutes steady

Day 5: 30 minutes easy

Day 6: 60–70 minutes, including 10–15 one minute fast, one minute slow

Day 7: Warm up, then half-marathon race or 90 minutes steady

Week 11

Day 1: a.m. 30 minutes easy

p.m. 50–60 minutes steady

Day 2: 75–80 minutes steady

Day 3: a.m. 30 minutes easy

p.m. eight 90-second runs, two minutes uphill with downhill recoveries

Day 4: a.m. 30 minutes easy

p.m. 50–60 minutes steady, plus eight 150-yard fast strides

Day 5: 30 minutes easy

Day 6: 10 minutes easy, 20 minutes brisk, 10 minutes easy

Day 7: 120–140 minutes at marathon speed

Week 12

Day 1: a.m. 30 minutes easy

p.m. 40–50 minutes steady; start slowly, finish faster

Day 2: a.m. 30 minutes easy

p.m. 50–60 minutes fartlek

Day 3: a.m. 30 minutes easy

p.m. eight 1,000-yard fast runs with two-minute recoveries

Day 4: 75 minutes steady

Day 5: 30 minutes easy

Day 6: 40 minutes easy, including six 200-yard strides

Day 7: 10-mile or half-marathon race, with extra running to total 16–18 miles

Week 13

Day 1: a.m. 30 minutes easy

p.m. 45–50 minutes steady, starting slowly

Day 2: Warm up, then four one-mile fast runs with three-minute recoveries

Day 3: a.m. 30 minutes easy

p.m. 40–50 minutes easy, including a few surges

Day 4: 50–60 minutes, including two three-mile runs

Day 5: 30 minutes easy

Day 6: Warm up, then 20 minutes brisk. Cool down

Day 7: 60–70 minutes marathon pace

Week 14 – race week

Day 1: 40 minutes steady, including six 150-yard fast strides

Day 2: Warm up, then two miles at race pace. Cool down

Day 3: 30 minutes easy

Day 4: 20 minutes easy

Day 5: Rest or 20 minutes easy

Day 6: 30 minutes slow in racing kit

Day 7: Race day

The Final Week

If training has gone well, and your target race is a week away, then this is the time to make sure that all your hard work does not go to waste. You've done the main thing – preparing your body for the rigours of 26.2 miles – but there are still plenty of things that could go wrong if you're not careful. Assess realistically that you *are* fit to run. If you have a temperature, or are taking antibiotics, or have suffered an injury recently, don't do it. Even though you

may have training partners, or a charity, depending on you, it's not worth the risk in these cases.

If you haven't put in the miles in training, now is not the time. Rest, rather than training, is going to be of more use, although if you really are ill prepared you should be ready for an uncomfortable and painful experience. If you are well prepared use the final days for a couple of slow runs of no more than four miles, with at least one in the kit that you're planning to wear during the race.

Don't wear new shoes for the race, or kit that you

Race Day Checklist

1. Race number
2. Safety pins
3. Race vest or T-shirt (pin your number on before you set off)
4. Shorts
5. Socks
6. Shoes
7. Petroleum jelly (for nipples, arm 'crutches' and inner thighs, not feet)
8. Plasters or dressing for feet
9. Medical supports or other medication you may need
10. Pint bottle of water
11. Snack for travelling to race
12. Old T-shirt or bin-liner (to wear and discard at start)
13. Toilet paper
14. Wristwatch
15. Waterproof top and bottoms for before start (if you have a helper)
16. Clothes to change into at finish (if applicable)
17. Post-race snack
18. Loose change for bus fare or phone call
19. Travel documents to get away at finish if necessary
20. Towel

---

haven't worn before. Seams that chafe will come back to haunt you at 20 miles.

Don't try any new foods or drinks in the days before, and if you're planning to take anything other than water on board during the race, make sure you've experimented with it during training.

As your training tapers down your carbohydrate intake should increase. The full 'bleed-out' diet popular 20 years ago (when you starve yourself of carbohydrates until four days before the race, then load up) is not advisable; far better just to gradually increase your carbohydrate intake to 17.5–21oz per day (roughly 70 per cent of your total food intake). Watch what you eat on the day before the race – too much fruit could give you diarrhoea. Try not to have a heavy meal in the evening as you may still feel bloated the following day. Keep drinking, preferably water, and avoid caffeine or alcohol. Breakfast, at least two hours before the race, can, on this occasion, include cereals, toast and juice.

Go For It!

After a year or two of marathons you may develop itchy feet and move on to long-distance orienteering, for which navigational skills are added to cross-country speed and endurance. You might find a liking for gradient running and, after checking out the various UK hill and mountain races, graduate to international events. Sky-runs (see page 194) are the pinnacle for runners reaching for the sky. Wherever sky meets mountain ridge-line – the Alps, Tibet, Nepal, Kenya, Colorado, Mexico – is where the sky-runners race. Races are usually staged between 14,000 and 17,000ft above sea-level, so the runners need to acclimatise. Some sky races cover the full 26-mile marathon distance, whereas the course for another may be only 1 kilometre long but it might rocket up 3,000 exhausting feet within that distance.

Another way of reaching for the sky is to join the climbing fraternity (see the Further Information section for details). There are climbing clubs all over the UK which teach the basic skills on a climbing wall in a local gymnasium. Fees are usually modest and often include the rental of the necessary gear: harness, carabiners, chalk bag and shoes. Later you may head out to the nearest quarry face, sea cliff or rock face for the real thing. If you enjoy the experience, you can join forays to mountain ranges all over the world and become one of the elite who tackle virgin Himalayan peaks, new routes up terror slabs like El Capitan in Colorado, or merely relish long, hard approach marches and relatively easy ascents requiring few, if any, technical skills, such as

Everest, Mount McKinley in Alaska or Mount Vincent in Antarctica.

At school I spent many happy nights with a succession of climbing partners ascending vertiginous school buildings and church spires. This pastime, known as stegophily, is not overburdened by safety gear since jangling equipment hinders one's escape from interfering police. As a Brighton-based student I extended my range to cover tall steeples all over England. Many climbs required the cover of moonless nights and bad weather. Untrustworthy drainpipes, wooden tile edges and ruler-thin lightning conductors often proved precarious holds for nine-hour climbs. Stegophily was my first experience of a semi-endurance sport, but neither that activity, nor, in the course of some 20 years, 70 parachute jumps from aeroplanes, helicopters and balloons, by static line and freefall, by day and by night, have cured me of my fear of heights. I have to concentrate hard on some nearby object – anything other than the drop below. I never look down. Night climbing is a great help, of course, since you cannot normally see the void.

In summertime I enjoy Alpine rambles with a group of expedition friends. We have included Mont Blanc and the Matterhorn, both of which have easy ascent routes as well as vertiginous walls. The Matterhorn kills an average of 16 people annually and ironically most of them die as a result of not taking enough care on the easy route. Mountainbased endurance races often involve far more difficult climbs, but deaths are rare because the organisers, wary of bad publicity, ensure that stringent safety rules are enforced.

Whether you decide to go in for mountain-climbing or mountain-racing, you will almost certainly need the quality of endurance, both mental and physical, to some extent. It is not always safe to assume that the shorter the climb, the less endurance you will need, because things do not always go according to plan on a mountainside and the weather in

mountain regions is unpredictable. You may be out there a lot longer than you had intended.

Whether you go for climbing, marathon-running or some other outdoor sport, you will be vulnerable to a number of hazards, including skin cancer, hypothermia, hyperthermia and hypoglycaemia.

Life on Earth exists only because of the sun's presence and we can become unhealthy through too little sunlight. Sunny days have as good an effect on our morale as fog and rain can make us gloomy. Suicide statistics in northern latitudes are far higher than in sunny, southern climes. But because of our largely manmade problems with the ozone layer, too much UV and blue light penetrates the protective ozone layers than is acceptable to the good health of our seven thin layers of skin.

To avoid sunburn, and all its associated ills:

- Never allow your skin to be exposed to UV light for too long. On a sunny summer's day (and outside the three danger hours around noon), it is safe in a Mediterranean climate, at sea-level, to expose the skin for 20 per minutes per day. If you have red hair, fair skin and/or known skin troubles, you may find even 20 minutes too long for you.

- The burning power of the sun increases in its effect by 5 per cent for every 1,000ft you climb above sea-level. Reflective surfaces like snow, sand and water increase UV radiation, as does your proximity to the sun. So, such factors as how near you are to the Equator and the season of the year must be considered when using the 20 minutes' daily exposure rule.

- Even for this 20-minute period you should apply a trusted sunburn protection treatment at a level recommended by your chemist. Remember to treat your lips (and your scalp, if your hair is thin). After being in the sun, apply a moisturising cream if you are fussy about retaining baby's-bottom skin texture.

- Keep your children well informed about the

dangers of sunburn. The younger they are, the more susceptible their skin.

- Apply sun protection half an hour or so before you are exposed – it takes that long to sink into the skin. Use the correct sun protection factor (SPF). SPF2 will allow you twice as long before you burn, so, if you would be burned in five minutes with no protection, you will be burned in 10 minutes using SPF2, or 20 minutes using SPF4, and so on. SPF15 is the strongest screen: any numbers higher than this are irrelevant.

- Do not allow sunscreen to give you a false sense of security. There is no such thing as a safe tan, whether you acquire it from the sun or a sunlamp. Some screens do allow potentially lethal UV rays to penetrate the skin. You can get skin cancer – now the most common of all cancers in men under 50 – in Britain just as you can on Bondi Beach.

On polar expeditions we make sure our skin is as well covered as possible. When I was unable to cover my lips, I found they quickly cracked and developed deep, suppurating sores. I devised an elasticised 'beak' to cover them but which allowed me to breathe.

Sun Damage to Eyes

Your eyes need protection from the sun at all times. Bad sunglasses are worse than no sunglasses at all because they fool the pupils into opening wider than they should while failing to provide the proper screening of damaging rays. Be sure to use well-known brands with UV protection of at least Class-400 rating against UV and blue light.

My eyes have suffered from too many years of intensive glare in the polar regions. Because I need to scrutinise the distant horizon when sledging over the Arctic pack ice, trying to spot areas of open water or high-pressure ridges, I find that goggles, which tend to mist up, prevent correct assessment of

> ### Environmental Pollution
> Most people accept that the ozone hole kills people through skin cancer. The nearer you live to the actual holes in the Earth's atmosphere, the likelier it is that your personal risk factor will be high. The holes are located close above the poles and the southern hole is currently the larger, allowing more harmful solar rays through the Earth's protective ultra-violet (UV) filter layers.

ice conditions, so I often remove them. In 1991, for the first time, I found myself going blind, or so it seemed, on an expedition. I had to follow the blurred outline of my colleague through the pack ice. Two or three weeks after my return to England my vision slowly came back. An ophthalmic surgeon later diagnosed retinal sunblindness. I was warned that further glare could cause me to go permanently blind so I have worn UV 400-rated eye protection ever since, even on cloudy days in the UK.

Hypothermia

Hypothermia is a problem all outdoor-activity enthusiasts should be aware of. It occurs when your body's core temperature drops below 37°C (98.6°F). This can happen if you become too cold in bad weather, or through sheer exhaustion, which can lead to lowered core heat even in mild weather, or through gradual core heat decline due to long immobility, as experienced by old people lying alone in bed. Symptoms can include shivering, drowsiness, mumbling speech and slow pulse.

I have dealt with many cases of hypothermia when travelling with small, isolated groups in the polar wastes. On one expedition, my colleague Mike Stroud succumbed to hypothermia three times in the course of a single 1,400-mile man-haul journey.

Mike Stroud in Antarctica in 1993. Author

I noticed something unaccountably different about Mike's behaviour. This was lucky for, had I moved off for the next 90-minute push, never looking back, he would have died. 'Are you OK?' I screamed at him, and struck his shoulder. There was no response and his head seemed to loll. I had seen him like this years before in the Arctic. With frozen hands I erected the tent while he stood swaying in that great deep-freeze. I forced him into the tent, into his bag and gave him hot soup. Then hot, sweet tea and chocolate. He slept for an hour. His memory of the last few hours had entirely gone. An hour later he returned gradually to normal.

My own state of poor health was at that time similar to Mike's but I never became hypothermic and, in 30 years of extreme cold-weather endurance activities, I never have. My method is never to push myself beyond a certain feeling of coldness, when the brain begins to close in on itself and the body feels utterly weak.

If I feel there is a chance that I am nearing the danger point, I repeat complex sentences aloud to myself, over and over again, and check that my words are neither mumbled nor slurred. If they are, I stop to consume energy drinks, chocolate, or both.

I swim in the sea whenever I find myself somewhere with ocean access. Usually I swim out for 45 minutes, then back. After the first 30 minutes, I often feel cold, so I start invoking my mental system then, too.

For long, cold swims, such as crossing the Channel, it is advisable to apply body greases and, unless you hate the idea, imbibe a prepared solution of calcium salt of pantothenic acid (vitamin B5). This improves endurance and reduces the likelihood of hypothermia. If you ever need to treat a hypothermia case:

Mike had seen, over many years of arduous expeditions, dozens of hypothermia cases and had often taught students how to recognise the symptoms in one another. This is important, since it is not possible to detect symptoms in your own body, and hypothermia is quick to kill.

In 1993, some 25 miles short of the South Pole at an altitude of 10,000ft, the wind-chill factor was –92°C (–167°F) and Mike and I were both dangerously exhausted and malnourished. I wrote of this experience in my diary at the time:

- Administer sweet drinks.
- Keep the patient completely still.
- Remove wet clothes and wrap the patient in insulation material. Keep him or her out of the wind. Add warmth by pressing your own body against his or hers inside the insulation barrier.
- Send for help as soon as you can.
- Reassure the patient and never leave him or her alone.

Hyperthermia

Hyperthermia, or heat stroke, is the opposite of hypothermia in that it occurs when the body core temperature rises above about 42.5°C (108.5°F). Death can follow in minutes.

At risk are people involved in marathons in hot weather, in prolonged aerobics in rooms with inadequate ventilation, or in taking violent exercise in too-warm clothes, even in quite mild temperatures.

As with hypothermia, the symptoms of hyperthermia may include stumbling, incoherence, irritability and cramps. The chest may feel warm and dry to the touch. Treat the patient as follows:

- Prevent further exercise.
- Lie the victim down and raise the legs slightly.
- Give liquids at slight intervals.
- Apply tepid water all over the prone body.
- Summon help if possible, but do not leave the patient alone.

Avoid heat stroke by wearing clothes which, whether wet or dry, keep you comfortably cool rather than warm when moving. Drink more than you think you need.

If possible acclimatise yourself to hot conditions before you begin your activity. Very fit individuals can prove extremely tolerant to circumstances which would quickly reduce lesser mortals to hyperthermia, but it takes a fit person 10 days of heat exposure combined with exercise to significantly reduce the risk of heat stroke.

Hypoglycaemia

Violent and prolonged exercise can lower your body-sugar level to the point where your brain becomes sugar-starved. At this stage, symptoms you may show include fatigue, headache and irritability, leading sometimes to unconsciousness. Americans describe people acting with hypoglycaemic behaviour as 'bonking'. This terminology can cause confusion in Britain.

Mike Stroud wrote of hypoglycaemia during our 1993 Antarctic expedition:

Towards the end of our journey our blood-sugar levels were so low we should have been dead . . . Analysis showed that our blood glucose had been low from the very first day. During the last few days the levels appeared to be impossible. On one occasion Ran had a level of 0.2 millimoles, while I had one of just 0.3. In ordinary circumstances, this would have been fatal, but our bodies must have adapted in some way to cope with the situation.

In fact the normal range for blood glucose levels is 3.5–7.8 millimoles per litre of blood. Avoid hypoglycaemia by eating and drinking regularly when taking prolonged exercise, especially in extreme temperatures, to maintain your blood-sugar level. Treat hypoglycaemic patients with sweet drinks, rest and reassurance.

13

Ultimate Fitness

You are somewhere between the ages of 18 and 75 and you are very fit. Having followed this book's simple exercise and food-control practices, you are now in the top 2 per cent of the population in terms of fitness. But you want to progress. Since some 55 million other individuals live in Great Britain, there are over a million in the top 2 per cent with you, which may not sound very exclusive. You want to climb higher and there is no reason why you should not. I will soon be 55, but I have far less time than I would like to spend on keeping fit. I hope that this will change in my mid-60s when I will be freed from my desk and able to train more frequently. As a result I aim to compensate for my older bones by keeping as fit at the age of 75 as I am now. Barring injury and illness, this should be an attainable goal.

This final chapter is for anyone, young or old, who would like to at least dip a toe into the wonderful world of the ultra-endurance event. Having watched Vic Stroud at 71 and another septuagenarian, the American veteran runner Helen Klein (73), fight their way through the Eco-Challenge Race in the Rockies, I know that the human body can stay in a very fair condition well into the 70s and

perhaps beyond. So although this chapter on extreme endurance may have a particular appeal for individuals in their 20s and 30s, it is equally valid for those others – the majority – who may mistakenly believe they are over the hill at 40.

The very human need for ongoing targets to prevent the staleness caused by the repetitive nature of training to keep fit may tempt you to ultra-endurance. People keep fit for 20 or 30 years but, inevitably and sadly, all but a relative handful eventually fall by the wayside before they need to. Some gradually train less and less, then not at all; others reach the top 2 per cent, congratulate themselves on getting there, and on having attained various long-held fitness goals, such as a three- or four-hour marathon, and then rust away due to lack of further incentive. The ultra can save you from this fate, as it has saved me.

What Are Ultra-Endurance Events?

In Europe, North America, Down Under and in many other parts of the world, enthusiasts are starting new, extreme endurance races every year. I will not attempt to list them all. You can hear about them on the endurance-event circuit, whose 'old hands' will be keen to convert you. A good start for data on running competitions of all shapes and sizes is *Runners' World*. Events for mountain-biking, swimming and most other popular sports, as well as running, are advertised in specialist magazines, at your health club or on the Internet. Find out the dates and venues which suit you best, pay your entry fee or fill in an application form and you are on your way. If you do badly at first, there is great satisfaction to be had in improvement the next time.

The key activities involved in ultra-endurance are running, swimming and cycling. The first track-and-field-type biathlon was a running and swimming race held in the UK in 1968. Biathlon means 'two athletic events', so can combine any two sports. The Nordic Biathlon, for instance, involves shooting and cross-country skiing. Triathlons, which entail three sports, come in all kinds of shapes and sizes. The three most common varieties are:

The Sprint: 0.5-mile swim → 10–15-mile cycle → 3.1-mile run.
The Olympic: 0.9-mile swim → 25-mile cycle → 6.2-mile run.
The Iron Man: 2.4-mile swim → 112-mile cycle → 26.2-mile run.

A sensible approach is to aim your sights low at the beginning. Start with a marathon or two, move on to a couple of biathlons and then enter a short triathlon.

When you have had your fill of triathlons, you can take up the quadrathlon, which adds kayaking to the other three sports. Swimming and kayak-paddling demand upper-body strength, whereas cycling and running focus on your legs. Quadrathons have taken place in the UK only since 1992. A quadrathon sprint race may last one hour and the ultimate category, Diamond Man, takes over eight hours. Quadrathon stars are mostly ex-triathlon competitors who have learned the fairly tricky art of paddling a kayak in choppy waters.

To get the most out of any ultra-endurance event you should train with individuals experienced in the relevant sports. A good start is to contact Kelly College in Tavistock, Devon, which holds summer courses in swimming and triathlon. Suitable summer courses are held also at Crystal Palace in London and the Kidlington Sports Centre near Oxford. You will gain training tips and find out about the best equipment through listening to your fellow competitors. You will learn to focus your training on whichever relevant activity you are weakest in and, when each event is over, to cope with the mood swings which affect most ultra-endurance participants – the euphoria as well as the emotional let-downs when, despite months of training, you do not do so well. The important thing is to enjoy the event itself, the training and its effect on your health, but not to become obsessed.

Other ultras you may like to consider range from swimming the Channel to one-day UK events such as the annual Tough Guy Race in Wolverhampton. This charity event requires some 3,000 entrants to carry 30lb packs over a muddy, marathon cross-country course, usually in bad weather, and to negotiate a wicked obstacle course into the bargain. The event takes only a day (usually in January), so it can serve as a good marker in your annual ultra programme.

Many people go in for their own attempts on the big, traditional targets such as the Eiger, Mount Everest or the poles. These cost money and a lot of time, because sponsorship chances fall away once a particular feat has been achieved for the first few times in history. That does not of course lessen the physical difficulty for each new contender. Once you

The author aged 37 in Ellesmereland, pictured in 1981 during the three-year Transglobe Expedition. Ultra-endurance challenges help to keep you aiming for new targets. Mike Hoover

have reached the summit of Mount Everest (and you do not need to be a good climber in the technical sense to do so), you can move on to ascending the top peaks in other continents. If you are in your 60s or 70s you could become the oldest person to conquer your chosen target and, if you wish, you could probably raise worthwhile sums of money for a charity in the process. To date my ultra-endurance expeditions have raised over £5 million, which has been used to set up Europe's first multiple sclerosis research centre and to start the building of a specialist breast cancer research centre in London.

Knowing that success or failure will affect the amount of money raised is another great mental spur to the effort you put into your training and into the event itself.

After you have bagged the seven highest peaks of the seven continents, swum the Channel and enjoyed a few UK triathlons or quadrathlons, have a go at completing the Hawaiian Iron Man competition without walking or resting en route. Find out how many days your fastest predecessors took, and the details of their schedule, so that you do not slacken off along the way. Thereafter you will need to ease off for a while with a less energetic but still demanding endeavour such as canoeing or kayaking around the United Kingdom with a couple of friends.

This may all sound rather fantastic at first, but ultra competitors come from all walks of life, so your circumstances and your profession need not stand in the way of your ultra aspirations. Most people love to chop and change from one type of ultra to another, but there are those who prefer to excel at one discipline. Alison Streeter works in the City of London as a foreign-exchange dealer, lives with her parents in Surrey and spends many weekends each year swimming off Dover. She was 18 when she first managed to swim the Channel and, at the time of writing, she has totalled 35 crossings, including the first and only three-way non-stop swim. Alison now runs weekend training sessions for would-be Channel-swimmers: you can join her most weekends at 10am on the beach at Dover.

Whatever you decide to aim at in the ultra world, once you have taken the plunge you will find that life is never boring again. Nor will lack of motivation allow you to skip training sessions without experiencing sharp twinges of guilt. Keep your diary in a constant state of 'train for the next event', and whenever you see a famine coming up, reach for the telephone and order a batch of application forms for the coming year.

How I Train For Ultra Events

Food Control

In 1996, when I attempted the first unsupported solo crossing of the Antarctic continent at the age of 52, I had prepared with a year of fitness training and food control carefully designed for a non-stop, three-month endurance race. By the end of the first month of the journey I was in fine physical form and producing better day-to-day man-hauling results than

the two other men, a Pole and a Norwegian, also attempting the solo crossing. Both were top polar man-haul experts in their respective countries, in peak physical condition and half my age. I think that proves there must be a sound basis to my training methods, even though my mission was ultimately thwarted by a kidney stone.

Where my training system did pay dividends, and proved itself to be up to the most extreme of all ultra-endurance events, was in 1993, when, with Mike Stroud, I completed the longest unsupported polar journey ever recorded. I was in my 49th year – 11 years older than Mike – and prone to various recurring injuries. The secret of our success was not some special skill or even an unusual level of competence: it lay entirely in careful preparation, especially regarding food control, in the 12 months leading up to the expedition.

We knew that even fully supported attempts to cross the Antarctic continent had been thwarted and that the great Italian mountaineer and adventurer Reinhold Messner had only just managed to man-haul sledgeloads half as heavy as those we would need for our unsupported attempt.

Mike and I did have a head start in preparing our bodies for such long-term stress, because he was Britain's leading researcher in the specialist field of endurance nutrition. We had already completed four long Arctic expeditions together over a six-year period and Mike, in collaboration with my long-standing expedition nutritional adviser, Dr Brian Welsby, had developed ever-improved rations.

In the early 1970s, before I met Brian, I had searched hard for a reliable source of low-weight, high-calorie rations. In the 1960s I had used Horlicks packs, which were light to carry but not high-calorie. Much later my quest took me to the NASA base in Houston, Texas, where the person in charge of planning food for the astronauts in space took me on board the Shuttle. 'Our work during the previous Apollo flights, where there was scant space for any extras, did involve low-weight, high-calorie foods,' she explained. 'But now' – she waved her hand about the roomy cavern of the Shuttle – 'there's no shortage of storage space. Today's astronauts like their turkey and ice-cream, so we no longer work on miniaturisation.'

She suggested I consult the US Special Forces. They directed me to Starlite Foods in San Francisco, who produce the ration packs which are used on Green Beret and SEAL special operations. However, they told me that such operations average fewer than 10 days, and their rations were therefore tailored to that period of time. By the end of a week's man-hauling in Antarctica on Starlite Foods rations we would have been seriously down on our fat intake. I then tried hiking-food manufacturers in France, Norway and Germany, but nothing suitable was available anywhere.

The high-energy nutritional system subsequently devised by Brian, Mike and me is now used by a number of top athletes, including Denise Lewis (heptathlon silver medallist, 1997 World Championships), Chantal Daucourt (1997 European mountain-bike champion) and Shirley Robertson (world number two dinghy sailor in the 1998 Olympic Single-Handed Class).

To be very fit, not just fit, endurance-wise means one thing for short, tough events like the Iron Man, Mount Everest or even a 10-day Eco-Challenge race. It means something altogether more radical for a three-month, unsupported (no para-wings) Antarctic continental crossing. In 1902 Captain Scott and Ernest Shackleton found that 5,000 calories of polar rations weighed about 2.5lbs, so each man had to carry 250lbs for a 100-day journey. Despite all our work on modern rations, we have scarcely whittled 2oz off that figure. We do have dehydrated foods now, but these lose their advantage in areas like Antarctica where there is no water to rehydrate them. Lots of fuel is needed to heat ice into warm water, and fuel is heavy.

So the key to making available food count in terms of miles travelled is to train your body to squeeze maximum energy out of each ration. And energy means glycogen. Previous journeys had taught us that we must each increase our glycogen storage capacity. This takes a long time because the human body can store only limited amounts of certain vital chemicals. Vitamin C is a good example. Vitamin C tablets have to be taken twice daily for maximum effect because our bodies store such a very small amount of it. Once your vitamin C quota has been filled, all further amounts will simply pass through the body until your store empties itself. The same applies to glycogen, the key to energy.

In 1939 researchers found that if a low-fat, high-carbohydrate diet was consumed on the days prior to exercise being taken, the athlete's capacity for exercise doubled. A high-fat, low-carbohydrate diet with the same consumption timing resulted in a 30 per cent exercise-capacity reduction. For years this discovery was ignored due to the ongoing myth that protein was the key to strength and endurance. Nowadays all athletes recognise that glycogen comes from carbohydrates, and that glycogen depletion in muscles, caused by exertion, leads quickly to muscle fatigue. How quickly? During an ice hockey game, the muscle glycogen store of an active player declines by up to 80 per cent in 40 minutes.

In 1970 researchers asked six marathon-runners to run on a treadmill for two hours on three successive days at a pace equivalent to their best marathon performance. Each day they ate a then normal mixed diet (50 per cent of their calories coming from carbohydrates, 35 per cent from fat, 15 per cent from protein). On average the runners covered 20 miles in the two hours, becoming more tired each day. By the third day none of them could maintain the pace of the previous two days and all had to stop before the two hours were up. Follow-up muscle biopsies revealed that their glycogen levels were all too low to provide sufficient energy for the set exercise.

For short events, like an ice hockey match, speedy glycogen-depletion is unlikely to cause disaster to the team because the game will have ended before the players' stores have depleted to the point where this will drastically affect their performance. But with longer-lasting endurance events the conclusion is obvious. You must train your muscles to store as much glycogen as possible through long-term exercise followed by carbohydrate consumption. Endurance-trained muscles also contain more fat than untrained muscles. During exercise your muscles will burn this fat more efficiently and access it easily, and this will lessen the initial demands on your glycogen supply. Most reasonably fit individuals store some 15 to 20 grams of glycogen per kilogram of muscle. Through a programme of daily exercise, followed by carbohydrate consumption, you will increase this ratio and benefit accordingly when you attack your next ultra-endurance event. During long events I drink high-energy powder mixed with water. The best source of easy-mix carbohydrate load and fluid-replacement electrolytes is Science in Sport Ltd (see page 195).

People usually obtain their carbohydrates from a healthy mix of potatoes, corn, rice, beans, wholegrain products and fresh fruit. But for good results at long, drawn-out endurance events (which separate strong, fit individuals who peg out on the fifth or 10th day from those who are still progressing on the 30th), our own 10 years of research into endurance nutrition have provided additional advice. This was possible because the conditions of our polar man-haul journeys were unique. The resulting scientific papers confirmed:

The energy expenditures of Fiennes and Stroud are exceptional and probably close to what is physio-logically possible . . . The figures recorded for the period between days 20 and 30 of 11,000 calories burned daily (when the heavy sledges were dragged uphill from the ice-shelf to the plateau) are proba-bly the highest sustained energy expenditure levels ever documented.

As Mike Stroud wrote:

This was 5,500 calories more than we were eating – a deficit equivalent to total starvation while running a couple of marathons a day. By the 68th day we had lost 50lb apiece, a loss equivalent to a food deficit of around 120,000 calories.

In the polar regions the air is thin, which increases the effects of altitude. We travelled at some 10,000ft above sea-level, the equivalent of 16,000ft in the Alps or Himalayas in terms of altitude effects on our bodies, including rapid glycogen depletion.

Mike's theories on nutrition to give us maximum endurance capacity were tested to the limit in Antarctica. He knew that high-carbohydrate intakes optimise the availability of glycogen to working muscles, but he suspected that our bodies might adapt to a high fat intake through an improved ability to synthesise glycogen and to use free fatty acids as direct-muscle substrates (compounds which enzymes can act upon). We needed lots of fat in order to consume a minimum of 5,000 calories a day while keeping the weight of three months' rations to a total which we could manage to drag uphill in soft snow. Only by using a preponderance of fatty food could we achieve such a high-calorie, low-weight requirement. We ended up with a diet of: **57 per cent fat, 33 per cent carbohydrate, 10 per cent protein**. The recommended diet for athletes in normal training is **25 per cent fat, 60 per cent carbohydrate, 15 per cent protein**.

University and hospital studies produce many of the statistics and 'facts' you read in health books and magazines. Their research concentrates on the way athletes train for and compete in various events. There is, therefore, far less information about the body's capacities at very sustained lower levels of exercise, and almost no information relating to sustained exercise when the athlete is slowly starving (i.e., in negative energy balance). Our Antarctic crossing, meticulously monitored by blood and urine analysis throughout, yielded unique information as a result. I will not attempt to give a scientific analysis of the results, since Mike has done so in learned medical papers of great length. What follows, however, are the more obvious comparisons between our two bodies and their reactions to the enormous and sustained exertion while starving over a 95-day period.

In the table below, it can be seen from the pre-expedition comparison that Mike was much stronger than me all round (apart from in elbow power). Yet at the end of the expedition, after three months of performing precisely the same tasks and eating exactly the same diet, I was considerably stronger than Mike, because his strength decline was greater.

A possible reason was that he was working harder, which would of course be reflected in his energy expenditure. But Mike recorded our energy expenditure data scientifically throughout the jour-

ney, and it showed that my output overall was greater. This table shows the figures for the first 50 days of man-hauling.

Energy Expenditure (approx.)

Days	Me	Mike
1 to 10	39.8	26.8
11 to 20	26.9	22.0
21 to 30	44.6	48.7
31 to 40	36.4	26.7
41 to 50	29.9	23.3

Another possibility might be a difference in body-fat percentages. As noted previously the ideal body-fat percentage (BFP) for a fit man is between 10 and 15 per cent of his total body mass. At the outset in Antarctica my BFP was 17 per cent and Mike's was 16 per cent. At the end of the journey mine had dropped to 1.9 and Mike's to 2.5. This was not surprising, since we had each lost about a quarter of our total body weight, but does not explain the strength-loss conundrum.

The last possible explanation might be the effect of extreme cold on our bodies. If muscles are

Strength Loss

Strength Factor	Me (aged 49)		Mike (aged 38)	
	Before Expedition	After Expedition	Before Expedition	After Expedition
Elbow (flexion)	28.1	25.2	27.4	16.0
Elbow (extension)	23.2	14.9	20.2	14.0
Grip	46.1	45.4	64.9	40.0
Leg (extension)	121.0	113.8	142.1	85.0
Abdominal (flexion)	45.7	46.3	52.5	42.0
Upright Pull	144.7	131.3	183.2	113.0

exercised in a cold environment, they become weaker and fatigue sets in much earlier because the higher oxygen uptake and metabolic rate lead to faster depletion of energy stores. Before the expedition Mike's scientists immersed us both in cold baths for two hours and attached to us an array of electrodes, probes and pressure cuffs. The cold water was continually circulated around our bodies. We both proved resistant to cooling and, in my case, the resistance was extreme: my core temperature actually rose slightly during the course of the immersion.

The difference in our different abilities to resist the cold may have had some slight influence on our relative strength depletion, but the evidence is inconclusive. My own interpretation of the anomaly goes back to 12 months before our journey when I began religiously to consume 10oz of complex carbohydrates a day, one hour after taking a run of at least an hour's duration, in addition to my normal daily food consumption and irrespective of my appetite. On the few days when I did not exercise I still took the carbohydrates. I believe this regimen, which Mike did not follow for so long so consistently, enormously enhanced both my normal

The author in Mike Stroud's torture chamber at Farnborough, aka the Army Personnel Research Establishment. Mike's tests on our bodies took place before and immediately after our expeditions. Mike Stroud, APRE

muscle glycogen level and my ability to use fat as direct-muscle substrates.

Many athletes do well on a 50 per cent carbohydrate diet, which they increase to 70 per cent during the three days before an endurance race. This maximises their liver glycogen reserves and minimises their risk of hypoglycaemia. Two or three hours prior to the start they will eat an easily digested carbohydrate meal of between 200 and 500 calories. They avoid eating anything in the 60 minutes immediately before the event. During the race, carbo-loaded drinks with electrolytes are needed to maintain efficiency, strength and hydration. I averaged between 60 and 70 per cent carbohydrate intake for 12 months without a break.

I have used this system ever since because, despite my age at the time, it worked so well for me during the most physically demanding endurance experience of my life. I vary the length of time I follow this diet before an endurance event, but I never change the daily amounts of complex carbohydrates consumed. If an endurance event is to last two or three months (such as a North Pole unsupported attempt), I will adhere to it for a year. For a 10-day Eco-Challenge, I will follow it for six months. For an Iron Man (which I have not yet attempted), I would follow the diet for three months.

My greatest regret is that I did not discover the huge advantages I could gain from this diet at least 30 years earlier.

Exercise

If I was to stuff myself with my endurance-training diet without taking any exercise, I would put on useless weight, so the diet must go hand in hand with a hard physical training programme. Two things to remember before you start:

- Once you are already very fit, any further small gain in performance will only result from *hard* training at levels considerably higher than those required for mere health and fitness maintenance, as discussed in previous chapters.

- Your body's natural tendency is to stay at whatever fitness level you have reached. If you always run six miles three times a week, you will be no fitter after keeping up that regime for six months than you were after doing it for five. To increase your fitness and endurance capacity you must increase your workload. The greater your desire to achieve some specific goal, the more you will be able to increase your workload without falling prey to the ever-present danger of going stale through overtraining.

Overtraining, or overload, is chiefly a mental state and can be kept at bay by cross-training or alternating between activities like swimming, running and rowing. This has the advantage of alleviating boredom and of distributing training stress between more muscles, thus reducing injury potential. But there are disadvantages to such non-specific training.

Specific training for any endurance sport, such as running, results in unique structural adaptations to our bodies to enable us to perform further and faster. The only similarity between, say, running and cycling, is the involvement of the lower body in an upright position. Quadriceps are the main movers for cycling, calf muscles for running. Running is a complete, weight-bearing activity with different joint ranges of motion and involving a large muscle mass. So use cross-training sparingly, just enough to keep tedium at bay, but no more. If your main endurance event involves running, then at least 80 per cent of your training time should be spent doing just that.

I have described the details of my endurance-training diet for extreme ultra events. However, you will not necessarily wish to copy my own 12-month exercise programme (see pages 181–183) unless your own ultras are as formidable as three months hauling heavy weights over 1,300 miles. On the

---

Rules For Endurance

- **Maximum aerobic training is the number one key to increasing your ability to exercise without fatigue.**
- **Strength training is a great help and must be done regularly to fortify your body against injury and to help improve economy of effort.**
- **Occasional burst training (such as plyometrics and fartlek speed bursts) helps raise your lactic acid tolerance and your ability to improve your speed slightly.**
- **Economy of movement involves mental training and technique leading to more efficient use of oxygen as energy for performance.**
- **You can develop mental techniques to keep warm in a cold bath or to prevent panic setting in during a treadmill test when you think you cannot keep going. If you allow that panic to manifest itself in heavy breathing, you will give up. But if you calm yourself and force your breathing to settle down, you will keep going a lot longer on the treadmill. In long endurance races the same principle applies, and the more you train over longer distances, the more your own tolerance to exercise fatigue and discomfort will improve.**

---

other hand, it will give you a proven formula for extreme endurance fitness, and you could use it as a basis on which to build your own programme. You can slot into it at any point of the 12 months. Concentrate on the exercises most relevant to you, which will probably not include tyre-pulling with ski sticks.

As a rough guideline, you can compare my programme with the following outline on page 183, from a US-based endurance training programme for the Ultimate Athlete Contest.

Training with tyres (top, Daily Telegraph) for Antarctic man-hauling (below, Dyson). *The total sledge weight of our provisions and equipment was 485lbs per sledge.*

The Ranulph Fiennes 12-Month Endurance Training Programme

(prepared in collaboration with my fitness consultant Jonathan Beevers)

First Four Months

One hour run (hilly) six days a week.

One hour on ski machine seventh day.

Additional mainly plyometric circuit, three times weekly, consisting of:

Warm-up

Star jumps	× 15
Push-ups against wall	× 10
Squat thrusts	× 10
Crunches	× 10
Star jumps	× 15
Push-ups (knees on floor due to weak back)	× 10
Squat thrusts	× 10
Crunches with twist	× 10

One minute's rest

Star jumps	× 15
Push-ups against wall	× 10
Burpees	× 10
Crunches with twist	× 10
Star jumps	× 15
Reverse dips	× 10
Sprints (each leg)	× 10
Crunches	× 20

Do all this twice

Stretches.

Next Two Months

My training consists of three programmes, one for each of three consecutive days with a rest day on the fourth day before resuming the three-day programmes. The programmes were as set by Jonathan Beevers and altered slightly by me to deal with back and ankle troubles.

Day 1

Warm up.

Row for 30 minutes with the machine set at level 4.

Stretch.

Step-ups on to 12in box, a 6lb (3kg) weight in each hand, doing bicep curls for 25 minutes. Make sure you stand up straight on the box, then return to the floor with the same leg you stepped up with. Then change legs, alternating as you do the exercise.

4 × 20 sit-ups; 15 seconds' rest between each set.

Stretch.

Run for one hour (hilly).

Day 2

Warm up.

30-minute run and straight into 40 minutes on Nordic skier.

Stretch.

Circuit:

Star jumps	× 20
Push-ups against wall	× 15
Squat thrusts	× 15
Crunches	× 15
Star jumps	× 20
Push-ups (knees on floor)	× 20
Squat thrusts	× 15
Crunches with twist	× 15

One minute's rest

Star jumps	× 20
Push-ups against wall	× 15
Burpees	× 15
Crunches with twist	× 15
Star jumps	× 20
Reverse dips	× 15
Sprints (each leg)	× 15
Crunches	× 15

Do circuit twice, then record pulse (HR).

Row for 30 minutes.

Stretch.

Day 3

Brisk walk on treadmill or hilly terrain, 30 minutes with a 6lb (3kg) weight in each hand.
Stretch.

Weights circuit:

Fifteen seconds' rest after each set. This involves only dumb-bells with a total of four exercises standing up and three on the bench. Arms, shoulders and chest muscles are targeted.

Upright rows	3×12	
Crunches	4×20	
Stretch		
Crunches with twist	4×20	
Stretch		
Lat. shoulder raises	3×12	
Crunches	4×20	
Stretch		
Reverse dips	3×12	feet on a chair
Crunches	4×20	
Step-ups	4×20	weight in hands
Stretch		
Bicep curls	4×20	
Crunches	4×20	
Stretch		
Squats with weight in hands	3×12	go down to 90 degrees
Stretch		
Run one hour		
Stretch.		

Do ankle-strengthening programme at least twice a day (see page 103).

Next Three Months

Gradually intensify the three-day programme, length of runs, etc. (because of my back problems I changed from rowing machine to bicycle and ski machines). By the end of the nine months, I will be averaging two hours' exercise six days a week.

Next Two Months

An average of two and a half hours per day, six days per week, still following a three-day programme.

Final Month

Between three and a half and six hours daily, six days a week. Specific sledge man-haul training (hauling 100lb tyres and using ski sticks) included. Three sample days consist of:

Day 1

Step-ups on to 12in box or step (i.e., steps into gym shed). Hold a 6lb (3kg) weight in each hand doing a bicep curl for 30 minutes (alternating legs).
Bike for 60 minutes on hilly terrain.
Stretch.
5×40 crunches.
Stretch.
Ski machine – 90 minutes.
Stretch.
Tyre-pulling – two hours.

Day 2

Warm up.
One hour 45-minute run (hilly), straight into two hours pulling tyres with ski sticks.
Stretch.

Circuit:

Star jumps	$\times 50$
Push-ups against wall	$\times 40$
Squat thrusts	$\times 40$
Crunches	$\times 40$
Star jumps	$\times 50$

Push-ups (knees on floor)	× 40	Stretch.		
Squat thrusts	× 40	Sprints	30 each leg	
Crunches with twist	× 40	Stretch		
One minute's rest		Lat. shoulder		
Star jumps	× 50	raises	5 × 20	
Press-ups against wall	× 40	Crunches	5 × 20	
Burpees	× 40	Stretch		
Crunches with twist	× 40	Reverse dips	5 × 20	
Star jumps	× 50	Crunches	5 × 30	
Reverse dips	× 40	Step-ups	5 × 30	weight in hands
Sprints (each leg)	× 35	Stretch		
Crunches	× 40	Bicep curls	5 × 30	
Stretch.		Crunches	5 × 30	
Bike for one hour 30 minutes.		Stretch.		
Stretch.		Two hours pulling tyres with ski sticks.		

Stretch.

Run for one hour 45 minutes.

Day 3

Brisk walk for two hours 30 minutes with a 6lb (3kg) weight in each hand (or 30lb rucksack).

Stretch.

Stretch.

Weights circuit:

(20s, with rest after each set)

For the final two weeks prior to an expedition, taper down the intensity of the programme. The last four days involve nothing but stuffing myself with complex carbohydrates.

Single-arm rows	5 × 20	
Crunches	5 × 30	alternate with 5 × 30 dorsal raises

US Ultimate Athlete Training Programme (12 months)

First Four Months

Run a total of 22 miles each week, spread as you wish, but one run should be at least 10 miles.

Final Four Months

As for the second four months, but add one three-hour run each month.

Second Four Months

As for the first four, but add a longer run of about 18 miles once every two weeks and a 40-minute hill run every two weeks.

Throughout the 12 months, do 30 minutes' strength training three times a week.

Updating Your Gear

The other factor which will affect your chances of success in ultra events is your choice of equipment, be it running shoes and power bars or bicycle and helmet.

Still training hard at the age of 54, this time for the 1998 Eco-Challenge Race. I'm wearing full climbing gear to exercise on the Versaclimber machine to simulate actual conditions. The Times

You will nearly always be competing against some individuals whose fitness and ability are on a par with yours, so the question of which of you wins may well be decided by who has the most appropriate gear.

Do not be satisfied with kit that has served you well for many past races just for the sake of it: you might be missing out on some great new alternative which could improve your performance dramatically. Take trade magazines dealing with the latest innovations in your sport and try out new equipment to ensure all your training, time and effort are not being handicapped by second-best accoutrements. In 1997 I was introduced to the Versaclimber, a machine which I now use three times a week for simultaneous upper- and lower-body-strength sessions (see page 194). It saves a great deal of time previously spent exercising different muscles separately, and I wish I had discovered it years ago. The machine fits into a small floor space but it does need a 9ft high ceiling.

How to Use Mind Over Matter to Keep Going

In an endurance race you may be inclined, through discomfort and weariness, to slow down or, worse still, to give up altogether. As with most other things, you can, through practice, improve your own chances of resisting such temptations. The more times you run 'through the wall' during a long run, the better you will become at dealing with it next time round. You need ammunition to call upon to fight the wimpish voice of self-pity. Sports psychologists trot out various helpful phrases, including:

'The psychologically well-prepared athlete is characterised by efficiency of thought and deed.'

'An efficient athlete adopts a task-relevant focus, not wasting attention on task-irrelevant processes like worrying.'

'Tangible physical processes occur in the brain and body as a result of the athlete's thinking processes. These processes can cause changes in physical performance. To achieve this, a narrow focus of attention must concentrate on the activity itself. There must be a sense of personal control, but a disorientation of time and space which slows down time.'

These formulae for mind control help to banish pain and fatigue. A challenge which faces most marathon-runners at some stage is 'the wall' through which they have to push themselves after some 18 to 22 miles. They feel weak, dizzy, disorientated, even sick, and desperate to slow down to walking pace. If you grit your teeth and keep running, this 'running on empty' feeling usually goes away after 10 to 30 minutes.

On any long run, if you are not on top form, you will feel you want to drop your pace or have a brief rest. At this point you usually exercise the self-control necessary to push yourself on to the end of the run. The more you get into this habit on a day-to-day basis, the greater the likelihood of success when the real challenges occur during your ultra-endurance events. The self-discipline and control skills you hone during training and races will have useful spin-offs in other areas of your life.

My own ammunition to help fight the wimpish side of my nature consists of a number of 'mental bullets'.

- Expect to be tempted to stop. Know that you will feel lousy, inadequate, sore and exhausted and set out saying to yourself that the only reason you have entered the event is to fight and win the mental battle to keep going when the moment of truth arrives.
- Review, in advance, how ashamed you will feel afterwards if you do give in. Savour that shame, that realisation of failure, and determine never to have to suffer it just because you have yielded to self-pity when the going gets tough.
- Think hard about competition, about beating other competitors, about finishing the race. Think

positive thoughts. At any point your mind is focused on such matters, it cannot be simultaneously contemplating surrender. Think about good times you have had in the past and imagine the great things you can do in the future.

In Antarctica, suffering from gangrene, slow starvation and frostbite, to name just a few of our problems, Mike and I resorted to 'mind-travel' during our daily 10 hours of man-haul purgatory. It was a vital form of mental defence against the negative thoughts which would otherwise have crowded in.

- Be aware that mental strategies to coax yourself into a more relaxed state when you are running do pay off by actually making things easier physically. A more relaxed body state lowers the oxygen cost of running and so upgrades economy and improves performance.
- Another trick is to invoke mantras which you repeat endlessly to yourself to the tired rhythm of each step. Two of my favourites are 'Stick it out, stick it out, stick it out,' and 'Always a little further'. Working on the principle of self-hypnosis, any appropriate doggerel will help take your mind off the painful blisters and the great distance ahead.
- Imagine that someone you respect, and who you want to make proud of you, is watching you. You will not want to let that person down. In an international race a sense of national pride – succeeding for your country – can help you pull out all the stops.

However far you have come, whether you have discovered the marvellous world of the ultra-endurance event, or are maintaining your fitness at a less demanding level at which you feel comfortable, I hope the suggestions in this book will help you towards a long life of good health and enjoyment of exercise.

Appendix 1

Avoiding Illness

Throughout our lives, our bodies act as hosts to a teeming mass of bacteria (some harmful, some beneficial) but, being healthy and fit, we normally fend off all or most of the harmful invaders and escape with just the occasional chest infection and, perhaps, some light food poisoning. In the depths of Antarctica, and out in the Arctic pack ice, I have lived for months in temperatures ranging down to –122˚C (–258°F) wind chill. Such cold kills off exposed bacteria but not those already sheltering in warm human tissues and sharing the protection of our windproof anoraks. After a year in Antarctica my wife and I returned to New Zealand, where we instantly caught every virus breathed out by the welcoming committee because, through disuse, we had lost some of our normal immunity defences.

The awesome changes of the 20th century have produced new and unknown pathogens which can no longer be counted upon to disperse at the first whiff of antibiotics. This is because many of them are mutated reincarnations of older, known bacteria grown resistant to our entire range of penicillins. There is not a great deal we can do to stave them off – other than to keep our bodies fighting fit.

Your state of fitness is vulnerable to degenerative diseases and injury as well as to killer viruses and everyday germs. Whatever the affliction that comes your way there is nearly always something you can do about it in terms of prevention, or cure, or both. This section deals with some of life's 'nasties' which can sadly be described as common occurrences in even the most advanced societies, and are likely to remain so well into the new millennium.

To play safe with your life (and you have only one, not nine), be sure to have thorough check-ups with your doctor annually, or with whatever frequency he or she advises as best for your particular and genetic state of health.

Colds and Flu

'Feed a cold and starve a fever' is an old wives' tale based on common sense and observation. But feed it with what? The UK's Common Cold Research Unit – despite having had funds poured into it for over 40 years as successive governments have attempted to reduce the huge number of work days lost to the nation annually through the cold virus – has still not found a cure for the common cold. However, it does advise that people living stressful lives are far more susceptible to catching colds in the first place, and to be more debilitated by them, than less stressed people. I catch very few colds, even when working in London offices and travelling by tube and train, and despite having spent long periods in polar regions where I temporarily lost my immunity to many common germs.

These are my common cold avoidance rules.

When you know somebody has a cold, steer clear of them as much as possible and in case you have already taken a bug on board, start taking cold preventative action as follows:

- Do not continue taking hard exercise. Halve your normal regime in order to keep up your body's germ-fighting energy levels.
- Take the tablet equivalent of 3 grams of **vitamin C** and 1 **zinc** tablet daily.
- Eat, as available, **garlic, cloves, citrus fruits, eggs, onions, vegetables.**

If, after seven days, you have no cold coming on and have met no more cold-carriers, go 'back to normal'. If you do develop a cold:

- Drink plenty of fluids (at least six mugfuls daily). Before going to bed, I have a large mug of hot toddy consisting of **honey**, **lemon juice**, **whisky** or **brandy** and **cinnamon** in boiling water.
- Stop taking exercise until the cold has gone.

If you contract something more serious, such as flu or pneumonia, you should not exercise in any circumstances. **Vitamins C** and **A** and **zinc** foods, especially fruit and vegetables, should be eaten and dairy products, which increase mucus, should be cut out. Only when you feel fully recovered should you begin to resume training, and then you should build back to normal slowly so that at no stage do you feel dizzy, unusually sweaty or faint. A period of two months' abstinence following pneumonia is about average before you should begin to work back to your normal training regime.

Asthma
Asthma affects the lungs and respiratory system. Like pneumonia it can kill: there are 2,000 deaths from the illness every year in the UK. In Britain two million people have asthma, and many of them are keen runners. Moderate exercise can have a beneficial effect on the disease, especially pool-swimming, due to the often warm, humid air. Many sufferers have food allergies which can be identified and, after cutting out or avoiding the culprit – often **milk, yeast, colourings, sulphites** and house dust or pollen – they can become asthma-free. When the weather gets cold keep your inhaler warm in an inside pocket because breathing the contents from a cold canister can actually bring on a worse bout. Exercise can itself act as a trigger, but usually, after careful trials, you will be able to find a sport, such as swimming, which suits you.

Diabetes
In Britain 1.4 million sufferers have been diagnosed, but a further million as yet undiagnosed are likely to be diabetic. The Diabetic Association predicts a figure of three million sufferers by 2010. Help yourself avoid diabetes by steering clear of refined sugars. Diabetics often think their condition prevents them from taking exercise, but this need not necessarily be so. Consult your nearest diabetes advice clinic and your GP. A great deal of research has been done on how to regulate your glucose levels to allow you a considerable range of trouble-free exercise options.

Diabetes need not be a bar to a long and successful sporting career: there have been many top sports people who are diabetic, including Gary Mabbutt, former captain of Tottenham Hotspur.

Anaemia
If you feel listless and everything gets on top of you, or if your lethargy has developed into breathlessness and palpitations, you have the classic symptoms of anaemia. If a blood test is positive you should stock up on **iron** through consuming plenty of:

- **Fish** and **lean meat**.
- **Fresh green vegetables**.
- **Vitamin C** drinks (orange juice, tomato juice, etc.) to help absorption of iron.
- **Iron pills** or **medicine** prescribed by your GP.

If you are anaemic you should cut out tea. Vegans and pregnant women often develop vitamin B12 and folic acid (folate) deficiencies leading to anaemia, and this requires a medically supervised regime of **vitamin** supplements.

Varicose Veins
If you suffer from varicose veins don't get into a hot bath or sauna straight after exercise. It is likely to worsen the situation.

Migraines
There are many reasons why migraine attacks occur, most often in women, but the best-known causes are thought to be food allergies. The most likely culprits are **caffeine**, **cheese**, **chocolate**, **citrus fruits** and **red wine**. Stress is another trigger. To alleviate the intensity of an attack, lie on your back with a pillow under your neck. To prevent attacks:

- Eat numerous small snacks instead of fixed meals (these allow your blood sugar-level to drop in between food intakes).
- Eat **salmon**, **sardines** and other **oily fish.**
- Take the herb **feverfew**, either as fresh leaves or in tablet form,which helps many sufferers.
- Take **ginger**, either as a tea or used in cooking.
- Only if you do not normally have caffeine in any form, you could try drinking a cup of coffee.

Insomnia

Everyone knows how many hours of sleep suit them best. I find between seven and eight hours keeps me at my healthiest and most mentally alert. For eight years, until his death at the age of 93, I worked for Dr Armand Hammer, the world-famous boss of Occidental Oil. In his 90s he was still running his worldwide business empire full-time, and the necessity of communicating with countries of varying time zones seldom allowed him a full night's sleep. He had become adept at catnapping at any time of the day or night, in a car or in an aeroplane, in a business meeting or a conference hall. He thrived on this sleep pattern for weeks on end, and advised me that any attempt he made to sleep in a 'normal' rhythm brought on insomnia.

If you desperately need to sleep and start trying to do so, your very anxiety will often only worsen matters. There are two basic causes of insomnia: stress and eating the wrong foods.

Avoid Stress

- Do not stimulate your mind shortly before going to bed. If you read a book keep to gently entertaining topics.
- Do not take violent exercise last thing at night. A gentle walk, however, may be beneficial.
- If sleep proves impossible, get up and read or write until you do feel sleepy.
- Actively avoid thinking about your business or domestic problems once you are in bed.
- Think actively about deep breathing, relaxing each limb one by one and floating on a lilo in the sun. (There's nothing even vaguely soporific about sheep leaping over walls.)
- As you get older, do not expect to sleep as much.

Dietary Advice

- Do not drink or eat anything containing **caffeine**, nor any other stimulants or greasy, heavy meals for four hours before bedtime.
- Do not **smoke** within an hour of bedtime.
- **Alcohol** can put you to sleep, but it tends to badly disrupt sleep patterns.
- Do not drink last thing before bed if you know you will then need to empty your bladder during the night. However, if you can drink a small nightcap and get away with it, then try the drink that works for me and all my expedition friends: two teaspoons of **Horlicks** and a dessertspoon of **whisky** or **brandy** dissolved in **hot milk**.

Other Insomnia Tips

- Keep fresh air circulating in your bedroom and avoid too many bedclothes.
- Ensure that your mattress is comfortable.
- Some people find a warm bath (with a few drops of lavender oil) is a great help just before bedtime.

If Your Problem Consists of Keeping Others Awake With Your Snoring

- You are obese and need to slim.
- You sleep on your back. Turn over to another position or try the special nose plasters, available at chemists, to help open your airways.
- You drink too much alcohol.

After years of forced wakefulness as a radio-operator on polar expeditions in the 1970s, my wife still suffers from insomnia simply because her sleep patterns were so badly disrupted for so long. Through observing the above rules she has at least improved her insomnia problems as much as possible.

Eczema

Although some people get eczema from the mere touch of wool, nylon, detergents and make-up, among other things, most sufferers have food allergy-driven eczema and can get rid of the ugly rash with its hellish itch by cutting out those foods to which they are allergic, once they have been identified. **Eggs**, **milk**, **shellfish** and **yeast** are the most common irritants. **Oil of evening primrose** and **fish oil** ointments can provide at least partial relief.

Cold Sores and Herpes

HSV-1 is the herpes virus which some children contract and this can cause intermittent cold sores (usually around the mouth) throughout their lives.

Women, just prior to menstruation, and anyone suffering undue stress are prone to cold sores. UV rays from the sun can also trigger sores, but this is less common.

Apply **Zovirax** (or any **vitamin C** and **bioflavinoid** ointment) to the relevant area when the initial slightly numb feeling occurs before the cold sore itself appears. To keep outbreaks to a minimum:

- Try to stay **unstressed**, whatever the provocation.
- Keep your immune system strong by sleeping well and eating **fresh fruit, vegetables, cereals (whole-grain), nuts, fish, lean meat and eggs, vitamins A, C** and **E** and **zinc**).
- Do not **smoke** or take **alcohol** or **caffeine.**

Cancer

Sixty per cent of all cancer deaths can be prevented by food control and by not smoking. Since one in every four humans dies of cancer, a ratio which seems to be worsening, we each have a good reason to avoid behaviour which is known to invite cancer risks.

Cancer does not normally develop suddenly. It is a slow process whereby certain cells in the body gradually lose their ability to function as they should. This degeneration often takes 20 to 40 years or more and is known as carcinogenesis. This mutation of sound cells into destructive cells can be due to high levels of toxins and poor immune systems. Changes in levels of exercise, diet and a patient's attitude can reverse the mutation process and eliminate the cancer cells.

Avoid
- All fatty **meats** and **dairy products.**
- **White sugar** and all **sweets, biscuits,** etc.
- **White flour, white rice, white bread.**

Eat
- Fifty per cent of your diet should be complex carbohydrates, including **brown rice** and **pasta.**
- Lots of **fresh fruit** and **vegetables,** including **cabbage, garlic, broccoli** and **lettuce.**

Heart Attacks, Angina and Strokes

Over many years fat deposited in arteries will narrow them until a mere blood clot can block the artery, causing a thrombosis. The narrowing process is known as atherosclerosis. When an artery in the brain is blocked, a stroke results.

If an artery in the heart is blocked, part of the heart muscle may die. This may cause death or merely permanent damage to one part of the heart. Warning symptoms of a heart-attack in the form of chest pains are known as angina.

Heart problems and atherosclerosis may be caused by many factors, including:

- High blood cholesterol
- Lack of exercise
- Genetic predisposition
- Age and gender (males are more prone)
- High blood sugar
- Being overweight
- Smoking
- Stress

Osteoporosis

Because oestrogen regulates the amount of calcium in the blood, women are likely to develop osteoporosis after the menopause, when their levels of oestrogen drop. Hormone replacement therapy (HRT) replaces oestrogen but can have side-effects, such as an increased risk of breast cancer.

Too little calcium weakens bones and renders them vulnerable to breakage. Because osteoporosis is often passed from mother to child, likely victims should, as children, be encouraged to exercise and to eat foods containing calcium.

Men can, and often do, suffer from osteoporosis as they grow older if their calcium levels are too low. Young women involved in marathon-running, ballet or gymnastics, or who have anorexic tendencies, are at risk as they are inclined to have low body weight and this puts less stress on their bones. This is bad because such stress increases bone density and because body fat promotes the production of oestrogen.

Osteoporosis in the USA has reached epidemic levels in women over 55 years of age, by which time they have lost one third of their bone mass. Their bones become brittle and fracture at the least trauma. Inactivity and high-protein diets exacerbate their problems. Excess protein contributes to calcium losses in sweat and urine, instead of storage in bones.

Until we are about 30 years old our bones grow more than they decrease in density. We expect loss of bone mass as we grow older at a rate of 3 per cent every 10 years. This is acceptable and painless until bones break at the least fall, or even due to too much body weight on a hip bone.

The earlier we start to try to prevent osteoporosis the better, but it is never too late to begin.

- Stop **smoking**, drinking **alcohol** in excess and take no unnecessary **drugs**. Cut down on **caffeine, salt** and **chocolate**.
- **Calcium** and **phosphorous** are major constituents of bones and teeth. They have a high rate of turnover and so need to be continuously replaced through diet. You should, therefore, take **calcium** and **vitamin D** supplements if you have osteoporosis already or think you may be susceptible. **Dairy produce, fresh, green vegetables** and **vitamin D**-rich **eggs** and **oily fish** are the best **calcium** foods.
- Expose yourself sensibly to **sunlight** in order to benefit from vitamin D through your skin.
- However old and fragile you feel, remember that **weight-bearing** and **weight-training** exercises will increase the density and tensile strength of your bones. Increases in strength and flexibility in elderly people, well into the 80s, are easily obtained through resistance exercises, no matter how gentle the training format. The corollary is that bones not subjected to a regular mechanical loading are vulnerable to 'disuse osteoporosis'.
- Exercises to prevent a stooping posture are especially suitable and these should concentrate on the **back muscles** (see pages 122–123).
- **Fitness activities** (like cycling or swimming), although good for cardiovascular fitness, are of little value against osteoporosis.

Arthritis

Arthritis has been around for quite a while: archaeologists often find traces of it in the bones of 50,000-year-old Neanderthal cave-dwellers and cave bears. It is Britain's most common disease and involves inflamed joints caused by a surplus of uric acid in the body. The excess

acid slowly forms deposits between your joints, on your bones and in your muscles.

Osteo-arthritis and rheumatoid arthritis are by far the most common of the 200 types. Muscular rheumatism can lead to excruciating pain at the least movement. It can affect young children and, in many Western countries, is increasingly doing so. Drugs such as cortisone are normally prescribed.

After many years of Army and SAS activities, followed by decades of expedition work, I developed arthritic pains in both hands and a hip. My mother, 74 years old at the time, was suffering from pains in her lower back which X-rays revealed to be arthritis-related. She read a book by Margaret Hills, *Curing Arthritis the Drug-Free Way*, and after six months of following the book's food-control advice, her condition improved dramatically.

I did not follow Margaret Hills' instructions to the letter but I did take up two of her main remedies. I began to eat a dessertspoonful of **black molasses** daily and, every evening after supper, I drank a mug of **cider vinegar** with hot water instead of my habitual coffee, tea or hot chocolate. After a while I grew used to the unusual taste and within eight or nine months my arthritic pains disappeared. That was 10 years ago, and I have been free of arthritic pain ever since, despite numerous old fractures, sprains, operations and a life of abusing every bone in my body as a soldier, parachutist, long-distance runner; sleeping on snow, ice and mud floors and, to top it all, living on Exmoor, which is famous for its damp climate.

Proper food control can cure you by using balanced nutrients which neutralise excess uric acid.

If you already have bad arthritis, I advise contacting the Margaret Hills Clinic (see page 195 and Bibliography). If, like mine was, your arthritis is still at the merely uncomfortable stage, you can rid yourself of it and stay clear in the future by observing this regime:

- Take **cider vinegar** and **black molasses** (see above).
- Take **dark honey**, not sugar (especially not white sugar).
- Avoid **salt**.
- Avoid **dairy products** that are high in lactic acid such as yoghurt, buttermilk and sour cream. Instead go for **vegetable margarines, dried or skimmed milk** and **cottage cheese**.
- Avoid **citrus fruits** and other acidics such as **strawberries, tomatoes** and **rhubarb**. There are plenty of

good fruits more suitable for arthritics such as **apples**, **pears**, **bananas** and **dates**.

- Avoid **red meat** if it is fatty or in any way processed (like **ham**, **bacon**, **sausages**, **corned beef** or **pâtés**).
- Avoid all **alcohol** (including wine), all **fries**, **white bread**, **cakes**, **biscuits**, **sweets** and **fruits bottled in syrup**.
- Eat three/four **eggs** a week, plenty of fresh **fish**, **wholegrain cereals**, **fresh fruit** (non-citric), **vegetables** and **soya beans**.

- Check with your GP that your arthritis is not at least partly **allergy**-related. If it is, then avoid the foods responsible.
- Remember that **obesity** worsens arthritic pains due to excess pressure on joints.
- **Stress** alone can cause serious relapses in arthritics, so stay as unstressed as possible.

Appendix 2

Further Information

General Exercise/Fitness

General

The Central Council for Physical Recreation (national governing body of sport), Francis House, Francis Street, London, SW1P 1DE. Tel: 0171 828 3163.

Exercise Association of England, Unit 4, Angel Gate, City Road, London, EC1V 2PT. Call the three-minute Health TopiX message 'Starting an Exercise Programme' on 0891 633 499, code 1001. Calls are charged at 50p per minute.

Keep Fit Association, Francis House, Francis Street, London, SW1P 1DE. Tel: 0171 233 8898.

Information on Gyms

Fitness Industry Association, Argent House, 103 Frimley Road, Camberley, Surrey, GU15 2PP. Tel: 01276 676275.

My own tip for an excellent gym group particularly well represented in London is the Courtneys group. I often used their Victoria centre when I worked close by. Advantages of membership include no joining fee; use of your membership at all their UK centres; free Adidas personal training assessments to monitor your progress; plenty of friendly, well-trained staff on hand; wide range of facilities and top-of-the-range equipment; free parking; large swimming pools, saunas, etc. There are Courtneys centres in Llanelli, Basingstoke, York, Wembley, Croydon and 10 in London. For more details call their head office on 0181 336 2288.

Personal Trainers

National Register of Personal Fitness Trainers, Thornton House, Thornton Road, Wimbledon, London, SW19 4NG. Tel: 0181 944 6688; fax: 0181 944 0353.

Health and Fitness Magazines

There are many on the shelves. Three of the best worth subscribing to are: *Ultra-Fit*, *Health and Fitness* and *Men's Health*.

Children's Fitness Classes

Fit Club, Tel: 0990 133434;
web: http://www.fitpro.com/fitclub/

Sports

Canoeing/Kayaking

British Canoe Union, John Dudderidge House, Adbolton Lane, West Bridgford, Nottinghamshire, NG2 5AS. Tel: 0115 982 1100.

Climbing

British Mountaineering Council, 177–179 Burton Road, Manchester, M20 2BB. Tel: 0161 445 4747; fax: 0161 445 4500; e-mail: office@thebmc.co.uk; web: www:thebmc.co.uk

Cross-Country Skiing

British Ski and Snowboard Federation, 258 Main Street, East Calder, Livingston, Invernessshire, EH53 0EE. Tel: 01506 884343.

Cycling

British Cycling Federation, National Cycling Centre, Stuart Street, Manchester, M11 4DQ. Tel: 0161 230 2301; fax: 0161 231 0591; web: www.bcf.uk.com

Disability Sport

Disability Sport England, Solecast House, 13 Brunswick Place, London, N1 6DX. Tel: 0171 490 4919.

The Welsh Sports Association for the Disabled, 21 Keir Hardie Terrace, Fwffryd, Crumlin, Newport, Gwent, NP1 5EJ. Tel: 01495 248861.

The Scottish Sports Association for Disabled People (SSAD), Fife Institute of Physical and Recreational Education, Viewfield Road, Glenrothes, Fife, KY6 2RB. Tel: 01592 415700.

Disability Sports NI, 2 Annadale Avenue, Belfast, BT7 3JH. Tel: 01232 491011.

Eco-Challenge

Discovery Channel Eco-Challenge, 9899 Santa Monica Boulevard, Suite 208, Beverly Hills, CA 90212, USA. Tel: 001 310 399 3080; fax: 001 310 399 3584.

Expeditions

Expedition Advisory Centre, Royal Geographical Society, 1 Kensington Gore, London SW7 2AR. Tel: 0171 591 3030; fax: 0171 591 3031; e-mail: eac@rgs.org; web: http://www.rgs.org/ex/eac.html
You need to become a member of the Society to obtain advice on expeditions.

Golf

Royal & Ancient Golf Club of St Andrews, St Andrews, Fife, KY16 9JD. Tel: 01334 472112; fax: 01334 477580.
Ladies' Golf Union, The Scores, St Andrews, Fife, KY16 9AT. Tel: 01334 475811.

Mountain-Biking

Mountain Bike Rider Magazine. Tel: 0171 261 5588.

Orienteering

British Orienteering Federation, Riversdale, Dale Road North, Darley Dale, Matlock, Derbyshire, DE4 2HX. Tel: 01629 734042.

Pentathlon and Biathlon

Modern Pentathlon Association of Great Britain, Pentathlon House, 1 Mount Pleasant, Tadley, Hampshire, RG26 4JH. Tel: 0118 981 7181.

Rowing and Indoor Rowing

Amateur Rowing Association, 6 Lower Mall, Hammersmith, London, W6 9DJ. Tel: 0181 748 3632.

Rugby League (Amateur)

British Amateur Rugby League Association, West Yorkshire House, 4 New North Parade, Huddersfield, HD1 5JP. Tel: 01484 544131.

Rugby Union

The Rugby Football Union, Rugby House, Rugby Road, Twickenham, Middlesex, TW1 1DS. Tel: 0181 892 2000.

Running

To obtain equipment and the Running Directory, which gives details and dates of all major UK runs, contact *Run and Become*, 42 Palmer Street, Victoria, London, SW1H 0PH. Tel: 0171 222 1314, or in Edinburgh 0131 313 5300.

For details of your local official running club contact:

Scotland:	0131 317 7320
Wales:	01792 456237
Southern England:	0171 247 2963
Midlands:	0121 452 1500
North of England:	0113 246 1835
Northern Ireland:	01232 602707
Republic of Ireland:	003531 8308925/8309901.

Runners' World, 7–10 Chandos Street, London W1M 0AB. The magazine publishes monthly advance data on UK races with distance categories. Contact them on 01858 435343 (subscriptions).

To obtain the Ultra and Long-Distance Running Directory, published by the Road Runners Club, contact R. Fisher, 2 Hodgson House, Eton, Windsor, SL4 6DE.

Race Walking, Running, Cross-Country Races and Marathons (governing body for athletics; formerly the AAA). Tel: 0121 440 5000.

Marathon
Advanced Performance Endurance Coaching, 2 Graeme Road, Sutton, Peterborough, PE5 7XE. Tel: 01780 783958; fax: 01780 784040; e-mail: stuart.hale@virgin. net. Help for all levels of athletes.

Sky-Running
Skyrunners, Viale C Battisti 26, 13051 Biella (BI), Italy. Tel: 0039 15 350 6406. Ask for Lauri van Houten.

Swimming
For general information about swimming contact the Amateur Swimming Association, Harold Fern House, Derby Square, Loughborough, Leicestershire, LE11 5AL. Tel: 01509 618700. For specific inquiries about swimming activities or clubs in your area, contact your local pool.

Triathlon and Iron Man
British Triathlon Association, PO Box 26, Ashby-de-la-Zouch, Leicestershire, LE65 2ZR. Tel: 01530 414234.

Walking
Long Distance Walkers' Association, 10 Temple Park Close, Leeds, LS15 0JJ. Tel: 0113 264 2205.

Gym Equipment

New
Life Fitness UK Ltd, Queen Adelaide, Ely, Cambridgeshire, CB7 4UB. Tel: 01353 666017.

Precor, 17 Marino Way, Hogwood Lane Industrial Estate, Finchampstead, Berkshire RG40 4RF. Tel: 0118 973 3994.

The Ultimate in Fitness, 529c Finchley Road, London, NW3 7BG. Tel: 0171 435 5046; fax: 0171 435 5047.

Versaclimber UK Ltd, Oriffing Industrial Estate, Unit 10, Penncricket Lane, Rowley Regis, West Midlands, B65 0SN. Tel: 0121 561 2771; fax: 0121 561 2032.

Second-Hand
Gymquip Ltd, Unit 3.2, Apex Business Centre, East Lane, Wembley, Middlesex, HA9 7UR. Tel: 0181 904 3005.

Physical Training Equipment Ltd, Physique Industrial Park, Barrowford Road, Colne, Lancashire, BB8 9AJ. Tel: 01282 863300.

Bodystat (body-fat self-assessment)
PO Box 50, Douglas, Isle of Man, IM99 1DQ. Tel: 01624 629571; fax 01624 611544.

Concept II Rowing Machines
Vermont House, Unit 5, Nottingham South and Wilford Industrial Estate, Ruddington Lane, Wilford, Nottinghamshire, NG11 7HQ. Tel: 0115 945 5522; fax: 0115 945 5533.

Heart-Rate Monitors
You can buy heart-rate monitors from gyms and good sports shops. I have found the Polar models to be reliable.

Polar Heart Rate Monitors, Leisure Systems International Ltd, Northfield Road, Southam, Warwickshire, CV33 0FG. Tel: 01926 811611; fax: 01926 816102

Clothing and Equipment for Outdoor Activities

Blacks
For your local retail outlet, check with the head office, Blacks Retail Distribution, Unit 3, Stephenson Industrial Estate, Washington, Tyne and Wear, NE37 3HR. Hotline: 0191 416 2929.

Ski Gear
Snow & Rock, 150 Holborn, London, EC1N 2LC. Tel: 0171 831 6900.

Socks
Bridgedale Socks, Donaghadee Road, Newtownards, Northern Ireland, BT23 3QR. Tel: 01247 813461.

Sports Bras
Berlei, Tel: 01525 850088.

Dans-Ex, Tel: 01843 866300.

Elle-Active, Tel: 0171 436 0222.

Marks & Spencer, Tel: 0171 935 4422.

Rigby & Peller, Tel: 0171 589 9293.

Sportjock, Tel: 0113 258 8630.

Triumph, Tel: 01793 720232.

Sports Clothes and Footwear

Adidas, Tel: 0161 419 2500; fax: 0161 419 2655.

Nutrition

Food Drinks/Electrolyte Powders

Science in Sport (SIS) Ltd, Ashwood Laboratories, Brockhall Village, Nr Blackburn, Lancashire, BB6 8BB. Tel: 01254 24606.

Professional Sports Nutrition Advice

Brian Welsby, Be-Well Nutritional Products Ltd, 20 King Street Industrial Estate, Langtoft, Peterborough, Cambridgeshire, PE6 9NF. Tel: 01778 560868; fax: 01778 560872.

Royal Tokaji wine can be obtained from The Royal Tokaji Wine Company, 3 St James's Place, London, SW1A 1NP. Tel: 0171 495 3010.

Health Advice

Back Pain

For advice as to your local back specialist ask your GP to contact The British Institute of Musculoskeletal Medicine, Tel/fax: 01923 820110. Do not contact the institute yourself, as they can only pass on names to your GP. You could also contact the National Back Pain Association, 16 Elmtree Road, Teddington, Middlesex, TW11 8ST. Tel: 0181 977 5474.

Back Support Products

PROCARE Ltd, 100 Shaw Road, Oldham, OL1 4AY. Tel: 0161 678 0233.
Putnams, Langage, Plympton, Devon, PL7 5ET. Tel: 01752 345678.

Help with Arthritis

The Margaret Hills Clinic, 1 Oaks Precinct, Caesar Road, Kenilworth, Warwickshire, CV8 1DP. Tel: 01926 854783.

Help to Stop Smoking

Quitline, Freephone 0800 002200, Monday–Friday, 12 noon–7.00pm.

Bibliography

Carper, Jean, *Stop Ageing Now*, HarperCollins, London, 1997.

Fiennes, Rannulph, *Mind Over Matter*, Sinclair-Stevenson, London, 1993

Henderson, Joe, *Better Runs*, Human Kinetics, Illinois, 1996.

Hills, Margaret, *Curing Arthritis the Drug-Free Way*, Sheldon Press, London, 1985.

Karlen, Arno, *Plague's Progress*, Victor Gollancz, London, 1995.

Mindell, Earl, *The Vitamin Bible*, Arlington Books, London, 1982.

Reader's Digest, *Foods That Harm; Foods That Heal*, Reader's Digest, London, 1996.

Royal Canadian Air Force, *Physical Fitness*, Penguin Books, London, 1964.

Stroud, Mike, *Survival of the Fittest*, Jonathan Cape, London, 1998.

Index

Index

Index